CW00996023

Naked Option

By Joe Kolman

HARRIMAN HOUSE LTD

3A Penns Road
Petersfield
Hampshire
GU32 2EW
GREAT BRITAIN

Tel: +44 (0)1730 233870
Fax: +44 (0)1730 233880
Email: enquiries@harriman-house.com
Website: www.harriman-house.com

First published in Great Britain in 2007
Copyright © Harriman House Ltd

The right of Joe Kolman to be identified as author has been asserted in
accordance with the Copyright, Design and Patents Act 1988.

ISBN: 1-905641-47-8
ISBN 13: 978-1905641-47-5

British Library Cataloguing in Publication Data
A CIP catalogue record for this book can be obtained from the British Library.

All rights reserved; no part of this publication may be reproduced, stored in a retrieval system,
or transmitted in any form or by any means, electronic, mechanical, photocopying, recording,
or otherwise without the prior written permission of the Publisher. This book may not be lent,
resold, hired out or otherwise disposed of by way of trade in any form of binding or cover other
than that in which it is published without the prior written consent of the Publisher.

Printed and bound in Great Britain by Biddles Ltd, Kings Lynn, Norfolk

The author gratefully acknowledges the support of The Writer's Room, New York, NY.

This is a work of fiction. Any resemblance between the characters herein and real
persons living or otherwise is purely coincidental.

No responsibility for loss occasioned to any person or corporate body
acting or refraining to act as a result of reading material in this book
can be accepted by the Publisher or by the Author.

For Lenore

Chapter 1

I used to pity the poor souls forced to work in Exchange Place, New Jersey.

Then, on September 12, 2001, I became one of them.

The day before, we watched the whole horrific scene over our shoulders as we fled from our offices in the World Financial Center, a few hundred feet west of the Trade Center. The headquarters of our investment bank was badly damaged by smoke and debris. But while we were still staring at the TV replays, the bank was leasing space in a building across the Hudson River that would serve as our temporary trading floor until things returned to normal.

Which they never did.

Monday, still shaky and haunted by our escape, we found our way to Exchange Place. Real estate developers like to call it "Wall Street West," but it's nothing more than a dozen corporate office buildings plunked down on the other side of the Hudson River near an entrance to the PATH train.

When we walked into the new trading floor, we faced rows of new desks with computers, but most of them had never been turned on. We spent the first few days idly watching techies try to wire everything together. By Wednesday afternoon, they managed to get the main derivatives trading system up, but it was disabled a half hour later by the Nimba virus. We were all floundering in our own noxious brew of emotions, and this comic dumb show was a welcome distraction from the tragedy playing outside.

When people weren't infuriated, they fell into a generalized depression. The trading screens that we had spent weeks customizing defaulted to their bewildering factory presets. Data about the stock, bond and currency markets was unavailable, delayed or hopelessly unreliable. I'd jump on a guaranteed sure thing, then get back an error message: "This trade cannot be processed" or "Awaiting credit check" or my favorite: "Network error: Please resubmit using a different DLL." I could make outgoing calls to clients, but I couldn't give them a phone number because I didn't know it myself. No one even knew the combination to the bathroom, so we used the one downstairs for two days — until somebody finally karate-kicked the door open.

A week later, as things progressed from insane to merely loony, we received a warning from on high: The bank's earnings would take a massive hit in the fourth quarter, and our bonuses would be cut by 50 percent or more.

That was big news on the trading desk, because our salary is only a fraction of our total compensation. Most of it comes from our bonuses, which depend on a baroque and secretive calculation of how well each trader, his department and the bank have done that particular year. I had a pretty good 2000, and the first three quarters of 2001 were looking even better. I was making $150,000 in salary and due to earn a bonus somewhere near $500,000 if my trading profits held up through December 31.

The bonus announcement hit everyone like a sucker punch. The year was shot. All our hard work down the toilet. The only thing to do was hold on until the next year and hope the markets recovered.

Like most of the guys on the trading desk, I had already spent my bonus. But the money was not the worst thing. More dispiriting was the depression around me. When I was a summer intern in 1991, a trader walked onto the First Boston trading floor and shot another guy who had been sleeping with his wife. They moved the victim to the side and called the paramedics. Within minutes everybody was trading again. I saw one guy actually step over the body to get back to his desk.

This time it was different. Nobody cared about making money. Instead of trading, people watched the news on CNN. Guys with draconian exercise regimens stopped entirely; they blimped up, day by day. I'd spent the last couple of weeks trying not to get sucked into the general gloom, but I wasn't succeeding.

I stomped around in a foul mood, but so did everyone. Instead of my 20-minute zip downtown, I had to change to the PATH train at 34th Street, and then transfer again in New Jersey. Exchange Place existed solely as a utility: a system of streets that supported buildings that stored people. It had wide avenues but no traffic. There were no shops or delis, unless you counted the McDonald's, the Starbucks and the Au Bon Pain. Rush hour was unidirectional: In the mornings people rushed from the PATH train to their building, in the evening they rushed back. Its sole redeeming feature, a spectacular view of lower Manhattan, only increased the sense of exile. As I walked to my office, carrying my McDonald's Big Breakfast, I tried to ignore the mass grave behind me. On the way back it was unavoidable, the vanishing point of every street.

Exchange Place leached the glamour out of our lives. We were options traders at one of the world's largest investment banks. But when we walked out of that PATH station, we might as well have been actuaries in Cincinnati.

That was a relatively minor irritation, however, compared to my biggest problem — Ray Goodman.

When I arrived in Exchange Place the first day, I found myself assigned to the seat next to his. We were both options traders with similar responsibilities. In the Financial Center, my superiors were always trying to convince us to sit together, but I pulled every trick in the book to keep a safe distance. Now we were rubbing elbows.

I was a brilliant trader. I could glance at four numbers on two screens, spin them around in my head and turn a wicked gamble into a mathematical equation. I devised new option trading techniques by adapting scholarly articles in trade journals. The firm had put $40 million of its capital in my trading account, a huge portfolio, which I earned based on five years of consistent profits.

But Ray was a superstar.

Month after month, I plodded along, studying the market, studying my models, tweaking things here and there just so I would be prepared to go "Ready, Aim, Fire!" at the right moment.

For him, it was just "Fire! Fire! Fire!"

He didn't have to think, he just did it. I used to watch him from afar. He would slouch in his chair, check his screens, fly his flight simulator, call his options broker in Chicago, shop for a better stereo. Then, inevitably, there would be a short conversation with his broker, a few dead seconds of silence, and a victorious "Cha-CHING!" accompanied by basketball hand pumps and the monkey hoots of a primate overcoming his rivals in a coconut battle. The fact that he never read anything but the Daily News sports pages only added to his mystique on the trading floor.

In the Financial Center, I sat close enough to see him, but I'd been spared the soundtrack. Now I heard him brag about his winning trades to his brokers. I heard him discuss which New Jersey mall restaurant he and his wife should try on Saturday night. I heard him grill audiophile salesmen about speaker acoustics. I heard him hum his three favorite Eagles tunes, off-key and just loud enough to be irritating. When he was deep in concentration, his right thigh would bounce up and down in his chair, and he would start sucking on his left pinky. Goodman was born a runty little physics nerd and he'd die one, in spite of his contact lenses, his Ferragamo loafers and the funky designer shirts his wife bought him.

The physical contrast between us couldn't be greater. He called me "Moose," a name not unfamiliar to guys who are 6'2" and 220 pounds. For variety, he occasionally called me "Link," as in "Missing Link," because I had to shave the hair on the back of my neck.

I called him "Dickhead," sometimes "Dick."

In the Financial Center, I had been a relatively distant and obscure rival. Now I became his obsession. He memorized all my trades and rubbed them in my face when they went bad. I responded by talking to my brokers in a low mutter so he wouldn't hear. He retaliated by peeping at my trade slips and my spreadsheets like a high school student cheating on his math test.

He seemed to spend as much time monitoring my trades as his own. I'd be watching my screen, trying to hide my emotions as the biggest trade of my day fell apart before my eyes. Then I'd hear him tapping away on his keyboard. "The market's dropping like a brick!" he would exclaim. "That put spread you sold must be bleeding pretty bad, huh?"

He had plenty of opportunities to mock me. I lost money hand over fist, and he minted it. After he cashed out of a winning trade, he would lean as far back into his chair as possible and launch into a remarkably adept mimicry of Bobby Mercer and Tim McCarver, the Yankee announcers.

"Goodman has been having a stellar year and an even better September, wouldn't you say so, Tim?"

"Yes, Bobby. What's notable about today's big trade was the way it was executed. He's done butterfly spreads before, but not quite in this size. I should point out that Goodman's performance contrasts dramatically with some of his other team members, particularly David Ackerman. Ackerman has had some serious problems since he came back from the September break. In fact, if you ask me, he's looking at a negative October."

"That's right, Tim. Ackerman's been playing in the majors for a decade now, but I get the feeling management has been disappointed by his performance lately. Once they get their trading floor problems straightened out, they're going to start cutting out the dead wood. It looks like Ackerman is heading back to the farm team."

Ray and I sat amid a small group of options traders in a carefully stratified primate hierarchy. Ray was clearly the dominant gorilla. I was number two, and some younger guys made up positions three through five.

We all had strong math or science backgrounds. Ray and Gary Pricer had Ph.D.s in physics. Steve Carey, Henry Wilson and I were math majors. But on a Wall Street trading floor, our conversation rarely surpassed the level you'd find in a high school locker room.

Sports, of course, was always the favorite topic. Steve, the youngster of the group, was a chatterbox who relayed sports bulletins as soon as they appeared on his screen. Ray, to his credit, knew an awesome amount about the Yankees. And I was the undisputed king of sports statistics.

After 9/11, however, war and military theory made inroads as the favorite topics. Steve had grown up in a military family and knew a lot about strategy and tactics. Ray, however, spent two summers as an intern in the nuclear weapons lab at Los Alamos, and was the expert on weapons of mass destruction. He told us all about the challenges of milling anthrax before they appeared in the papers. One morning, as we sipped our coffee, he delivered a mind-blowing lecture on the physics of tower fires, complete with gruesome theories of how our buddies at Cantor spent their last few seconds.

Most of our other discussions revolved around the markets, our fucked-up trading system, and when the techies would get things back to normal. There were no women within earshot, so my colleagues considered it acceptable to compete over who could be the most sexist. Racism was out of bounds, but it was fashionable to be homophobic and politically incorrect in every possible way. I generally kept out of this end of things, but the comments seemed to get more virulent as the general anxiety level increased.

Atul, our Pakistani network technician, had suffered more than his fair share of teasing in the old office. Now it was merciless. The poor schmuck always seemed to be on his back under somebody's desk, attaching wires from one computer to another. He carried a large black Samsonite briefcase weighted down with techie stuff, and had started wearing a huge red, white and blue ribbon on his shirt in a heartbreaking display of patriotism.

"Look at Atul," Steve said one slow afternoon. "I think he's got one of the suitcase nukes!" He called up a picture on his screen of a Pentagon expert with the model of a nuclear bomb missing from the Soviet arsenal. It looked exactly like Atul's briefcase. Steve soon had a half dozen people gathered, laughing hysterically.

They had to shout across the floor to get Atul's attention. "Hey, Atul! Don't waste it on New Jersey. Go over to the Lexington Avenue office. You could level midtown!"

Atul looked up with a weak smile, not getting the joke.

"A suitcase nuke wouldn't level midtown," Ray said, with an irritated authority that silenced everyone. "There'd be a nasty hole for about six blocks and a lot of big buildings down in a two-mile radius, but a lot of stuff would still be standing. Downtown should be unaffected."

"You're crazy," said Steve. "There'd be all kinds of radioactive fallout from a bomb like that."

"It would only be serious for four miles downwind," said Ray. "Beyond that, the effects are pretty minimal. And radioactive fallout isn't like instant death. You don't want to inhale it. That's why you wear a gas mask. It's like any other kind of dust. You take a shower and it washes off."

He opened up his bottom drawer and rooted around in its depths. "We're six miles from midtown. Get yourself a good Israeli gas mask and rubber gloves and you'll be fine."

He held up a box of Playtex Living Gloves and a larger box featuring Hebrew writing and a curly-haired blonde wearing a bright yellow gas mask. Ray's outfit was going to be color-coordinated.

"You're going to put those on if a nuclear bomb goes off?" I asked.

"Yeah, and I'm going to walk home. A car would be useless. My wife will duct tape the windows in the basement and turn off the ventilation system. The kids will walk home from school. We're going to take showers, change our clothes and then wait for the whole thing to blow over. It should take a day or two. Less if it rains. We've got food in the basement, video games, the works. It's not that big a deal."

He glanced at his futures screen and hit a couple buttons. "Fucking Eurodollars. They're all over the place."

Steve looked like he was going to be sick. I checked my watch: 3:29. Maybe it was time to call it a day.

It took me two hours and 14 minutes to get from Exchange Place to my girlfriend Chris's apartment in the East Village, including a lovely half hour stuck in the PATH train tunnel under the Hudson River. After a few minutes, the electricity died and the emergency lights kicked in, casting an eerie glow through the packed subway car. You could hear every cough, every nervous mutter.

A little while later, a girl of about 12, seated at the other side of the car, began hyperventilating because she thought the concrete barriers surrounding the Trade Center had been breached and that the river would soon rush in to flood us. Her dad hugged her and patiently explained that the tunnel they were worried about was the southern PATH tunnel. We were in the northern tunnel, which now ended a half mile north of the Trade Center.

I realized that the girl was either emotionally disturbed or mildly retarded when she continued to panic, but her fears infected all of us. Ten minutes stuck under the river was almost routine, but after 20 minutes, I couldn't help but think that something had happened in the real world upstairs, and that we had either been saved from a nuclear incident raging above us or that we had been buried alive. When the train arrived at 33rd Street a few minutes later, we all rushed out of the car in near panic.

The cab ride to Chris's place in the East Village was mercifully quick.

"Terrific day," I said as I collapsed on her couch. "Lots of fun." I wanted to drown my consciousness in a plate of killer ribs at the Korean restaurant nearby, then come back for some sexual healing and a good night's sleep.

Chris, however, was putting fresh batteries in the backlit Palm Pilot she used to take notes during film previews.

"I tried calling you on your cell, but you must have been in the tunnel," she said. "Brian wants me to cover an indie video festival tonight in Queens. I got him to pay for a car service back and forth. Can you believe it?"

"When is the car coming?"

"Seven-thirty. Do you want to grab a slice of pizza?"

I lifted her sweater and put my palm over her belly button.

We both looked at our watches. Seventeen minutes. We had our 10-minute quickie down pat, and our extended-play version could take all night. But 17 minutes would be an interesting challenge.

I could have bought us a few more minutes by giving her money to take a cab, but that would have deprived her of the victory she had just wrested from her editor. The economics of freelance film criticism never made much sense to me. She had just spent $800 to fly to Miami to write a director profile that paid $400, and she always seemed to have enough money to buy pricey vintage clothing and occasional bags of high-grade pot. I guessed Daddy was writing monthly checks for five or six grand.

I wasn't quite cool enough for Chris. And she wasn't really deep enough for me. But great sex gave the relationship an extended life it wouldn't have otherwise had.

The immediate challenge was our 17 minutes. The only way to guarantee her an orgasm in that period was orally. Then we'd have a few more minutes for "ride 'em cowboy," which, in the right circumstances, might allow her to reach a second orgasm — "O2" as she called it — just as I was having O1. We didn't need to articulate this. The strategy was obvious.

We pushed her dirty clothes off her bed, unzipped our pants, and set a new speed record for O1, in order to give her as much time as possible for O2.

The whole thing required enormous concentration on her part, with only a 50 percent chance of success, but "ride 'em cowboy" was what she preferred. There never seemed to be any pattern to it. One moment she loped rhythmically across the plains, the next she crouched into a gallop. Then she'd take a break and sit upright, do some yogic breathing for a few seconds, and try something else. It struck me as a noble struggle. She was never sure she'd get there, but damn it, she would go all out every time.

I wasn't about to complain. In fact, it required almost equal concentration on my part just to make sure I didn't come. I had an uneven track record the first few times, until I went out and bought the thickest condoms I could find.

I kept my eye on the VCR clock. At 7:25, as O2 was just within reach, the car service guy rang the buzzer.

"Wait, wait," I said, "We've got five minutes."

"Sorry cowboy, I gotta go." She grabbed my buttocks and did an irresistible little swivel thing that ended our western adventure right then and there.

"Black jeans," she said with satisfaction as she zipped up and headed out the door. "Nobody's going to see the wet spot."

My brain had been twisted inside out for a few minutes. Now I was back in New York City in November 2001, a space/time coordinate I wanted to leave.

Chapter 2

The next morning, Steve was noticeably quiet. I had vibes that it was going to be a bad day, but I didn't think it was going to be the day that changed my life.

After the morning meeting, we all returned to our seats in silence. Steve looked awful, as if he had been up all night. The weather was beautiful, in the upper 60s with clear skies and a velvety breeze, but the war news in the papers was bad: The commando raid in Afghanistan, proclaimed as a great victory the day before, was looking like a big failure.

"Hey, Ray," Steve said suddenly. "I was thinking about what you told us yesterday." Then I realized he was about to ask Ray another question about the goddamn suitcase nuke. I tried to stop him with a grimace — *Don't encourage this asshole* — but it didn't work.

"If a suitcase bomb goes off, we're all going to be cooked by the radiation," said Steve, rubbing the knot of his tie nervously between his fingers. "A gas mask isn't going to protect you from that."

"We're eight miles from midtown" — Ray shook his head, momentarily lost in thought. "It shouldn't be too bad." He did some figuring on a scratch pad as if he were calculating a restaurant tip.

"They're one kiloton each, a tenth the size of Hiroshima," he announced after double-checking his calculations. "It's not like you're going to glow or anything. How many chest x-rays have you had in your life? You've already probably had 10 at 25 millirems apiece. So this is going to be 30 more."

"Ray, shut the fuck up!" I bellowed, loud enough to be heard across the trading floor. "Can't you see you're scaring everybody shitless?"

"Fuck all of you," he said, slapping both palms fiercely on his desk. "It's not my problem if you guys have completely lost it. All you do is sit around on your ass, complaining about the fucked-up trading floor, the fucked-up markets, and the fucked-up bonus. None of you have made a winning trade since we moved here. And you know why you're not making money? Because you suck.

"If you just looked at your screens for once, instead of pissing and moaning, you'd realize it's great the markets are fucked up. Everything's out of whack. People are leaving millions of dollars on the table, and nobody here knows it because you're just as fucked up as they are. We're in the golden age of option arbitrage and you guys don't have a clue."

He swiveled 180 degrees in his chair and studied the Chicago Merc option page for a few seconds, then looked back at us over his shoulder in disgust. "Making money in good markets was easy. Now it takes talent."

Insults salted practically every sentence we uttered. But expressions of real emotion were an unacceptable breach of the rules. Ray's outburst was met with silence. The gorilla pack was going to isolate the miscreant.

But we all knew he was right. Struggling actors can look up at some movie star on the screen and tell themselves, "I could have done that." But trading is a pure meritocracy. The markets were coming back to normal. We all had the same opportunities, but Ray was making money while the rest of us were sitting on our collective ass.

I wanted to pound his little body into the ground.

It was not about money. I didn't mind making less money than Ray. I know that's hard to believe, but it's true. I was proud that I never got completely caught up in the Wall Street thing. I played basketball every Thursday night with my college friends, most of whom were still making five figures. In women, I tended to favor liberal arts types of various persuasions who wore little or no makeup. My clothes were acceptable, but never flashy. I had a nice car, a nice apartment, I bought good tickets to sporting events and went on quirky, expensive Caribbean vacations.

But I found that somewhere beyond $300,000 a year, economic value is governed by the law of diminishing returns. A two-bedroom apartment is a nice luxury, but a three-bedroom apartment isn't appreciably better. The same went for cars or coffee or Caribbean resorts.

My sin wasn't greed. It was pride. When I was a high school math whiz, I dreamed of finding the answer to Fermat's Theorem and leading the glamorous life of an impossibly wealthy math professor. When I actually met some math professors in college, I quickly transferred my fantasies to Wall Street, where I knew numbers could make you rich.

Options trading seemed to be created specifically for me. It was part math, part athletics — it required me to keep my eye on three screens, talk on the phone and juggle equations at the same time. I did my job, kept my nose clean, and made money for my employers. And after 9 years of hard work, I had become an extremely successful options trader.

But success is not greatness. I was 31 and I had not yet set the world on fire. A tiny part of me, however, still believed that if I pushed myself in the right direction, took the right risks, and had the right wind at my back, I, too, could become truly exceptional. I needed to trust my gut, just as Ray trusted his. I would find my true talents when I ingested the numbers and turned them into instinct. I needed one brilliant kick-ass trade to shove in Ray Goodman's face. Something that would shut him up for good.

The index futures on Globex were flapping around much lower. At 9:30, the teeming S&P pit at the Chicago Board Options Exchange would open for business, reflecting what several hundred screaming maniacs thought the value of the stock market was at that moment. At 10:00, the Commerce Department would announce last month's industrial production numbers.

It was time to make my move.

If a trader knew in advance what would happen before the number came out, and bought and sold the right options, he made millions by lunch. If he made the wrong moves, of course, he lost the same millions and more. Since we never knew what would happen, we tried to make educated guesses, based on screens and computer models, risking enough to make money, but not so much we would lose our shirts. That was the game. The game Ray Goodman played better than I did.

If you were going to do a big trade, you might as well do it with options. Options were financial rocket fuel, Wall Street's most powerful weapons. If the stock market went up 5 percent, you could set up an option portfolio that would go up 50 percent — or 120 percent or whatever number you chose. But if the market went the wrong way, the losses would come at you with breathtaking swiftness.

Everybody expected a bad number. If I bet that the number wouldn't be quite so bad, I could make a lot of money. It was a simple one-way bet on the direction of the market — precisely the opposite of what I usually did. In most cases, I devised elaborate combinations of trades that gave me a built-in safety net in case the market went the wrong way.

Trading options without this protection was what people called "punting," or "going naked." I called it "trading like a moron." Over the years, I had seen dozens of my colleagues get greedy, make one-way bets and blow out.

Ray made these kinds of bets routinely without getting burned. "Let the force be your guide," was his motto. In options markets, it was stupid advice. But it helped Luke Skywalker destroy the Death Star, and it worked for Ray.

To pull off a really stupid trade, you usually had to do a bit of flying under the radar. Before September 11, the radar was Armand Bisserian, the guy who was supposed to prevent traders like me from blowing up the bank. Armand was a physics professor who left his tenured position to try options trading. He never made much money, but he knew most of our tricks, and that made him particularly valuable to the firm.

In the Financial Center, he'd sat two rows behind us, in a desk littered with electric train magazines and Triscuit crumbs, monitoring every move we made. If we put on a particularly risky trade, a little flag popped up on his screen. A few clicks later, you'd get a call. "Interesting move, Dave," he'd say through his thick Armenian accent. "But it's a little too fancy for me."

The day before somebody said they saw Armand in the elevator, going to an office on a different floor. He had been assigned other duties while they rewired the elaborate connections between our trading system and his risk system. In other words, we had the freedom to do whatever the hell we wanted.

I had eight minutes before the markets opened, plenty of time to call Jeff, my favorite Chicago options broker, and put my plan into action. Our first conversation was an important part of my morning ritual, as I could often tell more about the mood of the market from his voice and from the background noise than from the numbers he quoted me.

"Hey, it's Dave," I announced. "See the game?"

"Yeah," he grunted. "The Bulls suck. What else is new?"

"Man, the Celtics were looking good. Awesome defense."

"What's up?"

"I need to sell 500 Dec 1050 puts at market on the open."

"Okay, selling 500 Dec 1050 puts market on the open. Ticket number 47. I'll call you with the fill."

The call went to dial tone and I was alone with my trade. Bad mood, bad day. I had just made a big bet that the American economy would look slightly better after the 10:00 industrial production number. A mistake? I could still reverse the trade and get out. I carefully punched the numbers into the firm's trading system and created a new workbook in my spreadsheet to track today's big trade, naming it "Goofy."

After a little puttering, I realized that Goofy wouldn't do what I wanted it to do. If the market moved my way, it would make some money, but not enough to really stick it to Ray. I had to call Jeff back and pump up the trade.

I punched the speed dial, but got Jerry at State Street in Boston instead, who was programmed into the button below Jeff. Jerry was my biggest client and a rabid Celtics fan. "Could you believe that fourth quarter?" he said, as he launched into a euphoric play-by-play. I listened as long as I could before interrupting him. "Jerry, I've got to book a trade before the open," I said, "Catch you later."

When I finally got Jeff, it was five minutes after the opening, and I couldn't hear the prices he was quoting me because of a sudden burst of noise on the trading floor. My stomach was rumbling and I had to pee. It was going to be a rough morning.

"Sorry I missed the opening. Where'd I get filled?" I asked him.

"You sold 300 1050 Dec puts at 9.40 and another 200 at 9.30."

"I can barely hear you. What's going on?"

"Everyone's hyped about the number. Premium's getting kinda pumped."

"Good, let's sell another 500."

"500? Checking new order. Selling 500 Dec puts at the market."

"I'll wait for the fill."

I waited while he signaled his floor trader in the center of the roiling S&P pit 30 feet away. Then he took another call while we waited to see what prices I'd get on the contracts I sold.

"Sold 500 Dec 1050 puts at 9.20. Ticket 18," he said.

Another sickening dial tone. Nothing I could do but pray for the American economy.

My neighbor, meanwhile, had called in his morning's trades and was sitting with his feet up, reading a summary of the Bulls-Celtics game online. Ray considered my continuing allegiance to the Bulls and the White Sox as a sign of romantic feeblemindedness, and never missed a chance to read choice selections of their failures.

"How the mighty have fallen," he said, clearing his throat theatrically. " '*The Bulls hit their nadir in the fourth quarter, when Charles Oakley received a technical foul for spitting in the vicinity of the referee.*' Pathetic. Steve, did you see that spit last night?"

"Shut the fuck up," I said.

"That team is out of control. A disgrace to the NBA. What kind of city are they from?"

We were both waiting for the number at 10:00. I thought I even detected a touch of anxiety as Ray checked his screens. I puttered some more with my spreadsheet, closing everything but a little window that told me Goofy's net worth. At the moment, my trade was down about $100,000, but if the numbers were good, Goofy would be earning seven figures in a hurry.

And then, at 10:00, right on schedule, the news hit, first from Reuters, then Dow Jones and Bloomberg a millisecond later: "COMMERCE DEPT. REPORTS INDUSTRIAL PRODUCTION DOWN 1.9 PERCENT."

That was good news. The investment geniuses on Wall Street were expecting something much worse, so everybody decided it was time to buy. Goofy was aloft, trembling at first at $225,000 then quickly doubling and tripling as the market data from Chicago fed into my spreadsheet. $400,000 quickly became $1.2 million, then $2 million soaring to $4 million, hitting a peak of $5 million and settling back into the $4 million range.

I felt the way I did the first five minutes in my friend's Piper Cub, before the noise of the plane gave me a headache. Options fed a dangerous kind of grandiosity. Trading put you right up there, close to the Options God, his lightning all around. He allowed you to soar high above the schmucks that could only trade stocks. But he was also a vengeful God who waited for a moment of pride before flinging you back down to earth.

I knew all about these dangers, but I needed to savor these moments in the heavens to sustain me through all the mundane expanses of the trading day. I stared at the minimized Excel number in the corner of my screen, screaming to myself: "Up, baby. Up, up, up!"

Goofy was all about luck, not skill, but I didn't care. This was going to be the day I knocked the smug smile off Ray's face.

"Are you the guy who sold 1000 at-the-money puts naked?" he said, staring at his screen.

"Yeah." I waited for my congratulations.

"Watch it, Link. Vol is pretty pumped and your puts are on the moon."

"Kiss my ass."

It was a rare piece of advice, something your older brother would tell you only when you were in serious danger. I would have been surprised by the gesture if I wasn't terrified. Casually, without a care in the world, I tapped a few keys and took another look at Goofy. Sure enough, I had been watching the futures price, but my puts weren't going down as much as my model predicted.

Trading options was like cooking four delicate sauces on one stove. You had to keep careful track of each one, or you'd ruin the dish. And Goodman was right. I had forgotten the béarnaise. In fact, if I didn't do something soon, it would bubble over and curdle into a god-awful mess.

Instinctively, I looked behind me to see what Armand was doing. Then I remembered I was in New Jersey, not Manhattan. It was November 2001. Nobody was watching me. I could do whatever the hell I wanted. But I was still very vulnerable. All it would take was one little market hiccup...

I punched Jeff in Chicago, knowing Ray would be dying to eavesdrop, and wheeled myself back to the end of my phone cord.

"Jeff, it's Dave," I said as quietly as I could.

"What've you got?"

"So I'm looking at my screen and the volatility on those puts... Is the screen off?"

I heard Jeff punch his keyboard.

"Shit." That was as articulate as he got, but it was enough.

"Yeah, shit is right," I said. "So I'm thinking about what I can do."

I glanced to my right. Goodman was in a huddle with Henry, no doubt discussing my stupid trade. The gorilla pack was concerned. Ape in trouble. Grunt. Nothing to do.

"You weren't naked, were you?" asked Jeff incredulously. "Selling 1000 puts before a number? Why'd you do that?"

"Because I wanted to be a fucking genius," I said. The honesty must have surprised Jeff, because he fell completely silent.

"You could get out, but it would cost you," he said.

"Yeah, I know."

"Hope the plane don't crash!" he said, quoting an old Bill Cosby line.

"Yeah, thanks." I said. "Me, too."

The only thing I could do was hope the market would stay where it was, or rally. It was only 10:12. The day was still young. Anything could happen. I kept my eyes glued to my screens, but I suspected the news about my position was being transmitted down the line of traders, no doubt distorting as it spread.

I did what I usually did in times of crisis: I went to a bathroom stall with my calculator and a notepad. People walked in and out, made noise, turned on and off the faucets, but I was completely focused, sketching out possible scenarios and trades. I had pulled myself out of the '97 collapse of the Thai Bhat and the Russian default of '98. Hell, I had been in worse shape in the lead-up to the NASDAQ crash. If the market stabilized, and I did a few trades with a smattering of luck, I could walk away relatively unscathed. And if the market rallied, I might actually make a killing.

Just when I'd started to breathe more easily, the bathroom door flew open, and I heard a sickening burst of shouting from the trading floor. Good news? Bad news? My toes curled up in my shoes. I ran back and checked the number racing across the digital screen on the wall. The S&P was down three percent.

"What's the big deal?" I asked Ray while I scanned my news screen.

"Murdoch is off his numbers big time," he said, staring at his monitor, where a redhead wearing black stockings and not much else was displaying her rump.

"Is that all?"

A pixilated harem of 10 redheads appeared on his screen. The Web filters were down, and Ray was using a porn search engine to find redheads that looked like his wife.

"The trend is your friend," he said.

The S&P index had reversed and was dropping like a brick. I could jump on the trend, and make it my friend, but I had already made a big bet the other way. The trend was my enemy.

Though it was just one earnings report, the markets were easily spooked and running in a herd. I wanted to scream at them as they rushed by: "You lemmings! It's just one earnings report! Shake it off!" But they wouldn't listen. In fact, the stampede only intensified when United Airlines released an ominous earnings warning.

I averted my eyes from the little number in the corner of my screen and tried to keep my head clear. I straightened my back and sat up in my chair. Then I looked. Goofy, my beautiful $4 million creation, was diving deep in negative number land... -$1.5 million, -$1.9 million, -$2.7 million…I couldn't watch.

Then I had the idea that changed my life. If I made Goofy really goofy, made him really sensitive to every market movement, the next up tick would send him bounding out of negative number land like an astronaut on a moon walk. As soon as he was profitable, I would sell out. And then spend the rest of the day at the movies.

I knew it was an extremely risky thing to do, but it had a certain impulsive charm. I punched Jeff's speed-dial before I had a chance to change my mind.

"Jeff, I've got a ratio spread. Buy 1000 Dec 1050 puts, sell 2000 Dec 1030 puts at market."

"But that's going to leave you short 2000," he said.

"Correct."

"All right, if that's what you want." He sighed like a bartender handing a drunk a double.

My stomach lurched to the top of my chest cavity and stayed there, like when an airplane drops suddenly in a patch of turbulence, and my heart seemed to move north as well.

I tapped the numbers into my spreadsheet, but I wasn't going to enter this lunatic thing into the trading system. Instead, I wrote the details down on a scrap of legal pad and put it in my drawer.

Then I waited for the market to turn around. If I had a seat belt on my chair, I would have snapped myself in.

I watched Goofy nose-dive for a while — -$3 million, -$6.5 million, -$18 million — then closed my spreadsheet. The newswires buzzed with the endless, mindless debate: Are we poised for an economic turnaround? Is it still premature? Another bullshit day, turbulent for no reason.

I fed a dollar into the soda machine in the hallway, read all the employee notices on the bulletin board, and tried to ignore the shouting from the floor. On the way back to my desk, I stopped to flirt with Annie, our chesty NYU intern.

"What's new, Anna Banana?"

"Same old, same old," she said, one eye on her screen. "What's happening to the market today?"

"Something wrong?"

"It dropped another two percent in five minutes. You got any ideas?"

"If I was so smart, I wouldn't be working, right?"

"You got a point there." She flashed me a distracted smile.

I went back to the bulletin board and studied the minimum wage notice again. A two percent drop on top of a three percent drop? All in a few minutes? I had seen it before. A wild early morning rush downward, sparked by a bit or two of bad news. My plan was to hold on until lunch, in the hope some other bit of news would stop the descent in its tracks, reinspire the bulls and turn the market around.

I did some rough calculations in my head. Goofy was down at least $61 million by now. Armand might not be watching, but a loss like that would trigger alarm bells somewhere in the bank. Somebody might even be monitoring the risk from London.

I had to come up with Plan B in a hurry. I walked back to the bathroom with my notepad and calculator, then knelt in front of a toilet and vomited as quietly as I could.

Suddenly, I remembered: My really goofy trades weren't even in the system! They were on a one-inch sliver of legal pad in my drawer! According to the system, Dave Ackerman hadn't lost $61 million dollars. He was only having a bad day!

At some point, of course, my bad trade would catch up with me. At some point, maybe an hour or two, somebody would get a call from Chicago: "Hey, did you know your guy Ackerman is down 61 mil in S&P options?"

But if I dumped the trades into a client account, I'd have time to turn things around. The trade accounting systems were so screwed up they wouldn't find out for at least a couple days. By then, the market could snap back and save my ass. And if that happened, my losing trade would be worth ten million dollars, maybe fifteen. Then I would transfer it back into my account and hope nobody would be the wiser. It wasn't much of a plan, but it was the best one I could think of.

The only problem was that it required me to commit securities fraud.

If I wanted to hide a $61 million loss, I'd have to dump it into a pretty big account. Jerry at State Street had $2 billion. That was big enough. I washed my face in the sink, walked back to my desk with feigned confidence and casually assigned the trade in my drawer to Jerry's account at State Street.

I looked around the trading room to get my bearings. It was 11:21, too late for breakfast, too early for lunch. I had to get out, get some fresh air. If the market rallied, I'd call Chicago, close out the trade and put this morning behind me.

If the market didn't rally... My breathing became shallow just thinking about it.

I had my cell phone in my pocket, but I needed a Market Feed, a little pager designed to display prices for the contracts I traded. But my Market Feed had been sitting on my desk in the Financial Center, and it was impossible to get hold of a replacement.

Ray had one in his pocket, but I couldn't ask him. I glimpsed one by Henry's phone, serving as a paperweight for a couple message slips.

"Henry, I need your Market Feed," I told him as calmly as I could. "I'm going out to lunch."

"Sorry, man." He grabbed it protectively. "I'm going out to lunch too. I really need it today."

"Yeah, but I really *really* need it."

"No can do, buddy."

"Henry," I said. "I would like to rent your Market Feed from you for two hours. Here is..." I reached in my wallet and counted out everything I had. "Four hundred and twenty one dollars."

Heads turned. I was losing my cool.

"Okay, a hundred dollars an hour," he said, neatly picking two hundreds from the pile on his desk. "Two-hour minimum."

I grabbed my coat and stopped at Annie's desk on the way out.

"I'm going to lunch," I announced.

She looked confused. It was 11:36 and the market was going to hell. "Is something wrong?"

"It's nothing serious," I said.

That made her even more confused.

"Call me on my cell phone if there's an emergency," I said. "The number's in the database."

I walked outside and down two buildings to the Au Bon Pain. The sandwich guy was spreading baguettes with mayo and stacking them in a neat pile. He looked at the clock: 11:43.

"A little early today?" he said, fixing my turkey club.

"I got hungry. What was I supposed to do?"

"Hey, my uncle made $900 in Security Identification Systems. SIS on NASDAQ. It went up 20 percent in one week."

"Is that so? Good for him."

"Now he's going to buy another company that makes generic smallpox vaccines. Massachusetts Biotech. You know anything about that?"

"I don't know anything about stocks, man. I trade options."

"What do you think he should he buy?"

"A Lotto ticket looks pretty good to me right now," I said, grabbing the sports section from somebody's leftover Post.

I tried to bury myself in the sports pages, determined not to look at the Market Feed until noon. The day's big story was Steinbrenner's housecleaning following the Yankee's World Series loss. The Knicks were having a hard time pulling out of a four-game losing-streak. Then I read the story on the Bulls-Celtics game and my stomach contracted around the turkey club I'd wolfed down. What was Jerry going to do when he found out I'd dumped that crazy trade in his account?

The pager seemed to tremble in my pocket. I pulled it out and peeked at the gray numbers: I was down $87 million and change.

I raced to the bathroom stall. But this time my stomach wouldn't move. I tried putting a couple fingers down my throat, tried thinking about the spotted stains at the bottom of the bowl until I nearly suffocated. Nothing worked.

Outside, I started taking deeper breaths. The streets were empty, no cars, no people. A newspaper truck drove by, ignorant of my plight. I was going to take this day a half hour at a time.

The weather was in the upper 50s, with cloudless skies. On a slow day, I used to go girl-watching in Battery Park on a bench overlooking the river. They got off the boat from the Statue of Liberty and followed their guidebooks to the park. My favorite game was "Guess the Nationality." I formed a hypothesis based on clothing, features, whatever, and then tested it against their conversations as they passed by.

Today there was nowhere to go, nothing to do but sit on a row of concrete benches facing the collapsed skyline of lower Manhattan. I sat for a few moments, the sun on my face, before I got a jolt of adrenaline: You idiot! You committed securities fraud a few minutes ago. That's a federal crime. A felony!

What the hell could I do?

Plan A: I could go back to the office, switch the trade back into my account, and then throw myself at the mercy of the powers that be. But that wouldn't work. When they found out about State Street, I'd be fired on the spot.

Plan B: I could stick with my original plan and sit tight until the market came back. Not all the way back, but until my losses were at some acceptable level, say $5 million or $10 million. Then I could go back, switch the trade and swear it was a mistake. I would become a reformed trader, chastened but honest. But that assumed the market would climb most of the way back. And at the end of the day, I might still be out of a job.

My cell phone rang.

"Armand and Vladimir are looking at your portfolio," Annie said, murmuring close to mouthpiece. "They're asking where you are."

"What did you tell him?"

"Au Bon Pain. They sent me down to look for you, but you'd left."

"Good. What are they doing now?"

"Standing around your desk. Armand is really pissed."

"Don't tell them about my cell phone, okay?" I looked down the street to our building, which towered over me belligerently. "I'm going to straighten this out in a minute."

"Dave? Do you know what's happening to the S&Ps?"

"Don't tell me. I've got to run," I said and clicked off.

I stowed my cell phone and took the Market Feed out with exaggerated care, like it was a bomb ready to go off. I pressed the on button, pressed the code for S&P December options and held my breath.

While I had been playing with numbers, the market had gone to hell. I was down at least $110 million. Maybe even more. The sun turned the river into a blinding sheet of glare. I blinked and pictured my 9-year career: The undergraduate years busting my ass, the years in B-school, the years of apprenticeship. The yearly struggle for more responsibility, a bigger trading book, and finally my trophy job at a major investment bank.

Then I prayed, in my fashion, before the Trading God, as I had done during other periods of crisis. This time, truly, my transgressions had taught me a painful lesson. If I could just get my position back to zero, I would never envy my neighbor. I would put up with his daily jibes. I would accept my place in the ranks of very talented, and bear Ray's taunts with humility.

My prayers went unanswered.

What really bothered me was that I wasn't even blowing up in a market crash. The Dow might be down a few percent for the day, big news in the financial section, but nothing that would make it to the front page.

I heard them in my head:

"Dave blew out in that blip we had last November."

"Which blip?"

Then the cell phone rang again. The caller ID read State Street. It was Jerry in Boston. A fresh flutter of nausea. Did I tell him the truth?

Yes? No?

"Dave, it's Jerry," he said. "I'm sorry to call, but this is an emergency. Annie gave me your number."

"Just a minute, Jerry. The reception is breaking up." I heard the beep indicating he was calling on his recorded line. Somewhere at State Street, a multi-track tape recorder was preserving all of this for posterity.

I put my palm over the mouthpiece and walked around the bench to collect my thoughts. A huge barge from the Trade Center floated by, not a hundred feet away, hauling rubble to Fresh Kills for sorting.

Yes? No?

"Sorry, Jerry. I'm in the middle of lunch. I can't hear you very well."

"Dave, the audit guys just told me about some S&P puts that are booked to…"

"I know all about it," I said. "It's a system error. They're installing a new reconciliation system and they're screwing it up worse than before."

"I just want to make sure this isn't my trade," he said, chuckling nervously. "It shows me down 80 mil on these puts."

$80 million seemed a little low. I thought the losses were over $110 million. "How much did you say you were down?"

"$80 million. It was over a hundred a few minutes ago, but the market's coming back."

I checked the Market Feed. The S&Ps were rallying. A violent upswing at last! If it stayed on course, Goofy would be shooting back up into the whole numbers like a Saturn 5.

"I don't know Jerry," I said, trying to make a joke out of it. "This trade could look pretty good in a few minutes. You sure you don't want it?"

"I wouldn't touch those babies with a 100-foot pole," he said. "They're radioactive."

"I'll be back in the office in a few minutes and clear this thing up," I said. "You coming into town next week? The Knicks are playing Chicago."

"Two shitty teams playing each other? I got better things to do with my time."

"Okay, catch you later."

I sat down on the concrete bench and did some quick arithmetic. He was right. Instead of a $100 million loss, it was now $72 million and dropping fast.

Maybe it was time for Plan C: Sit tight until the multi-million-dollar loss turned into a multi-million dollar profit. Then go back to the office, switch the State Street trade back to my account and swear it was an accident. It was a stupid plan, of course. But at the moment it didn't seem impossible. Maybe things would be all right. Maybe I'd even have a big trade to throw in Ray's face.

Briefly, it was a beautiful November afternoon again. Then a Newark Fire Department boat passed twenty feet from shore, its blue emergency light spinning. Where the hell was the fire?

Another call came in, this time from a phone somewhere on the trading floor, probably Armand. He was going to demand that I come back and close my position at a loss.

I let it ring until it kicked into voicemail. It rang again.

I ignored it and sat on the bench, cupping my hands around the pager to shield it from the glare. Every minute or so, the LED would rearrange itself in a happy new pattern.

"Come on, Goofy," I said aloud. "Up baby, up!"

Across the river, the windows of the late-model skyscrapers sparkled in the sunlight. Unlike most people I knew, I loved my job. I wanted to spend my life working in those gleaming office towers. But if I went back to my office right now, I would drop instantly from the ranks of the very talented into the ranks of the hopelessly unemployable. I never knew what happened to traders who blew out and lost their jobs. I suppose they did something else with their lives, but what I couldn't imagine.

The phone chirped again. I was not going to walk in there with a big loss. I could imagine that particular prison yard drama all too clearly: The long shuffle from the reception area to my desk, past the stares of my friends and enemies. The funereal cardboard box, loaded with my personal effects. The security guard nearby, in case things got nasty. And Ray Goodman, forlorn at the prospect of losing his favorite source of amusement. I didn't want his pity.

Another call rang out, this time from Annie's phone.

"Dave, I think you better get back in here right away."

"What's going on?"

"There are four or five big shots standing around your desk. One of them is talking to a lawyer about your trading book."

"They can't close out my position. It's on its way back up!"

"They already did. Twenty minutes ago. Pretty close to the bottom. Right before the rally."

I closed my eyes against the glare for a second. I couldn't feel the pain, but I knew it was coming. When I opened them, I was a 31-year-old ex-trader on a concrete bench in New Jersey with his ear stuck to a cell phone.

A voice twittered, like the Good Fairy in some Disney cartoon. It was a soft high female voice from the Thirties. "Congratulations, Dave," she crooned. "A $112 million loss! You really went out in style."

"I think you better get in here," said Annie. "They're really pissed."

Chapter 3

That was the end of my trading career. At 4:00, the market closed a few points above its opening number. The next morning, the Wall Street Journal published an hour-by-hour chart of its collapse and recovery. But it was just another particularly volatile day, soon forgotten.

The investment bank lost a total of $112 million on my option trades. A few weeks later, on Christmas Eve, I walked into the Securities and Exchange Commission offices on Broadway and wrote out a check for $612,000, almost my entire net worth, in return for a release from prosecution for securities fraud. I also accepted a permanent suspension of my Series 7 license, which prevented me from ever trading securities again.

There was never anything quite as bad as that winter. In the desperate months that followed my crime I became a Wall Street pariah, slinking around the edges of the financial world, trying to find a way back in. I reinvented myself first as a software salesman and then as a recruiter, without much success. I spent three months in a series of temp jobs, constructing Excel charts. I ate my paper bag lunches in employee cafeterias, checking my e-mail and voicemail for responses to one of my resumes, predictably lost in the blizzard of resumes blanketing Wall Street that season.

Occasionally, I quit temping for a day to attend a conference in the hope of meeting people I knew. But they'd be carrying a little stack of resumes as well. The guys in suits were "consulting" and looking for any way back into the business. The guys in business casual were afraid of layoffs and looking to move somewhere more secure.

One day, on my way home from a particularly humiliating PowerPoint assignment, I ran into one of the guys from my former trading desk coming out of a sushi joint.

"Dave Ackerman!" Henry Wilson exclaimed, pumping my arm as if I were back from the dead. "What are you doing these days? Are you okay?"

"I'm all right, thanks," I said. "I can't trade any more, but I'm picking up a consulting job here and there."

He nodded, then looked at my jeans and sneakers and the backpack slung over my shoulder. I might as well have said: "I'm living in a Bowery flophouse, drinking a lot of Dago Red."

"How are Ray and the rest of the guys?" I asked. "I hear you're still in Exchange Place."

"They are, but I left in January," he said. "I'm at Goldman now."

"Congratulations!"

What I really wanted to say was: "Goldman? You don't deserve to be at Goldman. We're in the midst of a Wall Street bloodbath! Talented traders are getting fired left and right. And you get a job at Goldman Fucking Sachs?"

"You heard about Steve, didn't you?" asked Henry, fear darkening his eyes.

"No," I said slowly. "Bad news?"

He glanced up and down Broadway a couple times. "Steve died in February, a few weeks after I left."

"Of what?"

"AIDS."

"AIDS?" I repeated in disbelief, lurching backwards a step. "AIDS?"

We both stared at his bag of sushi, as if we were considering eating it right there on the street.

"It wasn't some weird blood transfusion mistake, was it?" I asked.

"No, I guess Steve was gay. He kept it pretty well hidden from all of us."

Steve? Steve Carey, the Army brat who argued, quite convincingly, that a great-looking ass was rarer than a great set of tits? Steve, who gave us detailed reports about his long-term relationship with a sexy marketing rep from Ann Taylor?

"He didn't look like he was sick," I said after a while.

There was not much more to say. We exchanged e-mail addresses and went our separate ways.

Chris and I were going to meet at her apartment that night and then go out to dinner with one of her college roommates. I decided to walk uptown to clear my head. I was having a hard time recasting Steve as gay. I knew gay guys who made partner at major New York law firms. I knew gay MBA types in high positions at Fortune 500 corporations. Then I racked my brain trying to think of one person on any of the trading floors I'd known who was gay.

I couldn't.

Granted, Wall Street trading floors were one of the last bastions of macho. But it was 2002, for God's sake! Were all these gay traders still in the closet?

As I walked uptown, I chanted some Army calling cadences Steve taught us one Friday evening in a bar:

I don't know but I've been told,
Army wings are made of gold.
I don't know, but it's been said,
Air Force wings are made of lead.

If I die in the combat zone,
Box me up and send me home.
Pin my medals on my chest,
Tell my Mom I've done my best.

Chris was on the phone when I got to her apartment, arguing with Brian, her editor in L.A., about their favorite topic: money.

"You're going to have to come up with something better than that," she said. "L.A. is a very expensive town."

I decided the conversation was going to last for a while, so I started rummaging around in her refrigerator for a beer.

"I can't do it for that," she said. "We're going to have to start talking 40 pretty soon."

I threw her a quizzical look, which she waved off.

"Okay." She shot a victorious fist high in the air. "Then it's 40. I'm okay with that. Are you?"

Brian appeared to be okay with that.

"Great. We'll talk tomorrow. My boyfriend just walked in."

She grabbed the beer from my hand, and took a long chug. "Shake hands with the new second-string film critic for the L.A. Reader," she said, and proudly held out her hand.

"Second-string film critic... in L.A.?" I asked, my voice cracking.

"No, in Akron. Of course it's in L.A., you wanker. I'm finally legit. Aren't you going to congratulate me?"

Chapter 4

Things got colder just about the time they started peeling the missing-person posters off the phone booths. Every morning, as I joined the line of bundled tourists walking down Broadway, I brooded over what had happened to my life. One night I dreamed I was trying to type with amputated hands. I knew I would never trade securities again, but I wanted a job that made some use, however remote, of the skills I had mastered.

In March, an acquaintance told me about a Mr. Edward Lewis, who worked at an investment bank and needed a trader to help out with an auditing project. I didn't expect much. I'd been on a half dozen interviews with auditors, most of whom were housed deep in the windowless depths of bank back offices. Wall Street had reams of securities to process, and they were usually eager to hire anybody with a trading background. Inevitably, however, their interest evaporated when Human Resources dug into my background.

This time, it was different.

Mr. Lewis' investment bank was the first to move back into its headquarters at the World Financial Center. To get there, I navigated a rat maze of concrete barriers that ended abruptly at the glass and steel entrance. Then I went through a time warp. The spotless, dustless lobby, the gleaming escalators were just as they were. What once seemed like '90s excess became a poignant artifact from another time. The place had a Saturday feel to it; no cross-traffic from the other buildings, no shops, no tourists coming to ogle the palm trees in the Winter Garden, which had been crushed by Tower debris. The little harbor that once held sailboats teemed with dumpsters and backhoes, and the entrance to the other buildings was cut off by police sawhorses and yellow tape.

But the overpriced Japanese restaurant was open and ending what appeared to be a successful lunchtime rush. I saw the familiar Japanese grandma stacking menus by the entrance.

"Hi." I touched her arm to make sure she was real. "It's good to see you."

"Good to see you, too," she said and rushed off to the kitchen.

The visitor's entrance area bustled with people. "Mr. Lewis is on 57," the receptionist said, zapping the back of my driver's license with a bar code scanner. "Please wait for your escort."

A baby-faced black kid in an oversized uniform got up from a bench filled with a dozen other security guards.

"First time I've been escorted like this," I said as we waited for the elevator. "They usually just give you a tag and let you go up."

"It's a new thing," he said. "I got hired last week."

"I'm looking for a job myself. Wish me luck."

He glanced at my suit and briefcase and shrugged. "It's all fucked up," he said.

Lewis' office was just off an elegant little waiting room near the middle of a long, wide corridor that stretched the length of the building. At one end was the CEO's office; at the other was the boardroom. The place was decorated in what I call Edwardian skyscraper — expensive reproduction furniture fitted with computer terminals, hardwood floors, oriental rugs — anything to distinguish it from the bland corporate look of the rest of the bank.

The sign on Mr. Lewis' door identified him as corporation counsel, which made him some rarefied species of lawyer. He turned out to be a tall, gruff guy in his 40s seated at one end of a round glass-topped conference table covered with smudge marks. The shelves beside him displayed the usual collection of Lucite deal plaques and a photo of a 10-year-old in a judo outfit you wouldn't want to meet in a dark alley. All of the offices on that side of the building had views of both the Trade Center and the Statue of Liberty, but he had pulled his easternmost blinds to shut out Ground Zero.

He flipped through my resume. "Why did you leave your job as a trader?" That was always the first question. There were several ways to answer. The truth would get me nowhere.

"Lifestyle," I said. "After September 11, I decided I didn't want to live that life anymore. I'd saved up some money and decided to do something less stressful."

"Every job is stressful," he said. "Answering the phone is stressful."

I shrugged. "That's true."

"How old are you?"

"Thirty-one," I said.

"Have you ever committed a crime?"

"No," I said.

"Have you ever worked on an auditing project?"

"No, this would be my first."

He slipped my resume into a file and let out a sigh that filled the room. "We need an experienced options trader to take a look at our derivatives desk," he said. "There were all sorts of holes in our control systems when we moved to our backup site. We fixed some of them, but we found a lot more when we moved back here. We discovered what may turn out to be serious fraud, but we need some technical help to make sure we have a case. You would be hired for a month to help the auditor examine the books. When the whole thing is over, you'd go away and keep your mouth shut about what you found. That's the basic idea."

He paused and absentmindedly massaged his bony wrists, as if he had a bad case of carpal tunnel. When the silence became uncomfortable he asked: "Don't you have any questions?"

"Quite a few, in fact," I said, fidgeting as I tried to decode his comments. "What kind of fraud are we talking about?"

"I'm not exactly sure. Someone seems to be taking money out of some trades. The auditor found a lot of material, but I'm hesitant to jump to conclusions."

I found the whole thing a little disturbing. Some key component was missing. "If this is an auditing matter, why am I dealing with you?" I asked. "What do you do around here?"

"I'm the bank's corporation counsel," he said, lifting his chin proudly. "One of my duties is to act as the bank's liaison with the board of directors. One of the directors felt strongly that the derivatives group needed a special investigation and I'm acting on his suggestion."

"Can you tell me who this director is? Are we going to meet with him?"

"No," he said firmly, then softened a bit, tossing me a grim smile. "All that's irrelevant to your duties. You report to me and I forward the report to him."

Something was wrong with all this, but I couldn't nail it down. A derivatives desk at an investment bank would be a huge money maker, as well as a huge source of potential losses. At least two levels of people would be watching it: a group of risk managers who examined the trades and profits, and a team of auditors who would perform a series of spot checks at regular intervals. They would have no need for a lowly former trader to triple-check their efforts.

"I don't really understand why you'd want to hire me," I said. "You must have a fine collection of auditors and risk managers somewhere in this building."

"I don't really understand why I'd want to hire you, either," he said. "You've just lied to me about your past. How am I supposed to trust anything you say?"

I didn't quite know how to respond, so I shut up.

"What's the truth, Dave?" he asked, warming up to his job as inquisitor. "Why did you leave your last job?"

Miss Liberty was looking a little forlorn all the way out there in the river. As if holding up the lamp was not a job she particularly liked.

"I was fired," I said finally. "Last November, I sold some S&P puts which lost a lot of money. I made a stupid mistake. I blew out and now I'm here."

"You didn't just blow out," he said, smiling broadly. "You committed securities fraud."

The phrase made me wince. "Well, yes, that's true. I dumped some losing trades into a client portfolio. It was a momentary indiscretion."

"It cost your firm $112 million."

"The trade would have made money if they'd held onto the damn thing!" I regretted the comment instantly.

He picked up one of his Lucite deal plaques and studied it, as if drawing pleasure from the memory of the transaction. "If they hadn't hired you in the first place," he said, "their losses would have been zero."

Then I realized why Miss Liberty was bothering me. If she was supposed to welcome new immigrants to New York, why was she facing Wall Street?

He reopened the resume folder with a grimace meant to indicate some kind of disgust. "I'm not going to hire you because I think you're honest," he said, handing me a piece of paper. "I think it takes a crook to catch a crook."

He handed me an employment agreement. LVS Consulting would pay me $5,000 for one month as a technical consultant on various projects to be determined.

"Who's LVS Consulting?" I asked.

"They do a lot of work for the bank," he said. "I'm protecting myself in case you screw up."

"This contract says $5,000 for a month's work." I folded my arms across my chest. "That's not enough. How about $10,000?"

"How about $5,000?" he countered.

"What about a compromise? $7,500?"

He plucked the contract from my hand, and held it over the trash can. "How about no job?"

"$5,000 is okay," I said.

He slid it back across the desk. I signed because I couldn't see any reason not to. We both smiled politely at exactly the same moment.

"Now there's one thing I want you to understand," he said. "As far as the other traders are concerned, you're just another guy from auditing."

"I'm just some math geek who knows a little about options."

"Right." Lewis stood, indicating the meeting was over. He crossed to the window and peeked through the slats at the adjacent building, where I used to work. "Our tower was in pretty good shape. That's why we could move back as soon as we did. But your firm had fire damage. Everybody says they're not coming back."

"Why would they?" I said. "Exchange Place has great restaurants, theater, nightlife. Everything you'd want in a city."

Lewis was not in the mood for witty banter. "I'll take you down to meet the auditor," he said. "I wouldn't go into much detail about your last job. Auditors don't like to work with felons."

The trip from the executive floor on 57 to the auditing group on four was a dramatic plunge down the corporate pyramid. The area immediately off the elevator was under construction. The long rows of displaced desks had been stacked in a corner, but little notches in the linoleum remained where the legs had rested, and thick coils of computer and telephone wiring covered the floor like weeds. Lewis led me through a cheerless upscale cube farm. The auditor denizens manned their terminals, desks littered with computer printouts and spreadsheets. He found the right cubicle and knocked on the chest-high partition as if it were a door.

She was small and very thin, and pretty enough, but the most remarkable thing about her was her hair, which moved and swung as if alive. The lush dark mane fell almost to her waist, gleaming like a shampoo commercial under the fluorescent fixtures. I stared at it open-mouthed for a moment before I caught myself.

She was introduced as Susanna Cassuto, which sounded Italian but could also be Sephardic Jewish. Obviously she had experienced the hair stare before, because she quickly slid some of the silky stuff from her shoulder to her back with a quick flick of her fingers.

"I found you a trader," Lewis said, smirking at the dumbfounded expression on my face. "Dave here is going to find out what the hell's happening on that desk."

"Thank God," she said with an exaggerated sigh of relief. "I can figure out the interest-rate swaps and the futures, but options are a lot trickier. With the asymmetric returns and all that." The accent was New Jersey bleached through the Ivy League and delivered at blistering speed. She was way too skinny for my taste, and wore too much eye shadow, but those things could grow on you pretty fast.

She handed me a business card from her leather Filofax like a good little bureaucrat. Two of her neighbors tried to catch a peek at what was going on in our cubicle: One guy rolled his chair back as if to retrieve something from his file cabinet; another just popped his head over the partition like a prairie dog. I flashed them both a stupid grin. Back to work, chumps.

"I'm sorry I don't have a business card to give you," I said. "I don't even have a desk.

I was hired five minutes ago."

"Dave was an options trader at a major investment bank for about 9 years," said Lewis.

"That's interesting," she said, nodding to indicate she was impressed. "Why did you stop trading?"

"It's a long story," I said.

"He wanted a change of pace," Lewis said, before I had a chance to continue. "Dave has an MBA from Columbia and undergraduate math degree from Stanford."

"Dartmouth," I corrected.

"That's what I did," she said. "A math B.A., then an MBA. I passed the CPA exam when I was a junior."

"When did you get your MBA?" I asked. In a bar it would be tantamount to asking a woman how old she was, but in this context it had the guise of helping establish her expertise.

"Last June," she said. "I've been with the bank nine months."

That made her 24 or 25 by my calculations.

"I suppose I have no intellectual authority whatsoever now," she added with a coy smile.

That did it. I was gone. A woman capable of a snappy comeback had an express lane into my heart.

"I didn't mean that at all," I said, backpedaling furiously.

"Susanna is the rising star of the audit group," said Lewis. "That's why she's working on this project. The two of you are going to be working in an office on another floor. I'll take you up there in a minute."

I looked at the open Filofax on her desk. She had a big 5x7 photo of what I figured was her boyfriend in one of the plastic pockets you'd use to keep a calculator or a floppy disk. A handsome sonofabitch atop a mountain bike. A picture like that advertised some kind of serious commitment.

I tried to pull out the knife lodged in my heart. Five-one on tiptoes, a dressy dark suit, skinny legs in black tights, manicured fingers with no nail polish. The whole package might add up to 95 pounds, hair and all.

My college roommate once accused me of falling only for what he called "artsy chicks with big tits." Here was a scrawny thing who knew she wanted to be an accountant when she was still a teenager, who enjoyed going overboard on clothes and makeup, and who spent a lot of time taking care of her hair.

But she was also smart enough to pass the CPA test while her cohorts were taking Accounting 201, and she wasn't ashamed to let everyone know it.

Unattainable, but I could live with that. Everybody falls in love on the job. I knew what that particular masochistic pleasure was all about.

The office Lewis found for us was in Trading Operations on 17, directly below the bank's big trading floor. The place had the feel of a boiler room on a ship. Many of the ceiling tiles had been removed, revealing a multicolored jumble of wires and cables that connected the computer systems to the trading floor upstairs.

There was a sense of controlled panic in the air. I could see the legs of a few guys on ladders scattered throughout the floor, fiddling with the wiring overhead. Two of them shouted back and forth, trying to find a cable for a router that was on the fritz. Below them, other techies were busy at their workstations or bent over the guts of broken computers.

Our office was a conference room with a window facing a hallway. A paper sign taped on the door said "Post 9/11 Sun Parallel Support." Somebody had removed whatever was in the room before, installed two PCs and phones on opposite ends of the conference table, and dumped an old laser printer in a corner, stapling the cabling along the walls and across the jamb of the door so it wouldn't close. A dirty whiteboard and big schematic chart on the wall explained how a Sun computer did its thing, and snippets of wire and screws littered the carpet.

"We need to get this place vacuumed," Lewis snorted, tearing down the sign. "I wanted something private, near the trading floor. But they should fix this so you can lock the door when you leave."

He gave us the name of a person in Trading Support who would help us get access to whatever we needed. Then he tapped our new phone number into his Palm Pilot.

"You can ditch the suit," he said as he left, nodding to my blue pin-striped number. "You're a math geek, right?"

I gave him a military salute. "I get the picture."

He closed the door behind him, and we looked around our new digs. The whiteboard on the center of the wall had a single message from its previous life — "Bruce, I'm at lunch."

The room must have served as some kind of tech library. A stack of C++ programming magazines dating back to the mid-'90s lay in a carefully tended row at the edge of the conference room table, bookended by multiple copies of a paperback trading system manual.

Susanna poked the on button of the PC, and it pulled itself reluctantly from its hibernation.

"Let me show you something," she said. She clicked through her network folders to a particular PDF file and sent it to the printer.

One track in my mind was trying to concentrate on the business at hand, while a second track was soaking up all the details I needed to fuel my freshly-minted crush: The way she looked in profile, how she held her curved fingers over the keyboard, how she brushed the hair out of her eyes when she was distracted, her perfect posture.

What came out of the printer was a single sheet, a scan of a document that was originally square, perhaps from somebody's notepad. A trading system schematic, describing how a trade was born and what happened to it in the course of its short mercenary life. It was drawn quickly but with a certain flair, using block letters you might find in an architectural blueprint.

The diagram told its story with an arrow and a series of boxes, from left to right: A trade was sold to a client with a certain profit number built into it, indicated by the letter "P." But as the arrow passed through some other unnamed boxes — most likely legal approval, credit approval, trade execution — something happened to it. Instead of "P" at the end, it became "P -5%." And why? A new arrow, drawn with great force, blasted up till it hit the word "FRAUD."

I stared at the thing for a while, even turned it sideways to see if that gave me any insight.

"What is this?" I asked.

"It's a trading system schematic."

"I know that," I said. "But what is it supposed to mean?"

"It's the outline of the fraud we're supposed to find. It's the document that started this investigation."

"You're kidding me."

"That's all they gave me. I don't even know who wrote it."

We stared at the document together in a kind of glum trance, trying to wring whatever meaning we could out of it. When bankers first dream up a trade, they price how much the components would cost and the profit they'd get. Then they sell it to the client, execute the trade, and book those profits. According to this schematic, the fraud occurred while the trade was being completed.

"Here's what I don't understand," she said, pointing to the top of the sheet. "This arrow marked FRAUD is pointing outside the trading system. That means the trader is somehow taking the money out of the bank, skimming profits. But he can't physically take the money out. He can't write a bank check to himself. Or to a fake company. He doesn't have that authority."

The problem was irritating her. She stood up and began pacing.

"He doesn't have to steal money," I said, after thinking it through. "He can steal information. He can tell his partner, outside the bank, about a trade the bank's about to do, and somehow his partner makes money out of it."

She nodded quickly. "So the bank needs some components to do the trade. And his partner bids up the prices so the bank has to pay more?"

God, she was fast.

"That's one way to do it. You've got the idea." My crush descended into a robust sexual fantasy, with the usual bouncing-breasts scenario altering into one involving hair. She was sitting on top of me with her head down, dragging her hair sideways across my chest, back and forth, like a bridal train.

"It's like a baker making a cake," she said. "If the prices of the flour and sugar go up, he can't make as much money."

I wanted to unbutton her blouse and get the whole thing over right then and there. She smiled, proud of her analogy, and proud that she had put the pieces together so quickly.

I walked around to the other side of the table and sat down. I had to put some physical distance between us to clear my head.

"This is going to be a hell of a thing to research," I said. "Are you sure this is all we've got?"

"All Ed told me was that a bank director had gotten wind of the fraud and called for an investigation."

"And that bank director wrote this document?"

"Presumably," she said. "I don't really know."

"But we can't talk to him about it."

"No."

She looked up at me and tossed a skinny palm in the air, as if to say: This is all we've got. Let's make the best of it.

I started firing questions at her to get my bearings. How many traders were on the derivatives desk? What type of trades did they do? She produced a list of the firm's four dozen derivatives traders from a manila file and a sleek silver pen from her purse. I looked over her shoulder as we went through the list, crossing off names.

I was looking for a trader in a market that could be easily manipulated. You couldn't play tricks with prices in the Treasury market, a raucous arena where thousands of traders competed to make a few cents more than the other guy. Or currencies or interest-rate swaps, for that matter. You had to go someplace quiet. Some nice, obscure, thinly traded market, where a few people wandered in periodically, sniffed the merchandise and went on their way.

The chances of finding the bad trades seemed quixotic, bordering on hopeless, but

I didn't tell her. If the diagram was right, one of the bank's 50-odd traders had found a way to skim money from the bank by ruining the profitability of a trade, or a series of trades. The desk did thousands of trades a week. How were you going to find the needle in that haystack?

But we dutifully filtered the list down to eight prospects and made a trip to the Pepsi machine, where we came up with a strategy and a scope of work. We would divide the world in two, based on our skills. To Susanna Cassuto went the material world of contracts, the requisitioning of files from the bank's document storage warehouses in Hell's Kitchen and Queens, and the analysis of the letters and contracts in those files. To David Ackerman went the ethereal world of models, the copying of spreadsheets from the dozens of network drives scattered about the derivatives desk, and the analysis of the models buried deep in those spreadsheets. Did any of these guys look like they were playing tricks with their numbers?

I quickly developed a work rhythm — pulling up spreadsheets, giving them a quick check, and marking those that required further study. Across the conference table, Susanna was lost in her own hunt through the contracts. We worked quietly. The phones were silent, and the air conditioner vent, positioned directly above me, directed cold air down my shirt collar and my back with relentless efficiency. Occasionally, Susanna would say, "Here, look at this," and throw me the printout of a deal. I would take a quick look and toss it into one of two piles: clean or potentially dirty.

By 4 p.m., we had narrowed the field to two suspects.

Stuart Lister was the firm's emerging market options trader, and that alone should have made me suspicious. Emerging markets was Wall Street's label for countries that ranked in the economic nether regions between Third World basket case and industrial superpower. Countries like Brazil, Argentina and Thailand all needed to borrow money from international investors, but they had to pay up for it — often at rates of 20 or 30 percent or more. One of the big games of the '90s was investing in this high-yield debt, hoping the countries wouldn't default. When Russia did just that in 1998, the market collapsed virtually overnight.

But even before the crash, it was an area that was rife with backroom shenanigans. There were rumors of bribes to government officials, market squeezes, even mafia money laundered through off-shore subsidiaries.

Tim Scott, our second suspect, also operated in his own little world, in this case equity options on individual stocks. If investors liked a particular sector — energy, software or whatever — they'd buy baskets of options of the individual companies within that sector. It was a lucrative business, but you had to be a sharp trader to buy all the right options at once without getting ripped off.

Most of the options he dealt with were short-dated and allowed him to bet on the price of a company's stock price a few weeks or months from now. But some were long-dated bets on what the price would be two or three years in advance. There was a big market for the short-dated options, but the farther out you went, the thinner the demand. There were only a handful of traders interested in betting on the fortunes of a particular company two or three years from now. As a result, the prices could be manipulated more easily.

As our work was winding down, Susanna made a call to her friend Gigi and had an extended discussion about which trendy seafood restaurant Gigi should go to with her husband that night. They were both food snobs, and actually pulled up menus on some Web site before deciding on The Ocean Club and the lemon sole in puff pastry.

Meanwhile, I made a couple more desultory calls to realtors. The lease on my two-bedroom was ending, and in spite of the much-discussed downturn in the real estate market after September 11, all I could find was the usual collection of tenements with sky-high deposits.

"Would you take a sublet in Battery Park City?" she asked, after hearing me hang up in disgust on my third realtor.

"Anything in Manhattan with a bathroom," I said. "I'm not picky."

"There's a woman in my building who's being sent to Singapore for six months. She was going to let her studio sit empty because she couldn't find a subletter."

Before September, I had scorned the idea of living in Battery Park City, a planned landfill community designed for the convenience of Wall Streeters eager to yo-yo from work to home. Then, after 9/11, the place went from upscale enclave to beleaguered war zone. Windows were broken, wreckage from the site was everywhere, and you had to pass through National Guard checkpoints just to get in.

But Battery Park City was just five minutes from my new job. The views were astounding, as long as you didn't face the Trade Center. Plus I'd fallen hard. I wanted to see Susanna's apartment building, her gym, her mailbox, anything she touched. It was becoming that kind of crush.

"I haven't been there since September," I said. "What's it like these days?"

"Come see for yourself," she said. "Everything's back. Most of the stores are open, but a lot of people have moved out."

She called her friend, who was leaving in a couple days and wanted to meet me that night.

This was all promising, in a friendly sort of way. We walked south to Battery Park City along the edge of the West Side Highway, which sliced between the abandoned World Financial towers and the World Trade rubble. The last fires had been extinguished over the winter, but the pile still emitted the faint burned plastic smell I'd never be able to forget.

I gave her a creatively edited version of my resume along the way. At the corner of Albany Street, we passed a couple of National Guardsmen drinking coffee, but otherwise, the neighborhood seemed to be coming back to normal.

"I don't really understand why the corporation counsel is making such a big fuss about this," I said. "We're talking about a trading loss, not robbing a bank. It's a minor offense."

She stopped again and took her bag off of her shoulder, then looked down at the brass clasp as if it were the most interesting thing in the world. I had clearly said something wrong.

"What do you mean 'minor offense?' " she said, raising her voice. "Defrauding the bank is not a 'minor offense.' It's wire fraud, a federal felony. And grand larceny in state court."

I had stumbled onto a deep reservoir of auditor rage, a window into her secret soul.

"I'm not suggesting it wouldn't be a serious crime," I said.

"If some guy off the street robs a bank with a gun and steals half a million dollars, they'd put him in jail for 10 or 20 years," she said, her eyes on fire. "But if a trader steals half a million from an investment bank, they let him walk. That's not right. If you commit securities fraud, you should do the time."

Suddenly, we were a glamorous young couple stopping in the middle of the sidewalk to have a fight. Perhaps it was over money, or over our relationship, but it must have looked like a doozy to the people passing by.

"Those prisons are not country clubs," she snapped. "You sleep in bunks twenty to a room. You have eight hours of work detail, which can be pretty rough. Two months ago, the guy in one of my fraud cases was convicted and sent to the minimum security federal prison in Allenwood, Pennsylvania. I called up the warden and got him assigned to a detail in the maximum security prison a mile away." She smiled at her accomplishment.

"You put him inside a maximum security prison?"

"He was doing some bookkeeping, but he was there 8 to 5." She smiled even more broadly. "It made me feel great."

People scurried past us into the drugstore next door. She showed no eagerness to leave. I guessed that she didn't want to end the discussion with her new co-worker on a bad note.

"So is this going to be your new career? Auditing derivatives deals?" she asked.

"I don't know," I said. "But it's not a bad way to keep myself busy while I'm figuring what else to do."

"There's a lot of consulting work in forensic accounting if you pursued it. Most auditing people don't understand trading well enough to catch a real crook at work."

"It takes a crook to catch a crook," I said, under my breath, just quietly enough so she didn't hear.

Susanna's high-rise was built directly near the Battery Park esplanade, a long walkway along the Hudson at the southern tip of Manhattan. The supermarket, dry cleaners and restaurants that catered to the upscale Wall Street residents were all open for business. As we walked along the esplanade, we passed a stream of joggers going for their evening run, some of them with dogs in tow. The apartment buildings blocked the view east and the place managed to retain a clinical cleanliness that had nothing to do with the rest of retail New York. Homeless people had never set up shop here, and I expected they never would.

Susanna's friend Abigail on the 22nd floor turned out to be a mousy, pleasant-enough banker with a high voice who was overjoyed at the prospect of making a little money on a sublet. Her apartment was a large studio with a nice-sized living room, overlooking the Hudson. The decorating scheme was strictly Martha Stewart-by-numbers, but I liked it: white medical cabinets used as bookcases, ivory carpeting, a huge overstuffed couch in the center of the living room beside a nubbly flowering cactus plant. The only view of the WTC was from the bathroom window.

Her prize possession was a 40-gallon saltwater aquarium stocked with a couple thousand dollars' worth of exotic fish. I had funded my own aquarium in high school, and talked fish with her for a few minutes to reassure her about my maintenance skills. She had planned to leave them with a service for six months, but if I'd take care of them she'd lease me the apartment for half price. She was flying to Singapore Wednesday morning. Could I move in Wednesday night?

I told her it was a deal.

On the way to the elevator, Susanna asked if I wanted to see her place. I shrugged as if to say, "Sure, why not?"

She had a one-bedroom version of her friend's studio, on the same building line but six stories higher. She had the same view, but she eagerly showed me how you could catch a glimpse of Miss Liberty if you looked between a couple of neighboring buildings.

I was busy scouring the room for evidence of male habitation. Anything would do: another photo of Bicycle Boy, two tennis racquets nuzzling in a closet, a six-pack of beer, a 12-pack of condoms. It was clearly a single woman's apartment, upscale but not ostentatious, with yards of pricey off-white carpeting, a glass dining room table for two, and, marooned near the window, a white love seat placed to encourage the quiet contemplation of New Jersey.

A sculpted teak bookcase on one wall held a collection of vases, paperbacks and minimalist electronic components at well placed intervals.

"Can I get you anything to drink?" she asked.

"A beer would be great," I said.

"In spite of everything that happened, it's still really nice living here," she said from the kitchen. "There's a supermarket downstairs and a half dozen restaurants within three blocks. And not having to take the subway will add an extra hour to your day."

"The place seems to be recovering pretty nicely," I shouted, to make sure she heard me. "I like the promenade and living on the river, and the newness of the place. The only thing that bugs me is that everybody works on Wall Street."

"That's true," she said. "But it's very international. I know people from France, South Africa, Korea, you name it."

She emerged with a glass and a bottle of beer, one of those microbrews named after a large forest animal — the kind that a guy would buy.

"Everybody here has moved from someplace else, so they're very open and eager to make new friends. The sports club is the place where you really meet people. They just dropped their prices. I think it's only $1,800 a year now."

Sure, I smiled. Maybe I can sell some blood.

"Where do you live now?" she asked.

"On the Upper West Side, with all the other yups."

"I used to have a place on 92nd street," she said. "My three older brothers live up there. I lived with my brother's family for a while after September 11."

"Why did you move down here?" I asked. "A lot of people decided to leave Battery Park City for good."

"I love it here. When I lived on 92nd Street I kept running into my brothers all the time. They would tell my parents what I was doing, who I was going out with. Down here, nobody's looking over my shoulder. I can do whatever I want."

I took my new set of keys out of my pocket and stared at them with genuine pleasure. "I think living here is going to be okay."

"Are you really going to move in this Wednesday?"

"Sure, a few things. Why not?"

"Don't you have a lot of stuff to move?"

"It's my old life," I said. "My apartment is full of ugly furniture and exercise equipment. I'm sick of it all."

My eyes gravitated to a corner of the bookshelf that held a jewel-encrusted silver menorah, a cobalt blue Passover Seder plate and a fired clay tile with some words in Hebrew.

"Did you spend a summer in Israel?" I asked.

"Three years ago. I speak Hebrew pretty well. How about you?"

"A phrase or two. *Hava Nagila*, that kind of thing."

She laughed. "Do you know what *Hava Nagila* actually means?"

"All I know is that it's a song."

"It means, 'Let's have a party.' But it's very old-fashioned."

"What would they say now?"

"I don't know. Maybe *lanu atsmaut*, which means 'Let's celebrate.' "

"How would you say, 'Let's get down and get funky?' "

She smiled and lit into some Hebrew slang. "It's the kind of thing soldiers would say in a nightclub on a Friday night."

I smiled. An auditor who knew how to let down her hair.

"Sounds like fun," I said.

"So why are you so eager to start a new life?" she said, eager to change the subject. "What was wrong with your old life?"

I blew out a lungful of air, as if to exhale the last remnants of the trading floor from my lungs.

"I loved options trading, but the daily pressure was grinding me down. Particularly after the bank moved to Exchange Place. After a certain point, enough was enough. One morning I was a big-shot equity options trader. By 3 p.m. I was gone."

That, of course, only whet her appetite for more. What was my biggest success? My biggest loss? Did I have a particular trading style?

I constructed a plausible version of my own life — an iconoclastic, burnt-out trader who had suffered minor psychological wounds from his experience and was looking for a simpler way to live. I regaled her with war stories about my narrow escape from the Thai bhat crisis, my wild ride in Yahoo options in '97, my savvy handling of the Russian debt fallout in the summer of '98. After a while, I was beginning to feel genuinely battle-weary.

Then she asked about my family and I told her a few basics: my upscale childhood in suburban Chicago, my father's law practice, my older sister and her drug-induced crop of triplets.

"You look like you played college football," she said.

"That's what everybody says. But I'm just a math geek who did a little high school wrestling."

"Wrestling?" A smile crossed her face, but I couldn't tell whether she was impressed or amused.

"It's not like the kind on TV," I added quickly. "That's professional wrestling."

"I know the difference. My cousin did it in high school. He was always trying to drop to a lower weight class. Were you varsity?"

"I was captain of the team. We won the regionals my senior year and went downstate."

"Did you do it in college?"

"Nah. It takes too much time. I played basketball in my dorm league, stuff like that. What about you?"

"I went to a private high school where sports weren't very important. But I ran in the Marathon last year."

"Where's your Trek Pilot?" I asked.

"I keep it in the bike room downstairs. How did you know I had a bike?"

"I saw the picture on your Filofax," I said. "I used to have the same bike but I sold it."

She didn't blush, but her eyes dropped to the carpet and searched around for something interesting to look at. "It's an old picture," she said. "We're just friends now."

I managed to fend off a cynical smirk. *Really? It's all over? You just forgot to remove it?*

"Where did you grow up?" I asked.

"Over there," she said, tossing her head towards northern New Jersey, with the faintest hint of derision.

"What town?"

"Ridgewood. My dad is a CPA. He has an office at One Penn Plaza. My three brothers work with him in the same firm."

"So if you joined the firm, they could call it Cassuto, Cassuto, Cassuto, Cassuto and Cassuto."

"They talked about that many times when I was growing up."

"You know there's a joke..."

"I've heard that joke many times," she interrupted, a bit irritated. "I didn't want to go into the family business. I like being an auditor."

"You went to a private girl's school?"

"Yeah."

"Which one? I knew somebody that went to one in Short Hills."

"No. That was Catholic. You've never heard of this one, believe me."

"Isn't there one in South Orange?"

"You're not even close."

For some reason, that was a big conversation stopper. I thanked her for the apartment recommendation and the beer and made my exit.

In the elevator down, I tried to knit the new things I had learned about Susanna's personal life into a recognizable pattern, a cliché I could get my hands around. She had conventional tastes in expensive clothes and restaurants, which appeared to be funded by a combination of family wealth and her own paycheck, but she was also something of a rebel. She refused to join the family accounting practice in the face of obvious pressure, and she clearly relished the beat-cop functions of corporate auditing.

Plus she was definitely a party girl. No question. Not the downtown, leather-jacket kind, but the rich, Jewish, designer-handbag kind, who knew how to stay out late with Israeli soldiers and didn't like her protective brothers watching who she went home with.

Did I know anybody like that?

The closest I could come up with was Robin Meredith, a pal of a former girlfriend. By day, she was on the partner track at a prominent entertainment law firm. By night, she went off to meet her rich friends at the trendy restaurant of the moment, usually in couples. She flipped boyfriends every six months, eventually marrying into immense wealth. Robin wasn't quite as pretty as Susanna, but when she was deep into her second glass of wine, she could quote lyrics at length from forgotten Cole Porter musicals.

Was Susanna Cassuto a Robin Meredith with better hair?

Then, just to drive myself nuts, I imagined Susanna on the loveseat, minus today's dark pantsuit and almost everything else, her arms outstretched in a drunken post-coital reverie. I tried to turn this still life fantasy into a pornographic short by having the camera circle around her and move in. But the shot was ruined by a man's dirt bike that suddenly appeared parked by the love seat, its kick stand denting the carpet.

It was a long walk to the subway. As I passed the point on the sidewalk where we'd had our little fight about trading fraud, I stood frozen, stricken by a brilliant moment of clarity. Until then, I had been thinking of myself as a good person who had committed an unfortunate but momentary indiscretion and had been punished with undue severity. But in her eyes, and in the eyes of Wall Street, anybody that stepped over the line, even once, was a criminal forever. I could never be fully trusted.

By the same token, however, I'd been thrown a lifeline. I might never be able to trade again, but if I could hold onto this auditing job, and perform it well, I could build another career, make some money, raise a family, have a normal life. I had to make this job work.

Chapter 5

A thunderstorm broke when I was on my way to work, and I arrived a sodden mess of wet newspapers and soggy sneakers. Susanna came in a few minutes later in full rain battle gear: an adult version of a kid's classic yellow slicker, complete with big latch buttons, L.L. Bean boots tied halfway up in a smart bow, and a full-length umbrella with a black and yellow mallard duck carved on the handle. The interior outfit of the day was a wintry gray wool bolero jacket with matching skirt, and flats that appeared out of her purse.

She would have been perfectly groomed if the rain hadn't done a number on her hair. Rebel strands of frizz were shooting out here and there, and she headed straight to the bathroom for what I imagined as a vicious attack with a styling brush.

The first order of business was a close examination of Susanna's new profitability spreadsheet. A lot of Tim Scott's trades had come up as unprofitable that month, so he deserved some attention. There were four other traders who also dabbled in the same market, but Tim appeared to be the default guy for the longer-term trades that were the most susceptible to manipulation.

I had serious doubts about this line of attack. The markets for long-term options were dicey when you went out past two years. You could put a trade together, pretty sure you'd be able to buy all the pieces at the right price when it was time to pull the trigger. Then at the last minute some other trader in God-knows-where would fancy the same long-term option, and bid up the price. A sweet deal turns out not so sweet. Nothing you can do. It had happened to me a thousand times.

"My gut instinct tells me there's a good explanation for why these trades are unprofitable," I said, flipping through her report.

"That's okay," she said. "There's nothing wrong with rattling Tim's cage a little. And Stu's. That's what auditors do. Let them know we're watching."

I had suspicions about both traders, but my money was on Stu. I dug into his network drive and pulled up the biggest spreadsheet first.

"What the hell is this?" I asked aloud.

"Emerging Market Debt Instruments" was the damnedest thing I'd ever seen, a complete inventory of hundreds of emerging market bonds from more than two dozen countries. The guy had pasted little country flags in the left hand column of each row, and carefully tinted each of the horizontal cells in a slightly different pastel shade, so the thing looked like a color chart in a paint store. In case that didn't drive you nuts, he programmed the most attractive bonds of each country to blink on and off like the lights in a Christmas tree.

"What are you looking at?" Susanna asked.

"Stu Lister's master spreadsheet."

"Oh yeah. *The Artiste.*"

"He's not an artiste. He's a lunatic!"

The programming embroidery pointed to one thing: a trader with too much time on his hands. The whole thing had a certain poignancy. Emerging markets were pretty dead, particularly after September, and I imagined Stu burying himself in an Excel manual for hours at a time while he waited for his market to come back.

The situation was also the perfect setup for a fraud. Stu was operating in an obscure, immature market filled with exotic instruments that had no established price. He was also making a lot less money than he was a couple years before. If you were looking for somebody likely to fiddle with their numbers, you couldn't choose a better candidate.

"I spent two hours on that spreadsheet last week," Susanna said, without looking up from her screen. "It's a standard model."

"Standard, my ass. This thing is colored like a Crayola box."

"He added all the colors himself, but he bought the underlying model from a software vendor. The contact information is in the footnotes."

Bullshit, I thought. This guy's going down.

A few minutes later, she handed me a printout. "Look at this," she said. It was an e-mail with the message header: "22 Anne Street Group." Tim had received it a few weeks before. "We'll be meeting Tuesday and Friday nights, at the request of several people." The sender was bigdick99@hotmail.com.

"Who do you think he is?" I asked.

"If Tim is doing something wrong, maybe this is his accomplice."

A wild conjecture. Doubtful at best.

"All this proves is that he got an e-mail from some group, but we don't know anything about the group or what it does," I said. "Everybody gets personal e-mails at work. It could be something that was perfectly legal."

"Like what?"

"I don't know," I said. "Maybe a poker group."

"Tim may be scamming the bank out of thousands of dollars and he's received an e-mail from an anonymous source. Are you telling me the two couldn't possibly be connected?"

"They may not be," I said.

"So who do you think BigDick99 is?" she asked.

"I don't know," I said. "And neither do you."

"BigDick99 could be Tim's accomplice. Or one of his accomplices. Maybe he's got people feeding him information from other banks. Maybe that's what this meeting is about."

"For all we know, BigDick is a heavyset guy named Richard," I said.

"Sure," she said. "And maybe they're all meeting to wrap toys for the Red Cross."

We were at an impasse. I had more doubts than I was willing to admit, but I kept staking out my claim as a skeptic just to be ornery.

"Today's Tuesday," she said, her eyes lighting up with excitement. "We can go to 22 Anne Street after work and look around."

I shrugged my shoulders. I was happy to accompany her on any kind of post-work jaunt, but her grand survey of expected vs. real profits seemed a lot more promising.

It was an ambitious but tedious project. She had automated some of the drudgery with a series of macros that brought her to the relevant passages in each deal one by one, and would sit there for five or ten minutes at a time, staring and clicking — next, next, next — her face halfway between alertness and boredom. When she found the number she needed, she would squeeze her fist briefly and smile and mumble a particular phrase to herself. I couldn't quite tell what she said, but my best guess was: "I got you, sucker." Then she would write down the number on her printout and go on to the next trade.

At a few points during the day, she received what appeared to be personal e-mails. A couple mouse clicks would be followed by a broad smile. She would read it, nodding as if she were having a personal conversation with the person on screen, and then respond with a blast of furious typing.

Most of the time, though, she was a study in persistence and concentration. It was as if her monitor was a pool of water, and she was trying to stare through it for the truth that lay a few inches below the surface.

The mindlessness of my own tasks left my brain free to pursue its already overactive fantasy life, which was brimming with the new details I had picked up at her apartment the night before.

The general theme was: "Susanna, the party girl." I began embroidering a little romance of her at an Israeli nightclub. She and a girlfriend were sitting across from two Israeli soldiers at a table littered with beer bottles. They were tipsier than the soldiers, and subtly pairing off. Susanna was laughing hysterically at something he said, and kept tapping the instep of his boot with her sandal. It was late. What would happen next? Was she staying at a hotel nearby? Or did she kick out her roommate and bring him back to a skinny little bed in her dorm room?

It was absurd. My own fantasies were making me jealous.

At 12:15, she gathered her things to go out.

"You going to grab lunch downstairs?" I asked.

"I've got to run a few errands," she said, glancing at her watch.

I brought a sandwich back to my desk and did a little snooping into Stu's personnel file on the bank's human resource intranet. He turned out to be a math major like me, but with a slightly different trajectory. Instead of entering Wall Street through business school and the management trainee program, he got his Ph.D. in applied math and then was hired in 1991 as a lowly quantitative analyst.

In those days, banks would hire geeks by the dozen and house them in giant cube farms, adapting equations originally used in rocketry to the options market. The money was good by academic standards, but the more ambitious were always looking for their chance to jump from the "quant" ghetto to the trading floor, where the real money was made.

Stu got his chance when the emerging markets started heating up in 1994. While working on some South American debt models, he must have convinced somebody to give him a shot at trading. A rhesus monkey could have made a killing in those days. Every institutional investor worth his salt had to have a pile of high-yielding Brazilian, Thai and Russian bonds in his portfolio, and the bonds of even the dodgiest, most unstable governments were jumping 30 percent or more. But the market tanked after the Russian default in '98, and now he was the only trader left on the bank's emerging-markets desk.

Susanna returned a half hour later, carrying a paper bag with a lemon yogurt and a banana.

"This guy Stu is getting under my skin," I said, passing the file back across the table. "I'd love to get a look at the little runt before we grill him," I said.

"He's actually kind of tall, but why not? Let's go up to the trading floor. It's right upstairs."

Though she said it casually, I detected a touch of fear. She ate her yogurt quickly and gathered her papers, putting on her bolero jacket as if arming herself for battle.

"Stand up," she said, giving me a long critical head-to-toe look. "You should look more like a quant."

I sucked in my gut as discreetly as I could.

"Take off your tie."

I folded it up and put it on a chair.

She kept looking at me and shaking her head. "That's not enough. Take off your belt."

I rolled it up and put it on the table beside my tie.

Then she pointed a crooked finger at my crotch. "Pull out your... what do you call it? It's not your shirt sleeve. It's the part of your shirt that's in your pants."

"My shirttail?"

"Yeah, pull one side of it out."

I complied. I couldn't see myself in a mirror, but I certainly felt like a big quant in a wrinkled white shirt.

She was quite pleased with my makeover. "Good! Now follow behind me with a legal pad and you'll be fine."

Susanna led me up a narrow stairway and then, with a pause for drama, pushed the bars on a heavy fire door.

It was one of the biggest trading rooms on Wall Street and she was clearly proud of it. Most were built on metal platforms a foot or two off the floor, in order to accommodate the computer wiring underneath, and had a cramped feeling that only intensified the noise and activity. But this trading floor rose two stories high. All that space and light made it feel like a temple to the art of trading, and gave it a nobility it didn't deserve.

I stood in awe, surrounded by the sound of a thousand computers and a thousand phone conversations, broken by the constant chirp of telephones and voices raised in excitement or anger. The room, big as a football field, stretched the entire length of the building — a hundred yards of high-priced real estate that held more computer firepower than many foreign countries.

At first impression, it was a sea of sameness. Long rows of the latest ergonomic chairs faced desks jammed with telephone turrets and crazy stacks of computers and monitors. The close quarters enforced a certain collegiality: Even the biggest big shots sat at desks indistinguishable from their clerks. But, although no lines marked the floor, the trading room had been carefully carved up into a dozen different departments, governed by a dozen different managers. It was impossible to tell one group from another, though a practiced eye could make some guesses based on the quote machines and computers.

I found myself grinning at the whirring confusion of the place. I was back on a trading floor, not as a lowly temp hired to tinker with some trader's spreadsheet, but as a professional, hired to ferret out fraud. Was this the start of my new life?

The derivatives desk was off by itself at the far end of the football field. On the way, we passed the sterling and euro groups, the firm's huge government bond trading desk, a particularly raucous junk-bond group and, finally, U.S. equities.

The far side of the floor was a lot quieter. A six-foot inflatable Statue of Liberty perched on a chair in the middle of an area that spanned five rows of empty seats. Miss Liberty had deflated a bit and her torch arm tilted backwards at the elbow, as if someone had broken it. "That's the Asian currency group," said Susanna. "They got sent to Hong Kong after September. They're not coming back."

"What about those guys?" I gestured to a smaller group of empty seats nearby.

"Mortgage-backed trading. We're doing that from Connecticut now."

I trailed her circumspectly as I approached the analog incarnations of the traders I'd been studying for two days. The derivatives group was in full gear: 12 rows of dress shirts working the phones and the screens. Off in a corner, a few guys had moved their chairs into a semi-circle and were having a Diet Pepsi festival as they bent collectively over a document.

Tim Scott was sitting at his computer, staring at his screen while three other guys looked over his shoulder at something amusing. Blonde hair combed back over his ears, and the eyes of the office troublemaker. He looked up when we got into his line of sight and smiled broadly.

"Ms. Cassuto, we haven't seen you in a few days," giving her an appreciative full-body leer. "You aren't giving us the brush-off, are you?"

"I would never do that, Tim," she said, staring right back. "You guys mean too much to me."

"So what's happening in audit? You've got a wild and crazy crowd down there. You never invite us to your parties."

"Nothing special. Just trying to keep you guys honest."

"Impossible job. I'd give up."

She pointed out Rick Markowitz, the head of the trading desk, who was talking to somebody on his headset. It looked serious. Bad market news? He was a wiry guy with a small waist and a cartoonishly overdeveloped chest. A few years older than me and already at the top of the heap, pulling down three or four million a year, maybe more.

Markowitz caught sight of Susanna and raised two fingers: He wanted to talk, but give him a couple minutes. Then he pointed to his earpiece and turned his right hand into a chattering puppet: a guy who won't shut up.

She nodded at a trader sitting at the desolate end of a row of desks, all by himself. "That's Stu," she said.

As Susanna walked away to talk to Markowitz, I heard tinny disco music coming from a computer speaker. Tim had pulled up a Web site — "British Teens! 18 and Legal!" — where a jerky video showed a flat-chested high-school girl in a red wig doing an amateur bump and grind. The two guys on either side of him smiled.

I didn't think Susanna saw it, but it seemed to be displayed in her honor — a comment on her figure. When I approached Tim's desk and gave a dirty look, he turned flipping the screen back to his spreadsheet as if nothing had happened. I wasn't ready to let it drop, but I had to think through my next move. On his desk: a neat row of trade order slips, some earphones tangled in a vicious knot, and a coffee cup filled with stubby pencils. One of the pencils caught my eye.

"10-13-94?" I asked, picking it out of the cup and reading the date in red marker near the eraser.

"Lucky pencils from my best trades," he said, a little sheepishly. "Can't bear to throw them away."

Susanna returned, but it was clear she had seen something. She gave Tim a sweet smile that was all saccharine. "Have you got a few minutes to talk?"

"Sure," he said, returning his own version of the smile. "Anything special?"

"What about that conference room over there? In a half hour?"

Then we headed toward Stu's desk. He was deep in what was obviously a personal conversation, one hand pressing the telephone headset to his right ear, the other twiddling a blue felt-tipped pen in a way that left little spots on his palms.

He didn't see us as we approached and stood patiently a few feet away. He was a nerd through and through, but the tall gawky kind, and he would take his academic slouch with him to his grave.

"You waiting for me?" he asked, pinching the headset mouthpiece to mute it.

Susanna nodded. He finished his call pronto, and turned to us in what was clearly an attempt at feigned nonchalance.

"I'm sorry to interrupt you," Susanna said in a professional voice I had never heard before. "I don't think we've met. My name is Susanna Cassuto and this is my associate David Ackerman. We're from audit and we are trying to understand the emerging-market books."

"Great," he said with a smile. "When you figure them out, maybe you can tell me what's going on." He looked around, hoping one of his buddies had heard this brilliant witticism, but nobody was within earshot.

"It's all very new to us and a little confusing. We wonder if you could give us a crash course in emerging-market options."

"Okay," he said, "But I'm a little busy right now. I'll give you a call next week."

"Are you sure you can't find any time today?" she asked. "We want to finish this project as soon as we can."

"Sorry," he said and shrugged his shoulders. "I'll try to call you tomorrow afternoon."

Then we turned our attention back to Tim. We returned to our office on the floor below, grabbed some of our files, and set up shop in the glass-walled conference room just off the trading floor. Tim showed up a few minutes late, releasing a whiff of cold air and cigarette smoke.

"You just come from the smokers' garden?" I asked, referring to the grove of concrete-encased evergreens just outside the front entrance.

"I'm sorry, is the smell that obvious?" he asked, with exaggerated embarrassment. "It's a filthy habit."

He took a quick glance at our papers, and draped his suit jacket over a chair with a nonchalance that was meant to indicate his eagerness to help.

He was an attractive guy, 5-11, thin, in his late 30s, with light brown eyes decorated with crow's feet.

"I will say one thing for the smokers' garden," he said. "It's a great social scene. I know one guy who goes down there just to network. I swear he doesn't inhale."

He had the kind of face that would look good in the flattering light of an upscale bar. I knew plenty of guys like him in business school. The fast-living types who traveled in a pack. They smoked and worked out and didn't see a contradiction, drank their lattes with skim milk, and weren't above slipping into a tanning salon booth once in a while to pick up a healthy glow. Now, 10 years later, most of them were either divorced or single and still doing the same thing: spending their bonuses before they got them, going to Atlantic City in spite of the sucker odds, and trolling the Second Avenue bars for Ms. Right Now.

"So what can I do for you guys?" he asked, pressing his palms together as if in prayer. "Are my books in order? Can I teach you something about options trading?"

"Why don't you start by telling us what you and the other traders on the derivatives desk do," said Susanna. She was sitting at her place at the far end of the table, with her papers splayed out in neat piles in front of her.

"Okay. I'm one of four dozen overpaid white yuppies," he said. "We sit around all day watching the screens and being rude to each other. We get a steady stream of client orders to fulfill. Then we're supposed to make money for the bank in our own trading portfolios. But you know all that, don't you?"

"It's helpful to hear it from you," she said. "We get details we might not be aware of. Do you specialize in anything?"

"I'm an equities guy, equity options. There are other guys who specialize in currency derivatives and interest-rate swaps."

"So you place a lot of trades at the New York Mercantile Exchange?" I asked.

It was a stupid question, a trick question. You bought oil options at the New York Merc, not equity options. It made me look completely ignorant, but I felt like playing the fool. Big smart guys like me often get mistaken for the big dumb guys we play in movies and in hockey stadiums. I thought it might relax him a bit: Susanna might give him some trouble, but he didn't have to worry about me.

Tim and Susanna both smiled at my question, and started to answer, but she deferred the lesson to him.

"The New York Mercantile Exchange sells energy contracts," he explained, trying hard not to be patronizing. "You have to go to the Chicago Board Options Exchange or the Chicago Mercantile Exchange to trade equity futures or options. This stuff is very complicated. It's easy to get confused."

I was impressed. He was facing auditors for the first time, but he looked perfectly relaxed. In fact, he had real theatrical talent. I'd written the guy off as a macho jerk, but he was turning out to be quite charming.

"So how are things on the derivatives desk?" she asked. "Are you guys still making money?"

"Yeah, it's okay," he said. "Business isn't anywhere near where it was before September, but I think it's slowly coming back."

He bent his head down a bit, as if he were getting ready to tell us something, but he was searching for the words.

"Can we cut to the chase?" he asked. "I'm sorry about the porn screen. It was way out of line."

Susanna gave him a tiny little nod, enough to agree, but not enough to indicate she accepted his apology.

"Everybody's so goddamn glum these days," he said. "I was just trying to have a little fun. I won't do it again."

"Great," she said, and gave him a smile that was mostly grimace.

"Great," echoed Tim. The tension fell from his face and he began to stand up. "So we're done here?"

"No," she said.

It was one word, but it forced him to sit back down.

"So let's talk about what kind of deals you're doing these days," she said.

"As I explained before, I'm an equity options guy," he said. "I'll do swaps and currency trades if you twist my arm, but I'm only really comfortable with stock options. I do stock indexes, individual companies, short and long dates, you name it. These days, the only thing clients want is equity collars and baskets. Nothing fancy. Or they sell a position and do an equity-index play on the CBOE to keep up their asset allocation."

"And what about your own portfolio?" she asked.

"It's mostly short-term equity-option plays on listed and NASDAQ stocks, volatility plays, things like that. But it was impossible to make any money at our backup trading site, and it hasn't gotten much better since we moved back here."

"Do you ever get involved in the tax deals?" she asked. "Those usually involve equity options."

His eyes narrowed briefly. A sophisticated question he wasn't expecting.

"I don't do much of that stuff," he said, assuming a bored expression and tapping his fingers on the table. "They're not doing so many of those since Enron."

"Any need for long-dated options?" she asked.

"No, not really."

He turned to me briefly. "Stop me if we're using too much jargon."

I threw up my hands. Hey, I was just a big dumb guy. It was all beyond me. But I did have a question.

"Didn't you say earlier that you buy long-term options?" I asked.

"No," he said, turning to me, surprised. "I didn't say that."

"Let's see here," I said looking down at my notes. "*Stock indexes, individual companies, short and long dates, you name it*. So if you do all dates, you presumably do options that go out two or three years."

His eyes narrowed once more.

"That's right," he said. "Once in a while I buy long-term options, mostly for my own trading account. They don't cost a lot, so there's not much risk. It's like playing the quarter machines in Vegas. Long-term equity options are dirt cheap, and once in a while I get lucky."

A reasonable question. And a reasonable answer. But I was no longer quite as dumb as I first appeared.

"Okay, since you're an equity guy, let's talk about equity basket trades," I said, turning back to my notes. "A lot of your trades have turned out to be much less profitable than expected."

"What you do mean less profitable? Less profitable than what?"

"Less profitable than predicted."

He tried to focus on me, but his eyes kept jumping back to Susanna, who had started writing notes furiously in her steno pad.

"Well, the option markets are pretty crazy now," he said cautiously. "A lot of players have pulled out. The pricing is uncertain, so the profitability is uncertain."

"Uncertainty is when something is profitable one day and unprofitable the next," I said. "But in equity baskets, things are very certain. They're certain to lose money."

"We don't lose money on equity basket trades," he said.

"He's right," Susanna said, playing the objective intermediary and squinting theatrically at her printout. "We make money on equity baskets."

"But not as much as we expect," I said.

"There are plenty of reasons why some of those trades aren't profitable," he said with irritated authority. "What are you suggesting?"

"We're not suggesting anything," Susanna said. "We're just noting that they're not as profitable as they're supposed to be."

"You can project profitability on these trades all day long, but it's only an estimate," he said. "Shit happens. Some floor trader on the Amex smells a big basket order coming through and jumps on it. Or it's some sharp geezer sitting in his condo in Florida. You never know who's on the other side of those trades."

"Look," Susanna said, trying to turn down the temperature. "We're not accusing you of anything. We haven't found anything. But if we do find something fraudulent, it's not going to be good for whoever was doing it. If somebody explains a problem they've been having, or enlightens us in some way, they'd be much better off. It might not be a slap on the wrist, but it would be a hell of a lot better than the alternative."

Then she let the silence hang. We had set out to do what we accomplished.

"I don't know what you two are talking about," he said. "If you want to find out why these trades are unprofitable, discuss it with the guys in risk management. They're breathing down our necks every day about this stuff."

"Maybe we will," Susanna said, standing up to indicate the meeting was over. "I know you're very busy. We appreciate your time. If you want to come by and tell us anything else, we're all ears. We're especially interested in how we can improve the profitability of our equity basket trades."

He walked out the door in a huff. He was about to let the door slam shut, but he caught it just in time.

Susanna's mouth crimped with annoyance as she sat back in her chair.

"He's clean," I said.

She had her arms placed skeptically across her chest, but nodded in agreement.

"I don't mind pulling his chain," I said. "But he's right. We found a few bad trades. Shit happens. I'd be very surprised if he was playing games with us."

Still, you could never be sure.

We returned to our office and went over the data we had each collected, checking for anything we might have missed. A few minutes later, Susanna beckoned me to her side of the room.

She typed in a password and we entered some kind of high security network, where the bank kept the personnel records and archived e-mail files of all of its employees. A few taps later and we were staring at several months of Stu's correspondence.

"We're trying to gather information about Tim and Stu's trading practices," she reminded me. "We're not doing this to snoop into their personal lives."

But snoop we did.

Our troll through Tim's e-mails gave us a high-resolution portrait of a sex- and sports-obsessed trader, pretty close to the cultural mean. In spite of his fondness for online pornography, he seemed to be a very hard-working performer who ranked above the middle of the heap in terms of talent and responsibility. Judging by his extensive 5 p.m. e-mails, he appeared to expend most of his recreational energy meeting his buddies after work and picking up women in bars. If you wanted to believe his Monday morning e-mail boasting, he "got lucky" with some degree of regularity. He also seemed particularly eager to take clients to high-priced sporting events on the bank's tab.

His resume was not terribly revealing. A B.A. from the University of Texas at Austin surprised us because we hadn't noticed any Texas accent, but it was followed by a gold-plated entrance into investment banking via a Stanford MBA. He did boilerplate tours of duty at JP Morgan, Paine Webber and Goldman Sachs, before being hired in 1998. His earnings, at $610,293, were above the middle of the pack, but like everybody else, he had suffered in the great bonus hit of 2001.

Stu was a horse of a different color. He got a vocabulary word-of-the-day, an exercise-you-could-do-at-your-desk-of-the-day, and even a daily brain teaser contest, the winner receiving a $50 gift certificate to mathbooks.com.

Then there was a long series of emails from one Alison DiPiero, who appeared to be his fiancée. I grabbed Susanna's mouse and sorted messages by name, and we spent a few guilty minutes silently clicking through one email after another. We learned pretty quickly that they were moving from their New York apartment to a house in Westchester. Alison's great quest at the time was finding the perfect L-shaped sectional for the raised alcove area of their new living room. Stu, however, seemed to be getting a bit weary of the 7 p.m. appointments at furniture stores. He also hinted, on a number of occasions, that he found the weekend visits to her parents on Long Island a bit too frequent as well.

"The guy's got financial pressures," I said.

"He's moving into a new house with his fiancée," Susanna said, grabbing back the mouse like a schoolmarm closing a biology textbook with drawings of human genitalia.

"That's all we need to know."

That inspired me to figure out just how Stu had managed to transform a bland purchased model into his blinking pointillist masterpiece. I downloaded a trial copy from the software company's Web site, and dug in.

I spent most of the rest of the afternoon poring through an Excel manual, reconstructing Stu's embroidery techniques. Then I went through the entire spreadsheet, line by line, tracking the modifications he had made in the hopes of uncovering the technique he might be using to boost his numbers.

By the end of the day, I knew what I was facing: Two traders and two potential crimes. Both operating in thinly-traded markets. Both of which fit the diagram, more or less. Tim's trades appeared to be less profitable than they should be, but it was hard to tell. They could indicate some kind of trading fraud. They could indicate nothing. Stu's crime was much more plausible. All he had to do was inflate his option valuations a bit to make his portfolio look more profitable than it really was. A common enough trick. But I suspected he was doing it in a grand way.

I could theorize all I wanted, but guessing wasn't good enough. To really nail either of them, I had to analyze the data with real facts and figures. The final proof would require a Monte Carlo simulation. Monte Carlo analysis was one of the most accurate ways to value an option portfolio, but it operated on a very laborious and time-consuming principle. If you threw a stone, you couldn't be sure where it would land. But if you threw millions of stones and saw where they piled up, you'd get an idea of the most likely places. Monte Carlo did the same exercise with an option portfolio, but you needed a very powerful computer to calculate the millions of possible outcomes.

I looked up the number for mainframe administration. My call was answered by a beleaguered techie deep in a sub-basement who sounded like he was just ending a 12-hour shift. Yes, the firm's biggest computer was capable of doing advanced Monte Carlo analysis, but it was only available after 7 p.m., when it had finished digesting all bank's trades on the New York Stock Exchange.

"Then I'll need a 7 p.m. appointment for tonight," I said with as much authority as I could muster.

"Risk management comes in at 7," he said. "Their run lasts until midnight."

"I'm afraid we need that computer tonight for a very urgent project."

"You'll have to wait until the weekend," the voice said. "We've got some free slots then."

"Audit has priority over risk management. They'll have to wait until I'm finished."

Susanna flashed me a thumbs-up sign as encouragement.

"Okay," he said reluctantly, "Come on in at 7 and we'll set you up."

Chapter 6

Twenty-two Anne Street was an old sliver of a tower, wedged between a new office building and another clunker, with a Thai restaurant at ground level. The narrow block, just off Broadway, also hosted a 99-cent store, a cell phone emporium, a Radio Shack, and a couple of cheap clothing stores.

The building's security guard was watching Vanna White on a tiny screen at an ancient oak desk. Behind him were two brass elevator cages. The first door was closed, and the second was a manually-operated freight elevator.

"Do you want us to sign in?" I asked.

"No service after 6:00," he said, shaking his head and nodding to the open stairway.

The office directory had a little plaque that read: "This Building Owned and Managed by the Joint Catholic Mission." The names of a dozen or so occupants were listed in rough alphabetical order. In some cases, the names had been cut out of business cards and fitted into the metal slots.

My eyes fell immediately on a familiar name. "Derivatives Strategy, Room 406," I said. "That's got to be where they're meeting."

"What is it?" Susanna said.

"It's a trade magazine," I said. "A pretty good one."

As we walked up the stairs I began to have second thoughts about what we were doing. If this were some kind of conspiratorial group, they wouldn't be happy to see us. "Let's think about this a minute," I murmured. "We don't know what we're walking in on."

"It's a magazine, right?" she said. "Let me ask for some back issues. I'm not as threatening as you."

We stood outside the door for a while, listening for sounds of a meeting, but we didn't hear anything. Then Susanna knocked.

"Come in," a voice said wearily. "It's unlocked."

The magazine office was empty save for a guy in round spectacles throwing a stack of back issues into a canvas dumpster. Some beat-up computers and phones had been removed from the desks and were stacked in piles on the far side of the office. Network and phone wiring had been ripped from the walls and gathered in an unruly pile in the center of the floor.

"I want to buy a copy of the latest issue," Susanna said.

"We stopped publishing last month," he said. "I fired the staff last week."

"That's too bad," I said. "It was a good magazine."

"It was eight years of begging for ads," he said. "I was sick of it." He picked up a time clock from the shelf, considered it for a second, and then threw it into the dumpster.

"Do you know about any derivatives meeting that might be scheduled here?" Susanna asked.

"In this office?"

"Well, maybe in this building. A group that meets regularly to talk about trades, that kind of thing."

"You could try the Thai restaurant downstairs," he said. "Citibank bought the building from the Catholic Church last year. They're going to tear it down this summer."

We walked down the hallway, checking the names on the other offices. They belonged to a lawyer who claimed to be a financial advisor, a credit research firm that was probably a bill chaser, and a dental laboratory that looked as if it had been one of the original tenants. On the floor below, The Joint Catholic Mission had moved out, leaving its doors unlocked.

Our best shot was the Thai restaurant, which was one of those inexpensive places with paper mats that allowed office workers to grab a quick lunch and get back to work. It looked like it did a modest second rush at the end of the day with Wall Street types looking for free pad thai appetizers and a quiet place to drink.

We took a table in the corner and ordered a couple beers. The 22 Anne Street Group, whatever it was, didn't seem to be meeting that night.

I did a little eavesdropping to make sure. The guys at the table next to us were talking about the market, and three guys by the bar were talking sports. A third group was listening to somebody brag about how much he got his company to spend on tickets to a sold-out Broadway show for a visiting client.

"The e-mail didn't say when the meeting was going to be held," Susanna said. She sat quietly, taking little sips on her beer. During the day, she was in constant motion, but here she seemed preternaturally calm, as if the backlit photos of Thai forests and waterfalls were having their intended effect.

"I think this is a dead end," I said.

"You in a hurry?" she asked.

"I've got my Monte Carlo run at 7:00."

She looked at her watch. "Just sit here and keep me company. You've got half an hour."

Then she reached across the table and gave my hand a squeeze. A flirty squeeze? Or a reassuring, just-be-patient squeeze? Either way her hand was cold from holding her beer.

As she gazed at the multicolored racks of liquor bottles, I discreetly examined the cashmere turtleneck she was wearing under her jacket. This was okay. A little evening adventure, if not a romance.

SYSOPS Sub-B, as the mainframe support area was called, held a number of big computers. But the prize jewel of the systems department, the baddest and fastest, wasn't much bigger than a refrigerator laid sideways. You told it what to do via two Sun workstations with huge monitors that stood side by side on a long desk. A spiral steno pad that functioned as a signup sheet lay between the workstations, with my name written over that evening's 7 p.m. appointment.

I got there a little early so I'd be familiar with the Monte Carlo program the minute it was free, but the surly computer admin nearby said he was hardware, not systems, and couldn't help. After a few minutes of studying the help screens, I managed to figure most of it out. Then I sensed somebody behind me.

"Do you know how Monte Carlo works?" asked a voice that managed to be both helpful and condescending.

He was a quant's quant, a slightly pudgy, 30-ish Indian guy in a short-sleeve white shirt. The hems of his khakis were frayed and looked like they hadn't seen an iron since their manufacture. An empty plastic cell phone holster hung from his belt. I suppose he thought I was just another geek doing some recreational puttering.

"I think so," I said. "But I can't figure out how to take off the efficiency routines."

The comment immediately qualified me as his equal. He bent down beside me, grabbed the mouse and showed me the ropes.

"What are you using this for?" he asked.

"I've got a run that starts in five minutes," I said.

"No, you don't," he said, standing up abruptly and reverting to defense mode. "I'm Shivakumar Mehta. I have a standing reservation for 7 p.m."

"I made the reservation this afternoon. Everything was confirmed."

"I've never seen you here before. Where are you from?"

"Audit."

"What does audit need Monte Carlo for?"

"We're checking the portfolio of two derivatives traders."

"Which traders?"

"I'm afraid I can't tell you that."

He was silent for quite a while.

"Listen, my friend," he said diplomatically. "I'm the risk manager for the derivatives desk. I do the risk run every night. I know all the traders. We work for the same bank. And you can't tell me which two you're auditing?"

"I'm afraid not," I said. "Risk management reports to the trading desk, and I report to the Board of Directors."

"Are you an auditor?"

"I'm a consultant who works for audit."

"Who do you work for?"

"Susanna Cassuto."

"Oh," he said.

The name seemed to settle things. He dropped his shoulders and took a step back. It was a minor movement, but it signaled a retreat.

"I'll be done at midnight," I said. "You can have it then."

"She's very pretty," he said. "She has nice hair."

Yeah, I thought. And Michael Jordan plays basketball.

Shivakumar drifted to an abandoned desk a few feet away, and withdrew a book from his backpack. I got the sense that he had spent many long hours at that desk, reading and waiting for his daily runs to complete. A few minutes later, when I'd set up my own run, I was in the same situation.

"What are you reading?" I asked.

He showed me a book on options theory. "He's a very smart guy."

"Arrogant as all hell," I said.

"You know him?"

"I worked with him for five years."

"Are you an options trader?"

I stopped myself. *Keep your big mouth shut!*

"No," I said. "But I had to audit him."

He nodded.

"You sure there's nothing I can help you with?" he asked.

"I've got two projects. First I'm checking the profitability of somebody's trades. But I'm not sure I'm going to find anything useful."

"I run a profitability report every week. I send a report to Rick Markowitz every

Monday morning. What do you want to know?"

"There are some trades that aren't as profitable as expected. They run into some price spikes that destroy the profitability of the trades."

"Yes," he said. "That happens. So what?"

"I want to find out why the prices spike."

He made a short popping sound with his mouth, mostly air.

"That's the way option prices are. Predictably unpredictable."

"The price spikes are accidents?"

"Brownian motion," he said. "Randomness. Options are strange things. Sometimes they spike and you never know why."

I smiled and turned to my screen. Maybe. But maybe not.

"You want to figure out why some option prices spike?" he asked "It's statistical folly, my friend. And you didn't need to reserve a powerful computer like this for that problem. Your PC could do it."

I ignored him but, as I learned a few minutes later, he was right. I tried to analyze all the long-dated option deals where Tim had lost a significant amount of money. Most went out one or two years. A few went out longer but they all fit Tim's explanation: He liked to buy long shots cheap in the hope that one of them would pay off some day.

I had reserved the mainframe to analyze Stu's trades. Earlier that day, I had performed a simple arithmetic exercise a few times to get a handle on the price of Stu's options. How much would these options be worth in one month if U.S. interest rates moved up a bit and the dollar moved down a bit? In two months? In three? In five? Or if rates moved down and the dollar moved up? Or stayed the same? Or spiked upwards? That afternoon I had run through 10 or 20 scenarios and graphed the results before the sheer drudgery of the project forced me to give up. My twenty minutes of punching the plastic buttons on my calculator had told me very little about the price of Stu's options for one simple reason: The exercise did not allow me to predict the future. Only the future itself would tell me what would happen to the markets at a particular point in time and how much his options might be worth.

That night, I used the mainframe to help me prophesize. I programmed it to throw out every possible combination of market factors to calculate every one of the millions of possible outcomes the Option God might dish out. It was a task that could only be accomplished manually if I gave everybody in the bank a calculator and reassigned them to my task and made them spend their lifetimes and the lifetimes of their children, and their children's children, punching their calculators until their fingers were stumps.

I clicked the "Start run" button. The results began appearing as lines on a graph —

the first line starting low and moving high, the second, an instant later, starting midway up the chart and remaining unchanged, and so on until thousands and millions of lines flew across the chart and fell into place like a statistical sediment, forming summaries of lines and summaries of summaries. The most likely outcome was where the most lines fell.

I watched, awed with appreciation at the brute power being thrown at my task. A few feet away, the mainframe gave no indication that it was doing much of anything. The only thing moving was a number on my display that clocked the times it performed its calculations, jumping like a crazy odometer from the thousands into the millions of iterations.

Fifty minutes later, when it reached 50 million, I clicked the "Stop Run" button. The machine displayed a neat set of numbers at the bottom of the results chart.

"Maybe, maybe," I mumbled to myself.

Shivakumar looked up from his software manual.

"I'm done," I said. "Thanks for waiting."

"What are you going to do with the results?" he asked.

"I think I'm about to scare a trader shitless," I said.

"Good luck," he said, smiling and shaking his head. "That's something I've never been able to do."

The next morning, I got in early and spent more than an hour comparing the volatility estimates from my Monte Carlo run with the numbers published by Reuters and Bloomberg. In this particular set of trades, a higher volatility meant a bigger profit on Stu's books. And, of course, a bigger bonus. On February 7, the day the trade was booked, Reuters measured volatility at 24 percent. Bloomberg said it was 27 percent. And Stu Lister said it was 39.

"The scumbag!" I declared, slamming my hand on the table so hard Susanna jumped in her chair.

"What do you have?" Susanna asked, looking up from her screen.

"The little sucker is pushing his vols. They're off by 30 percent or more."

I explained how Stu's scam matched the diagram: He was taking money out of the trading system by inflating his trading profits. He couldn't make money in an out-of-fashion market, so he changed a number or two on a spreadsheet, hoping nobody would notice. The result? By my estimates, he picked up a $240,000 bonus instead of a $110,000 bonus. Or a $130,000 fraud.

Susanna nodded along with my explanation, then wanted to go through the numbers for herself. After she punched them into her calculator twice, an exultant smile broke across her face. She threw her shoulders back and stepped quickly to the white-board, where she wrote "$130,000" in huge letters. Then she took a step back, fashioned her finger into a pistol and took a shot at the number.

"Pow!" she said. "We did it." She paced back and forth for a while, staring back at it to squeeze all the triumph she could out of it.

I wasn't quite as juiced as she was. $130,000 was a decent amount of money. Our first kill. A fish of respectable size, big enough to keep. But maybe we'd find more.

She must have read something in my eyes.

"Don't kid yourself," she said. "If you stole $130,000 in a bank robbery you'd have 20 guys from the FBI after you. But we did it with two people. In three days."

"Stu was too busy to talk to us yesterday," I said. "He'll have to talk to us now."

We had a lot of work to do before we could tell Markowitz what we found. We spent most of the day assembling all the contractual and statistical evidence into Excel tables and charts. Soon after we started, the air conditioning shut off with a clunk. As the room warmed up, I peeled down to a grungy 1992 season Chicago White Sox t-shirt I never intended for public display. Susanna was wearing a very thick cable sweater and a plaid pleated wool skirt. It was a great retro fashion statement, but it looked insufferably hot.

A few minutes later, I looked up and found she had taken the sweater off, revealing a skimpy ribbed tank top that functioned as her sole undergarment above the waist. She gave me a quick smile, which seemed to contain a mixture of pride and embarrassment. Maybe this was my little present for helping her nail Stu. I savored it.

For the next 20 minutes, the only thing I was capable of doing was engage in vivid sexual fantasies. I was never big on originality in my fantasy life. I used a variation on an old standby: She was sitting astride me in my office chair, her pleated skirt spread around our hips, bouncing up and down with little screams of delight, etc., etc. Every once in a while I looked across the room at the real thing, in her skimpy tank top, picking through her hair for split ends.

The air conditioning returned to duty with a vengeance a few minutes later. I spent the rest of the morning patiently pasting numbers from one spreadsheet to another. Susanna, meanwhile, sought relief from her equally mundane scan through the deal folders by holding a marathon telephone conversation with her girlfriend.

She had a special affinity for the telephone. Her computer was treated as something to be mastered, but her telephone handset was a dear friend. On business calls, she held it like a walkie-talkie, the earpiece barely touching her ear. But on personal conversations, she cradled it in her neck, half covering it with her hair, and patiently flipped through file folders while her friend enumerated the plusses and minuses of half a dozen different Upper West Side preschools.

At one point she slipped into Hebrew, apparently to keep her conversation private. Was she talking about me? I had an Israeli roommate in business school and knew a few phrases, but couldn't decipher any she was throwing around.

I crouched behind my screen, closing my eyes in an effort to filter the Hebrew words from the white noise of the air conditioner. I typed a few phrases on my screen, transliterating as best I could. Then she slipped back to English. She hung up and took her half-hour lunch break a few minutes later.

While she was out, I squandered 12 fruitless minutes struggling to research her phrases via a Hebrew-English Internet dictionary. Then I remembered that I could call Doug, my basketball buddy, who had spent a few summers in Israel.

"Where've you been?" he asked. "I don't see you on Thursday nights."

"I don't have the money for the health club fees anymore."

"What happened?" he asked. "I heard you got fired for losing a million bucks."

"It's a long story, which I'll tell you sometime later," I said. "I'm calling because I need you to translate some Hebrew phrases for me."

"Does this involve some woman?"

"I work with her."

"How did I guess?"

"I think she said something in Hebrew about me to her girlfriend and I can't translate it."

"Okay. What's the phrase?"

"*Alti dag. Ani aseet.* Or something like that."

"Who said this to whom?"

"She said this to her girlfriend on the phone. I think she was talking about me. What does it mean?"

"It means 'Don't worry. I'm going to do it.' How do you know she's talking about you?"

"I don't. What about: *Ze lo beg deel etzli?*"

"It's not a big deal to me."

"The next phrase I know. *Ha leilah.* That means 'tonight.' What about '*Ani lo pochedet?*'"

"It means 'I'm not afraid.'"

"So its: 'Don't worry. I'll do it tonight. I'm not afraid.' "

"Does that help you out?"

"I don't know. Maybe."

"What's the context? You got a thing going with her?"

"I wish. She had a boyfriend who's some kind of securities lawyer. But she still keeps a big picture of him in her Filofax."

"Not a good sign. But aren't you still with Chris? She was a poet? Or an actress?"

"A formerly aspiring film critic," I sighed. "Now a real one. She got a job in L.A."

"So what's this one like? Big balcony?"

"Actually she's quite petite on top."

"Ackerman, baby! A little change of pace!"

"She runs her fingers through her hair and I get a hard-on."

"Ouch. Time for baggy pants."

"Look, I've got to hang up, she's going to come back from lunch any minute."

"Okay, but watch out for the work-related romance thing. Familiarity breeds contempt."

We made it down to the trading floor just as the market was closing. Markowitz's office was barely large enough for his desk and two visitors, but it had big windows onto the trading floor that allowed him to see his army on the move. His suitcase was parked outside the door like a guard dog and he was listening to a guy with a Liverpool accent tell the last leg of a story about a recent client meeting.

"So what happened?" Markowitz asked, eager for the punch line.

"He looks me right in the eye and says, 'Okay, Pete, I'll take the trade.' "

They both burst into raucous laughter, shaking their heads at the client's incredible stupidity. Then Markowitz spotted Susanna, and raised his hand in a greeting. She pantomimed a knock and then approached the door.

Markowitz turned his attention to me. Who was I? Another auditor?

"Rick Markowitz," he said, giving my hand a short squeeze. "Derivatives sales and trading."

"Dave Ackerman."

He turned to Susanna. "I haven't talked to you in a while. How did our audit turn out?"

"I'm still working on it," she said. "A couple of things have come up that I need to discuss."

"Oh," he said, glancing out towards the trading floor. He was trying to act like he didn't care, but he wasn't convincing anybody. "Anything interesting?"

"A couple of things Stu and Tim are doing don't look quite kosher," she said. "We have to do a little more work on Tim, but we're pretty sure Stu is playing a few games with his numbers."

He pivoted toward Susanna. "You're looking for trading fraud?" he asked, his eyes bright with disbelief.

"That's the assignment," she admitted reluctantly.

Markowitz morphed into the happiest man in the world. "Shit, I've got nothing to worry about. I was sure you were going to close down our tax business because of Enron. Or I thought maybe we lost some of our deal documents in the move."

"Nothing like that," she said. "We talked to Tim for a few minutes yesterday. We wanted to talk to Stu, but he said he was busy."

"Busy," he said with a snort. "What a jerk."

He looked across the trading floor as he punched the numbers on his phone.

"Stu. It's Rick. Can you haul your ass in here pronto, please?"

He stood up, and glared as Stu made his way across the trading floor to the office.

"Here's what you need to know about these two guys," he said. "Stu is passive-aggressive. Tim is just aggressive. Two sides of the same coin."

He rubbed his temples in frustration. We had just added another burden to his already overloaded shoulders.

"I've got 54 seats out there. Trading jocks or options nerds. Take your pick. There's nothing about any them that I don't know. Stu? He's just an options nerd. Tim? A generic asshole. If Stu is participating in some kind of serious trading fraud, he's out the door today. But I'd be very, very surprised. Same with Tim."

Stu lingered outside the door, like a kid caught smoking cigarettes.

"What's up?" he asked. Outwardly respectful. Inwardly fuck you.

Rick shook his head. "These fine people from audit said they asked to talk to you about your options book yesterday. Is that right?"

He nodded and blinked, ready to take his punishment: "I was busy."

"You're too busy to spend some time with an auditor? Are you nuts? Has the emerging-market debt market suddenly caught fire? Or are you just yanking their chain because you're hoping they'll go away?"

"I told them I'd talk to them," he said, then looked at us, trying to smile. "Name the time."

We made arrangements to meet in our office the next day at 11:00.

"You see?" Markowitz said, after Stu left. "One nudge and he falls over. Now let's deal with jerk number two."

He picked up the phone again and called Tim, whose desk was a few feet away.

Tim was having an involved conversation with a guy who looked like a college intern. When Tim got the call, he looked at the caller ID and swiveled toward us as he reached for the handset.

"I'm chatting here with the auditors," Markowitz said. "Would you care to join us?"

He heard something he didn't like. "Okay. Then finish up and come over here. We don't have all day." He took a deep breath. "Can't live with him. Can't live without him."

We watched Tim a few feet away, talking with the intern, gesturing with his arms, flinging them out expansively and smiling. It certainly didn't look like a work conversation.

"Enough of this shit," said Rick, bursting out of his office.

The intern looked up but Tim ignored us and continued talking. "So I said to her: 'Oh yeah?' So she says, 'Yeah.' So I said 'Oh yeah?' And she still says 'Yeah.' We go on like that back and forth for a few minutes..."

Rick stepped beside Tim and grabbed his shoulder, pulling his dress shirt askew. "Hey asshole!" he shouted.

They were both relatively slight, although Markowitz had a body builder's chest and Tim was a beanpole. Still, it didn't look like anybody was going to throw a punch.

Tim twisted away from Rick's grasp. "I'm in the middle of a *conversation!*" he said. A half dozen traders looked up from their screens and their phones as he walked away, eager to catch an episode of the Rick and Tim Show.

Tim straightened his shirt and took a seat on the edge of his desk.

"We got two people from audit who want to talk to you," Rick said, pointing his thumb over his shoulder at Susanna and me. "Have you ever had a colonoscopy?"

Tim ignored him and continued searching his loafers for scratch marks.

"I'm asking you a question, asshole," Rick said.

Tim wasn't going to dignify this exchange with a reply.

"Well, I had one three months ago and it's *nothing* compared to what these auditors can do to you. If they recommend a full trade audit, you'll have a dozen of their auditor friends crawling up your ass, examining every deal you ever did. You're going to feel sore for a week. You understand?"

Rick turned to us apologetically. "Excuse me, Susanna," he said, lowering his voice and gesturing toward the audience. "This is how civilized people are forced to communicate with each other on the trading floor."

Tim crossed his arms on his chest and closed his eyes into slits. "I spent half an hour with them yesterday," he said.

"Good," said Rick, turning to leave. "But if they ask for anything else, I want you to tell them whatever they need to know. *Capiche?*"

Rick guided us back to his office.

"A real prince," I said.

He stopped in his tracks and turned his attention to me.

"And what do *you* do for this bank, Dave?"

Susanna placed one petite hand on my shoulder. "Dave has come in to help me with some of the more technical trading aspects."

"That's great." Markowitz said, looking me up and down as if he was fitting me for a suit. I was much bigger than him, but he looked mad enough to make it a fair fight. "Done a lot of trading, Dave?"

"No, not really," I said.

Susanna raised her eyebrows in warning: Keep cool.

"A couple of simple option trades in your 401(k) account?" Rick asked. "That kind of thing?"

"Yeah, more or less."

"Well, you must know a hell of a lot about derivatives if audit is letting you judge my work and the work of 54 of the most sophisticated traders and quants in the world. You must be one of the smartest people on Wall Street."

Susanna's face turned to granite. I'd been through this before. It was going to be a classic chest-pounding duel. I could only win if I kept my cool.

"I don't have to be that smart," I said.

"No?"

"Once you know the games options traders play, you start looking for patterns, and it gets to be pretty easy." I tried to relax my shoulders and smile broadly.

"Such as?"

"Such as using the wrong underlying on a deal. Or understating the mark when there's some judgment involved. Or trying to convince somebody that a far out-of-the-money option has no value when it's really bleeding."

Markowitz shook his head. "Jesus Christ," he said. "Trading fraud again. That's the only thing that gets you audit guys horny." He looked up at the ceiling as if appealing to some higher banking authority. "You never get the big picture, do you? This bank took a $430 million earnings hit in the fourth quarter. It'll be a $150 million hit in the first quarter. It needs money — fast. I just came back from London where I made a few million bucks that will help keep this bank afloat. This trading desk is carrying you and everybody else on our fucking shoulders. We have no time for the penny-ass cheating you guys are looking for. If you want fraud, take a look at desks that are losing money. Go spend some time in mortgage-backed trading. They're losing it hand over fist!"

He picked up a file randomly from his desk and started reading it. He meant it as an act of dismissal.

"Tim Scott knows more about options trading than you ever will," he said, glaring at me derisively. "A little knowledge is a dangerous thing."

I found the whole episode disturbing, but Susanna was all smiles as we walked to the elevator.

"We've got them all running scared," she said. "We wanted to stir the pot. And that's exactly what we did."

"I just hope Markowitz doesn't try to get his revenge."

"He can't," she said. "We don't report to him. We did exactly what we were supposed to do. This is a big deal. Let's celebrate."

She punched the elevator button for the 46th floor.

"Forty-six?" I asked.

"I'll show you," she said.

The firm's executive dining room took up most of the floor. There was an area where secretaries could pick up fancy lunches on china for their bosses, and a broad hallway lined with smaller dining rooms, where company waiters were throwing white tablecloths into laundry dumpsters.

The last dining room was on the southeast corner of the building, with windows facing Ground Zero. The afternoon sun lit up a dozen multicolored cranes delicately picking over the rubble. The round dining room tables had been stripped to their wooden frames, and a middle-aged Hispanic waiter with a comb-over and a white uniform was sitting at one, doing some serious damage to the *Times* crossword puzzle.

When Susanna knocked on the open door, he put down his reading glasses and beamed. "My favorite auditor! I haven't seen you in months. Sit down and have some coffee."

"Issidro, this is David Ackerman, who works with me now," she said. "We were on our way somewhere else. I just stopped by to say hello."

"Nonsense. Stay a few minutes. How are you doing? How did you get out that day?"

"I took one of the buses to Brooklyn. Then I moved into my brother's place for a few weeks. What about you?"

"I got out on the ferry. I spent three days with my friend in Jersey City."

"Did the bank have you working somewhere else?"

"I'm not an employee of the bank," he said, shaking his head. "I work for the restaurant concession. We were laid off for six months. I'm back here just two weeks. Everything is just like it was."

He stopped a younger Hispanic waiter who was about to remove the chairs. "This is Susanna Cassuto," he told him. "She's head of audit. Or perhaps she will be, sometime soon." He tossed her a smile and a theatrical wink. "She takes a cappuccino. And Mr. Ackerman?"

"The same," I said.

He brushed some invisible crumbs from the table, took a folded tablecloth from a neatly stacked pile, grabbed one corner and flung it across the table with a windy snap. Then he adjusted the cloth until it made a perfect circle, all the while whistling the introduction to a song I couldn't place.

It was extraordinary whistling, with perfect vibrato, intonation and attack, and deep undertones that sounded more like a flute than something that came out of somebody's lips. In Susanna's honor, it was the chorus of a show tune: "A Pretty Girl Is Like a Melody."

"I've seen you in Central Park, near the zoo," I said. "You're the guy who whistles to the Paganini violin concerto. And you do the bird calls for the kids."

"That's me," he said, proudly. "I was the protégé of Manuel Vargas, the world's greatest classical whistler. I've performed with the Brooklyn Youth Chorus."

"You were selling a CD," I said. "I was going to buy it."

"I'll give you a copy," he said. "I have one in the kitchen. Any friend of Susanna's is a friend of mine."

The young waiter returned and placed the two cappuccinos and a small plate of cookies in front of us. Manuel glared at him.

"And where is the bowl? How is she going to add her sugar if she doesn't have a sugar bowl?"

The kid looked up at us sullenly, a teenager who had still refused to accept the adult world.

"My sister's boy, Miguel," he whispered when he left for the kitchen. He tapped his right temple twice. "A little slow."

Susanna took a sip and nodded thank you. "We're auditing Rick Markowitz's derivatives trading desk this month," she said. "We just left the trading floor. He and one of his traders were having a little disagreement."

"Mr. Markowitz is a very fine man," Issidro said. "You need people like that to run a big bank. *I* can't do it. *You* can't do it." He adjusted our teaspoons and the doily underneath the cookies. "A very talented man. They say he's going to be the new head of capital markets. In three months."

"Really!" Susanna asked. "Is Tony leaving?"

"He's going to take over London."

"And Rick's going to be head of capital markets?"

She looked at me and raised her index finger and her eyebrows simultaneously.

The nephew returned with a crystal sugar bowl and a wooden box which held packets of artificial sweeteners. He was gangly and slim, and looked barely 18. Issidro said something to him in Spanish and started to arrange the packets in neat rows. His nephew rolled his eyes defiantly, but arranged the rest of the box as Issidro took a seat beside Susanna.

"I've been here 19 years," Issidro said, speaking in something just above a murmur. "I went through the crash in '87. But I've never seen everybody so worried. The bank is in big trouble now. That's what I hear."

"We're investigating two traders now," she said. "Tim Scott and Stu Lister."

"Mr. Lister is a very nice man," said Issidro. "Very polite. If he's doing something wrong, maybe there's an explanation."

"It's possible," she said diplomatically.

"He's getting married soon," he said. "He brought his fiancée here last week. Very nice lady. And Mr. Scott is the skinny one with the blonde hair?"

Susanna nodded. Issidro made a face. Not his type at all.

We sat sipping our coffee and looking out the windows. A patch of dark clouds had dimmed downtown Manhattan, but the darkness hadn't made it out to Miss Liberty's part of the harbor, where she reflected the sunlight in her full American Express glory.

Cappuccino and sugar cookies. The sweet taste of victory. Susanna and I had caught somebody who had committed trading fraud, and tomorrow we were going to wrap things up and claim our first kill. I had a new apartment and a new career. And Susanna had suggesting grabbing some Chinese food at the restaurant near our building.

For the first time in months, and for a perfect fleeting moment, I allowed myself to be conned into thinking that all was right with the world.

Chapter 7

The restaurant was one of those upscale Chinese soup kitchens that fed the Wall Street crowd with the efficiency they had come to expect at work. Although it was right outside the entrance to her building, it seemed unfamiliar to Susanna. I sat her down at a small table in the corner and went looking for somebody who could get me a vodka and tonic. When I returned, she was standing at the cash register with her coat on, holding a menu.

"This place is too smoky," she said, handing me my coat. I looked around. I couldn't see anybody smoking. It didn't smell smoky.

"We can have dinner upstairs," she said with a sly smile. "I'm sure they deliver."

Upstairs was okay with me.

In the elevator it dawned on me that we weren't going to eat anytime soon. The moment is etched in my memory, as are all the defining moments in my romantic history. We joined a black dry-cleaning delivery guy carrying a half dozen suits on hangers and a banker type in a sweaty t-shirt just back from his run. When the banker got off at his floor, Susanna grabbed my hand and didn't let go. She held onto it as she led me down the hallway and opened the door with her key.

In a few moments we were smooching on her overstuffed white love seat, her shoes off, my shoes on.

Women had caught me by surprise before, and I always found it a little unsettling. My guiding principle in these matters was to let the woman choose the menu and set the pace.

Susanna on the couch was as quick as Susanna in the office. A flurry of flighty kisses, exploratory nibbles, and head gropes seemed to be driven more by sheer nervousness than by desire. Then a series of busy wandering kisses journeyed to ears and chins and foreheads but stopped at the neck. The territory was circumscribed. No hot flashes, no groping into pants, no frantic unbuttoning in the hunger for body contact.

The tempo was a little too fast. After days of collecting miserly bits and pieces about her, I wanted more time to study the flood of new information coming my way. The face I had been watching from 10 feet away was now microscopically close. I could see the roots of her eyebrows, her mascara, the pores of her skin. I could feel and hear and smell her quick breath against my neck. And most of all, I wanted to explore, in my own time, the bony and practically weightless body wedged between me and the couch pillows.

What was really driving me nuts were my shoes. I couldn't kick them off, couldn't plop them on her perfect white couch, so my legs remained awkwardly cantilevered across the arm of her couch.

Then without any warning, she slipped out of my arms and disappeared into the hallway, hitting the light switch as she left. The apartment dissolved into a series of shadows. Some ambient light trickled through the shuttered mini-blinds from the promenade 30 stories below, then an LED from a smoke detector near the door popped out like a beacon in the darkness. When my eyes adjusted, I became aware of an enticing glimmer of light in the hallway that I guessed was leaking from the bottom of her bathroom or bedroom door.

I was in the doctor's-office dilemma. How much do you undress? I took off my shoes, stowed them neatly beneath the couch with my wallet and keys, and reassumed my previous position on the couch, raising one leg to hide an enormous erection.

A minute later, she appeared around the corner. She had taken her sweater off, but was still wearing a silk blouse, which shimmered briefly in the darkness. Then she slipped back into the space between me and the couch pillows.

After some initial positioning, she wrapped her legs around the top of my thigh and started rocking sideways back and forth. She was holding me from the side, like a climber hugging a rock face. I was suddenly aware of the huge disparity in our body sizes. I slipped one arm around her as she pulsed beneath me, but it didn't feel like an embrace because most of her weight was carried by my leg and the couch pillows. And the locked-legs thing, it quickly became clear, was not a simple warm-up or a spontaneous erotic improvisation, but the first step in her master plan — one that led directly to an orgasm.

I thought immediately of Sandra Evans, my completely uninhibited sophomore year crush, who could climax in less than a minute by wriggling against the base of my palm. She liked to do this at the very beginning of our lovemaking, as if to clear her head and warm up for events to follow.

But Susanna was not Sandra. My job, as I understood it, was to help things out by tensing the muscles in my thigh, and pushing back at the right moments to the rhythm she was setting. I felt a little beside the point, lying there on the couch with my feet up. If the TV had been on, I could have watched the basketball game.

She didn't seem to be getting where she wanted to go, but it wasn't for lack of trying. I started pushing sympathetically on her ass, which fit gloriously into my out-stretched palms. A period of enormous concentration followed, like a car ignition turning over and over. Then she stopped as suddenly as she began, and sighed. But what kind of sigh was it? Happy? Frustrated? I couldn't see because her head was nestled into my neck.

I thought: Okay, that didn't work. We've got all night. Her blouse had silk buttons almost the size of capers, and little buttonholes to match. I wiggled the top button experimentally: Does this come off now?

She shook her head slowly, then settled deeper into my arms.

I was dying to turn on a light. What did we have here? Sexual embarrassment? A blissful pause? Did she stop pedaling suddenly in order to coast downhill a while? My own desire took second place to my need to make this a successful event.

Time to go back to mouth-and-tongue world? I tried an experimental peck on the lips.

No. Another shake of the head.

I used the pause to make a field study of her hair, selecting a handful from her shoulders. It felt surprisingly heavy as it slipped through my fingers. Every hair was long and coated. No short pieces, no frizzy rebels appeared. It fell off her shoulders in happy disorder, down the side of her back and disappeared into the couch pillows. I could smell the perspiration caught in it, but there was also a distinct chemical smell and another low note, like something had burned. Did she iron it?

"I don't think this is going to work," she said.

My breath stopped. *Sucker punch!* I tried to think over the din of alarm bells going off in my brain. *NO, NO, NO, NO! We never even got started! Unfair! Unfair! I must protest to higher authorities!*

Then a calmer mind dissected her statement: What isn't going to work? The leg-and-thigh thing? Us, tonight? Us, ever? My mind raced through a quickly assembled database of past seductions, searching for insight. Conversations on couches, beds, floors, in half light, in almost total darkness like this. Answers flooded in to fill the information vacuum: I had misread her signals. She went for skinny guys, like the guy on the bike. I was too passive, too slow. She wanted a guy to take control and push her over the edge, right away.

She was still buried into my side, holding tight to my chest. I couldn't turn to look at her without risking a neck injury. And my right leg, still dangling off the side of the love seat, had gone numb.

"Does it have something to do with that guy on the bike?" I asked.

She raised herself up on her elbow. Her face, suddenly illuminated in a rectangular plane of light, was confused, curious.

"Which guy on the bike?"

"The one on the big photo in your Filofax," I said.

"Oh," she said, before falling back into the darkness.

I took the opportunity to roll off the couch onto the carpet. Suddenly, we were two people lying flat on our backs, joined by our interest at some fascinating object on the ceiling.

"So where is he?" I asked.

"He's away. He's studying."

"Where is away?"

"He's overseas."

"What do you mean, overseas? Over which sea?"

"He's in Israel."

"Okay. The Atlantic. Now I know."

"And the Mediterranean."

"Terrific."

On the esplanade below, a little dog and a bigger dog had a barking match for a while and then went their separate ways. I looked at my watch discreetly: 7:14 p.m. It seemed like the middle of the night.

"When did he leave?"

"A while ago."

"Is it a temporary thing or are you going to go back to him when it's over?"

"We broke up," she said.

"But you still carry his photo around."

Silence. The mile-a-minute chatterbox was dispensing words like Chiclets.

"Can I ask you a personal question?" she asked suddenly.

"Sure."

"How many dates do you usually have with a girl before you sleep with her?"

I couldn't believe my ears. I was ecstatic. I was on familiar territory at last! This was the standard pre-coital interrogation, where the prospective lover takes a sober inventory of your romantic past and examines it for insights into your character. In law, it was called discovery — the litigator's broad request for intimate documents, and for the insights that might be revealed in the way I discussed them. Once I had answered the woman's particular concerns — Was I trustworthy? Discreet? Good in bed? — things might proceed to a court-appointed delay, or else directly to wild all-night fucking. Did I feel the edge of a condom package in the pocket of her blouse? Or was it just a silk inseam?

"What do you mean?" I asked. "On average? Statistically?"

"Yeah, statistically."

"Well, it's not a lognormal distribution. There are fat tails on both sides."

"But what's the mean of the distribution?"

"The mean? Maybe the fifth or sixth date," I said, immediately regretting it. It was more or less accurate, but it was the wrong answer for that particular moment.

"Of course, there are a lot of qualitative issues," I said quickly. "If you know somebody in another context, the numbers are going to be skewed downward."

"How big is the sample population?"

"I don't know," I said, stalling for time. It was a sneaky question, but one I always got asked, one way or another. I thought it was best to revise things downward. "Maybe 10 or 15. But there's a problem with the sample definition. How do you define the event? Do you include just messing around?"

"I think that's a good way to describe things," she said, slipping off the couch and turning on the light.

The evening was over.

Her blouse was a beautiful neutral beige, which was almost no color at all, and, in spite of everything, perfectly pressed. After a couple of quick flutters of her hands, her hair fell back in place, as if nothing had ever happened. She waited, heartbreakingly patient, as I put on my shoes and stuffed my wallet into my pants, then led me to the door.

She wore a smile that would have pleased a sphinx, a smile that meant nothing, or could mean many things: This was a fun first start; we'll continue later. Or else: This was a big mistake; let's forget about the whole thing.

I didn't ask for a kiss goodnight and didn't receive one.

"I'm very good as a secondary boyfriend," I said, turning to her for my final pitch. "I work cheap."

"You don't know the first thing about me, do you?" she said, shaking her head as she closed the door.

I moved to Battery Park City that night. I took a cab back to my old apartment, packed most of my life into moving boxes and deposited them in the basement storage locker. Then I hopped in a taxi and made a grand entrance to my new downtown apartment at midnight, carrying four suitcases and three garbage bags full of clothes.

I woke up several times that night. Although I found the surprise seduction exhilarating, I found our victory over Stu deeply disturbing. While part of me was celebrating, another part of me was stricken with enormous guilt. What were we about to do to this poor schmuck? He was just trying to make money to buy a new sectional for his fiancée.

For a while, I was surprised by my reaction. Then I realized a horrible truth: There was an enormous moral gulf between Susanna and Stu, and I was stuck on the wrong side. In Susanna's world, you chased after bad guys who needed to be apprehended and punished. In Stu's world, you took what you could get away with. Cop logic versus criminal logic. In spite of my eagerness to nail him, Stu and I might as well be partners in crime.

I vowed to keep my moral ambivalence as a secret, shameful remnant of the life I wanted to discard. This shame and this desire also helped explain Susanna's overwhelming attraction. I wanted to see the world as she did. I wanted some of her moral certitude to find its way into my own polluted soul.

I had seen a variation of that in women I'd dated. Many of them, struggling with their own ambitions, were attracted to my success as a trader and clung to me, not so much to share in my wealth (although there was plenty of that), but in hopes that some of my success would rub off on them. Now I was on the other side and it made me even more desperate for her approval.

Chapter 8

At 5:30, after several attempts at forcing myself back to sleep, I decided I might as well go into the office.

Susanna was there when I arrived, her eyes glued to the screen, a supersized latte steaming beside her.

She was acting as if nothing had changed or was going to change. If it was all over, I told myself, I'd find some way to work with a knife in my heart. And if it wasn't? Well, that alluring prospect walked into my brain and set up shop.

Stu arrived promptly at 11:00 for our meeting, nervous as hell, but determined not to show it. He'd gotten a haircut, but looked a little haggard, as if he didn't get a good night's sleep, either. I motioned him to my chair, which I positioned at the head of the table, and grabbed a busted secretarial chair we hadn't bothered to throw out. It collapsed comically to its lowest position when I sat on it, but nobody smiled.

"As I said yesterday, this is strictly routine, but we do need to examine some trades in depth," said Susanna.

"Whatever I can do to help," said Stu, smiling as graciously as he could.

"David knows something about trading, so I'll let him start," she said.

The semiotics of the room were all wrong. His chair was all the way up, while mine was halfway to the floor. I started shuffling through my papers to create a little breathing space. We knew he was pumping up his bonus by a couple hundred grand, and we had a massive Monte Carlo run to prove it. But a smart quant trader could always wriggle his way out of that kind of jam with one technical point or another. I'd done it myself on a couple of occasions. The next best thing — the only thing — was to catch him in a lie, to get him to talk about his methods in enough detail so we could use it against him.

"So what's it like in emerging markets these days?" I began, trying for a casual tone we both knew was fake.

"Nobody's doing anything," he said, shoving his long legs out under the desk.

"Everybody got burned in '98. The hedge funds that tried to buy at the bottom got killed when the market dropped again in '99. And it got even worse after September."

"So if I worked at a hedge fund and I told my boss I wanted to buy emerging market debt..."

"He'd have you committed," he said, smiling at his own cleverness.

"But in spite of that, you've been able to make a decent amount of money." I meant it as a compliment, but it came out as an accusation.

He was no fool. No matter what we told him, this was going to feel like an inquisition. I needed a change of mood, a different approach. I remembered that Stu had a few good trades on his books — real trades where he didn't bother to play with his numbers, and where he made real money. I pulled one of them out of my file.

"Okay, look at this great trade you did a few months ago," I said. "You've got a three-year option on Brazilian paper here. When you bought into the trade, it was worth $240,000. Now it's worth $1.4 million. How did you manage that?"

"Emerging markets are not like the Treasury bond market," he said. "It's not about math, or economic logic. These days it's all about fear. This trade happened last March."

"March 19," I said.

"Yeah. The International Monetary Fund put Argentina and Thailand on its watch list. That doesn't mean much, but a lot of guys who didn't know any better saw this come across the screen and said, 'Shit, Argentina! That's near Brazil! I got to sell.' "

"And you were standing on the other side."

"Yeah. I knew this watch list thing was bullshit. But I saw the panic coming and I started scooping things up as the prices dropped. I went right up to my limit by noon. Then I went to Markowitz and said, 'I've got this terrific opportunity. I need another $20 million.' He said fine. But the next day, prices kept dropping. Risk management was all over me to sell. I went to Rick and said, 'This trade is going to be a big fucking moneymaker. Give me another three days.' "

I stole a glance at Susanna. She was busy taking notes, but she had pushed her chair back against the wall, trying to be inconspicuous.

"That was a Friday," Stu continued. "Then on Monday, everything fell in place. People calmed down over the weekend. Guess what? Brazil didn't fall into the ocean. And these options were in the money, big time."

He was beaming. He looked almost handsome. He was a successful young trader after all. He had found somebody who could appreciate his great success.

"And they're still in the money," I said, grinning back like a fool.

"That's right," he said, folding his arms to savor the conclusion. He finally knew where the discussion was going. We wanted to talk about his big swinging dick.

"I suppose those numbers are from Bloomberg," I said, as if merely crossing a "t."

"That's right."

"So the moral of the story is: 'If you have a good trader, let him have the courage of his convictions and everybody will make money.' "

"Something like that."

I put away the papers, and then absentmindedly, as if I had just happened to think about it some more, opened the folder again.

"Are the vol numbers coming out of Bloomberg pretty accurate in this market?"

"Yes. Pretty much."

"So, in your portfolio, the volatility estimates are based on Bloomberg or Reuters or some other published number." In a court of law, you might have called it "leading the witness."

"No, not in every case," he said, somewhat warily.

"But you generally prefer to use published estimates."

"Yeah, usually."

"So your policy would be: Whenever they are available I use Bloomberg."

"Sure."

I put the folder away, satisfied with the answer. I wanted to swivel on my heels, face the jury and say: "I rest my case, your honor." His statement was completely at odds with his practice. If it wasn't an outright lie, it was pretty damn close. Time for the handoff.

Susanna flashed Stu a coy smile to indicate it was her turn, then rose quickly from her chair and crossed the room, standing a little too close. I had been trying to defuse the tension, but she was playing it somewhere between "Perry Mason" and "L.A. Law" — the prosecutor out to contradict the witness.

"Okay," she said. Then she paused, brushed her hair out of her face, and began again a few notes lower and at half her usual speed. "You prefer to use volatility numbers coming out of Bloomberg or Reuters. Let's test your hypothesis."

"Not quite," he said. He didn't like where things were going. "I said, 'in most cases.' "

"Fine. In most cases. On December 19, 11 days before your year-end portfolio valuation, you purchased an option on a Malaysian sovereign debt issue. On December 31, you booked a profit of $339,394 on the deal. Bloomberg estimated the volatility of this bond at 32 percent. You had it at 39." She shoved a piece of paper at him.

"I thought Bloomberg was wrong," he said, ignoring it.

"Okay. Fine. On December 27, just before the end of the year, you bought a Brady bond option that Bloomberg valued at 29 percent volatility. You valued it at 41. This happens over and over again. You buy something right before it's time for your portfolio to be valued and simply dump in your volatility estimate. That pushes up the price and pushes up your bonus."

"Bloomberg numbers aren't God," he said. "I develop my own volatility estimates, based on my own models. I have my own program. It lists every bond from 23 emerging-market countries and it allows me to value every option..."

"I've seen your model," she interrupted. "It's very beautiful. It's the underlying volatility assumptions I object to."

The insult caught him off guard. She flipped through her legal pad, picking up speed. "You say you like using your own model to value your deals. But just a minute ago you said something different. Question: *'You generally prefer to use published estimates.'* Answer: *'Yeah, usually.'* Question: *'So your policy would be: Whenever they are available I use Bloomberg.'* Answer: *'Sure.'* "

He was about to respond, but she interrupted him: "Do you want to alter those statements now?"

Stu took a breath and gathered whatever equanimity he could muster. "My estimates are based on something called Monte Carlo analysis," he said, in a patronizing academic tone. "It's a stochastic modeling routine used in a number of engineering applications, including financial engineering. I do an abbreviated version of it on my own computer using my own models. My numbers are checked every night by the risk management group. If I was off base, they'd report it to my boss. But nobody has ever objected to my valuations. And if you bothered to do your own Monte Carlo analysis, you would discover the same thing."

He turned to me, as a potential ally. "If you need more help, I'm sure Dave can explain how it works," he said.

But I was no longer the good cop.

"I ran the Monte Carlo last night on the mainframe," I said quietly. "I ran it without any of the efficiency routines, at 50 million iterations. It took an hour and a half. Your valuations were still way off. You were paid $342,323 last year. You only deserved to make $209,932."

Stu looked at me with venom. His face said: You tricked me.

"What's going on, Stu?" asked Susanna. "Why are you lying to us?"

"You people don't know what you're talking about," he said, rising from his chair. "You're not qualified to judge what I do. You're not traders. You're not risk managers. I don't have to answer to you."

"I'm afraid you do," she said, turning a little shrill. "You made $132,391 more than you deserved to make last year. You knew the bank's controls were screwed up and you thought you wouldn't get caught. But we can't have you writing yourself a check whenever you feel like it. There's a word for what you're doing. It's called bank fraud."

"I'm talking to a lawyer," he said, walking towards the door.

"This is not a trial, Stu. We're not lawyers, we're auditors. We want to find out the truth. Why are you lying to us?"

"I'm not going to discuss this any further until I have counsel."

"Don't flatter yourself," she said, dropping her files on the table with a thud. "You don't need a lawyer. You need a recruiter."

We burst into smiles when he left the room, and then noisy high-fives when he was out of earshot, the giddy kind of elation you feel after your first high school theatrical, complete with spontaneous clapping and fake bows.

This time I had no chance to feel ambivalent. Our performance was brilliant. We were a team. And I was in love.

Markowitz was alone in his office this time, looking beleaguered. It was 15 minutes after the close, and he was idly watching his traders leave to catch their trains while he stayed late to clean up. His cell phone rang just as he was closing the door behind us. He turned it off with a grimace to show us he was serious about listening to what we had to say. Then he placed it carefully between us on his desk as if it were a tape recorder or a gun.

"Okay, what do you got?" he said.

Susanna paused for a moment, as if gathering herself for a performance. "Stu Lister has been using a fraudulent scheme to increase his bonus," she announced, passing him a copy of our report.

She went through the evidence very methodically. She described how we had tracked the modifications he'd made to his purchased models, how we had questioned the inputs and how we compared them with published numbers on Bloomberg and Reuters. She went through the Excel charts that described his portfolio by date, by country, and by the amount of the misstatement. Then she gave him an abbreviated description of this afternoon's interview with Stu, and of his conflicting explanations for his practices.

She ended with the results of my late night Monte Carlo run. "Based on our Monte Carlo analysis, we believe the amount of the fraud to be $132,391," she said. "We have not attempted to go back to estimate the fraud from previous years, but its likely that this pattern predates this period."

Markowitz listened quietly to her presentation, without questions or interruptions. When she was done, he picked up the report and turned to the last page. Then he flipped the report over to the blank back page, as if looking for more information.

"Is that what you've found?" he said. "Nothing else?"

"This is the first incident of fraud we've discovered on your desk," she said.

"Is there any evidence that he colluded with any other trader on this desk?"

"No."

"So this is what you're telling me: The guy wants to earn 400, but he only deserves to earn 200. So he pumps up his vols to get a bigger bonus. Is that the basic idea?"

"Yes," she said. "He defrauded the bank of $132,391."

"Do you think this *shocks* me?" he asked, suddenly standing up and grabbing his cell phone tightly in his fist. I wasn't sure if he was going to crush it or throw it across the room. "Do you think this is something new? Something I don't know about? Like I'm going to wake up in the middle of the night in a cold sweat thinking, 'Oh, my God! Stu Lister is pushing his vols!' "

He fished out a report from the pile on his desk, and flipped through it until he came to a particular page. "Does this look familiar?" he asked, placing it in front of us. It was a Monte Carlo report, printed from the same program, with the same charts. The title was: "Lister Volatility Analysis" and it reached pretty much the same conclusion.

He grabbed the report back. "Every night this guy Shivakumar from risk management does a Monte Carlo run testing the numbers of all of our option traders. And every Monday he e-mails me a hysterical note about how half a dozen traders, including Stu, are off their numbers by this or that percent. He even uses the urgent button so it comes in my e-mail with a red flag."

He flipped to the next page and began reading with an Indian accent. "Based on my Monte Carlo analysis of March 6, Lister's position continues to vary significantly from published volatility estimates."

He suddenly scanned the trading floor until he found a particular person, then picked up the phone and rang his extension.

"Yo, Jim. Can you come here a minute?"

We watched in silence as Jim approached the office. I stole a glance at Susanna. Her body posture was pure defense: back straight, arms folded, knees together.

"Jim, this conversation is between you and me and these two auditors," Markowitz said. "It's about Stu. We never had this conversation. You understand?"

"I understand," he said, nodding and studying our faces to pick up some clue about the discussion.

"We all know Stu is a great guy, right?"

"Right, sure," said Jim. "Stu's a great guy."

"Okay. But between you and me and these wonderful people from audit, is there anything that bothers you about him? That we discussed the other day?"

"His goddamn wingtips," he said. "He wears these ugly brown wingtips."

"Okay, I know. But is there anything related to his job or his trading or his bonus? The thing we discussed the other day?"

"He pushes his vols, and he thinks he's fooling us."

"Thank you, thank you very much." Markowitz broke into a goofy, Jack Nicholson smile. "Sorry to bother you, Jim. You can go back to whatever you were doing."

The smile disappeared the moment Jim left.

"Stu Lister is not the world's greatest trader," said Markowitz. "He's not the world's worst. But he knows a tiny little bit more about emerging-market debt than anybody else. And that's why he's here. Right now the emerging markets are in the crapper, but one of these days they're going to come back. In the mean time, I need a body to keep the chair warm.

"Okay, he pushes his vols. But what would happen if I fired him? I'd have to hire somebody else. I'd have to pay some recruiter a fee equal to 30 percent of his first year's compensation. I might have to pay a signup bonus. And the guy I hired might be worse. He may be some kind of flake. With Stu, I know exactly what I'm getting."

He paused, staring at the cover page of our report, and looked away in disgust.

"I've tried to explain this to you guys before, but you don't seem to understand: *There is nothing about these traders that I don't know.* I have one professional goal: to make money for this bank. A hundred million. Maybe 200 million if we have a good year. That kind of money. And I get angry when the money I make for the bank gets pissed away by people like you, who are duplicating work that's already being done by my people in risk management. You are worse than the regular idiots in audit. You actually think you know enough to evaluate what we're doing here."

He paused again. His speech was over, and now he was contemplating his next move.

"I'm going to e-mail the head of audit," he said, glancing at his computer screen. "This was a complete waste of bank resources."

"This is not an audit project," Susanna said quickly. "If you have any complaints about our work, you can direct them to the corporation counsel." She wrote down his phone and e-mail and handed it across the table. He grabbed it eagerly.

He stared at the paper for a moment, as if trying to remember if he knew the corporation counsel, but then smiled. He folded the paper a couple times and wagged it back and forth, as if he had the instrument of our destruction in his hands. "I certainly hope this ends this investigation," he said.

"We'll be reporting to him. He would be the one to make that decision," she said. Susanna's tiny fists were clenched with her thumbs tucked inside, like two mallets looking for nails to pound.

A bunch of traders watched us leave Markowitz's office, Tim Scott among them. They were all slouching in their chairs and sharing some private joke, trying to figure out what had happened.

We walked past trying not to pay them any attention, but I couldn't help but notice some titters and muffled laughs down one of the aisles. Tim had the same British teen on his monitor, dancing to the same tinny disco track. But this time the volume was up and she was moaning "*Fuck me... fuck me.*"

Susanna walked directly over to Tim's desk and stared at his screen. "That's really great," she said, as if evaluating the quality of the girl's dance performance. "Can I show you guys a cool site you probably haven't seen?"

She grabbed Tim's mouse. After a few seconds of angry clicking, one of the bank's internal pages appeared on the screen — "Filing Sexual Harassment Complaints."

"Here's where they define harassment," she said to Tim and the other traders looking her way. "They give you a checklist to help you figure out if a particular incident falls under the harassment criteria or not. This one definitely does. Then they give you this little form to fill out."

She clicked again and started filling it in. "I put in my name here, then your name, Tim Scott. Two t's. Then I put all the details of the incident here..."

She circled the mouse around the blank portions of the form, as if giving a software demo. "Then I hit the submit button and the form goes off to Donna Brodie, a bank attorney who works in human resources. Donna's a friend of mine. We belong to the same gym. Her job is to get you fired."

She smiled at the growing audience her performance was attracting. "I'd love to chat with you guys some more, but it's getting late," she said, closing the screen and looking at her watch. "Have a nice evening."

Susanna shot out the door before I had a chance to gather my things. Not a good sign. We lived six floors apart, but I was not walking her home. Was last night's episode the first and last chapter?

It certainly seemed so. It didn't take long to unpack because I hadn't brought much with me. I bought a few things at the grocery store, and selected a Led Zeppelin CD from Abigail's extensive collection for nostalgic effect while I ate dinner. I went for a long run down the esplanade to clear the cotton balls out of my head, following the route I imagined Susanna used every morning.

Then, in a gesture of goodwill, I decided to give Abigail's fish tank a thorough cleaning. Her particular setup required you to change filters, do a couple chemical tests of the water, and run a hose to and from the bathroom sink, 20 feet away. As I was rolling up the hose in its storage box, the phone rang.

"Hi," Susanna said matter-of-factly.

"Hi," I said.

"Are we on for tonight?"

I dropped the hose box on my toe.

"Sure," I said, as casually as I could. "You want me to come down?"

"No, I want to come up to your place."

"Okay. Soon?"

"Give me 20 minutes."

I did a frantic parody of a guy cleaning up his apartment for a big date, before realizing it didn't require much effort to restore the apartment to its Martha Stewart purity. I returned the Led Zeppelin to its place and, in a burst of optimism, straightened the down coverlet on the bed.

While waiting for Susanna to arrive, I tried out several casual poses — relaxing with a magazine on the couch, gazing moodily out the window at New Jersey — but they all made me feel like Hugh Hefner.

I stood by the door like a commando awaiting my signals, ready for whatever move was required. But she surprised me, brushing her hand against my cheek as she passed, as if to circumvent a kiss, and then walking past me nervously into the apartment.

"You haven't changed this place very much, have you?" she said, moving towards the aquarium, which served as a divider between the living room and the studio's bedroom alcove. She was wearing a cream-colored silk pants suit with matching suede loafers, and either no makeup or the makeup that guys are not supposed to see.

I couldn't think of anything to say, so I stood by the window, cultivating my Hugh Hefner silence.

She ran her hands along the edge of the fish tank then noticed the CD collection of the shelf beside it.

"Abigail's got all sorts of stuff there," I said. "Put on whatever you want."

The collection was a conventional one that meandered along the demilitarized zone between folk and rock, with particular emphasis on singer-songwriters. On the fringes, it made hesitant incursions into classic rock, Miles Davis and Mozart, but the theme was overwhelmingly low-key and relaxed — the kind of music that would that accompany a saltwater fish tank.

"Oh, I love this album," she said. I heard the clatter of the plastic case opening, then the opening bass line of Van Morrison's "Moondance."

I had to suppress a groan. My older sister had played that record incessantly when she was thinking about some guy or breaking up with him. Apparently, it was the ultimate romantic mood record, which had an amazing ability to leap generational barriers and appear in the collections of women born decades after its initial release.

Van was clearly doing something right. My guess was that he expressed a particular kind of coy, appealing sensuality that women did not find threatening. He didn't really want to have sex. He just wanted to lead you in a dance. Or so he claimed.

She surprised me again by snapping off the lights, first the halogen lamp by the couch then the light by the window, leaving the fish tank ablaze in the darkness like a Technicolor movie.

Within moments, we were back to our previous positions on the couch. This time, the foreplay was slower and more overtly inspectional. This is your ear. This is my shoulder. This is your earlobe. I was soon on my back, taking over the narrow real estate of the couch, with her on top, one of her legs wedged into the corner of the couch, the other between my knees.

I tried hard to record it all: the feeling of a new body, before it erased the lingering impressions of the other bodies I'd embraced. I was surprised again by how close her bones seemed to the surface of her skin. People who are married forget how lonely the single life can be. These glorious moments of sudden intimacy were the payback.

Her outfit sported a modest v-neck, which displayed her prominent collarbones and allowed me enough room to move the opening around the top of her shoulders.

Then I realized that her silk outfit, minus the loafers, could double as pajamas. Maybe that's what they were. They had padded buttons, and I tested the top one, but she shook her head. The rules of tonight's engagement were becoming clear. Yes, it was okay to move my hands under the back of her blouse, but not the front. Nothing was going to be unbuttoned. There would be no direct contact with primary or secondary sexual organs.

I worked with what I had.

She was trying a variation from the other night, but instead of wrapping herself around my leg and grinding away, she moved farther up and worked against the resistance of my hip bone. This time it felt like it was going to work. Her hair was in a ponytail, but it was slipping around every which way, some of it getting swept into her mouth.

Then I moved her off my hip to put pressure against my penis, which was flattened upwards against my lower stomach. That seemed to work better for her as well, and she immediately began rocking back and forth against it. I moved her leg out in order get all of her 95 pounds on top of me and wrapped my arms around her waist. Now we were talking!

She leaned up on her elbows briefly to put more pressure where she wanted it, and then bounced against me: bam, bam, bam. I grabbed her ass as if to say: "Yes, let's do that again!" But she was already closing in on her own goals.

All I had to do was make sure I didn't come. Van was helping a lot. He had finished his moondance and his ode to "Crazy Love." Now we were at "Caravan," the nadir of the record, where he told his sweet lady of the night that he wanted to hold her tight and mumbled endless mystic incoherences about merry gypsies playing around campfires.

Then Susanna stopped and slipped off me to the side, wrapping herself loosely around my leg. Did I miss something? Was that last little clutch it? She released a single but definitive sigh. Yes.

Okay, but I didn't have much to do with it. And I still had my erection.

Almost on cue, she unzipped by pants, grabbed my penis and gave it a few squeezes here and there. It was not particularly skillful, neither expert nor inexpert. But it was clear that intercourse was not on the menu tonight and that this was how it was going to end for me. As soon as I realized that, I flipped a little switch in my brain and a few seconds later, the ballgame was all over. As I came, I thought about a *New York Post* headline. Some ex-lover of Donald Trump was telling her story on the front page: "BEST SEX I EVER HAD!"

It wasn't the best sex, not by a long shot. There was no body contact, no sweat, no drama. But I wasn't complaining. It was only Thursday night. We had all weekend to practice.

She was staring at the fish tank on the other side of the room. It floated in the darkness, dominating the room like some kind of exotic window into another world.

"How are you?" I asked, throwing the couch pillows on the carpet to give us more room.

"I'm fine," she said, matter-of-factly, as if we were still in the office. "How are you?"

"I'm fine," I said in the same tone. Then we both laughed.

"What do you think Stu is doing tonight?" she asked, returning her gaze to the fish tank.

"Stu was the wrong guy," I said.

"Yeah," she said. Then a bitter sigh. "The wrong guy."

"Maybe the diagram was about Tim," I said.

"Or maybe somebody else," she said. "What do you think Tim is doing now?"

"Closing the Second Avenue bars, trying to get lucky."

"No, I don't think so," she said. "If he's committed some kind of fraud, he's freaking out. He knows we're onto him. He's already told his partners and they're trying to come up with a plan."

The aerator in the fish tank kicked into its hourly cleaning cycle and started burbling at double speed. I lifted her hair from her shoulders and ran my fingers through it. "Can I ask you something?"

"Sure," she said, lifting her head to look at me.

"Do you have any plans for the weekend?"

She squirmed a bit.

"Actually, I'm going away," she said.

"Yeah?"

"To a friend's house in New Jersey."

It didn't take much to put the pieces together. The rich party girl goes off to another weekend affair, leaving the weekday guy in the dust.

"A boyfriend?"

"No."

"A friend who's a boy?"

She seemed irritated by my insistence. She sat up, removed a rubber band from her pants and rolled her hair into a bun.

"It's just a group of people I hang around with," she said. "It's not what you think. Can I ask *you* something?"

"Go ahead."

"Why did you quit trading?"

I should have been expecting it, but it caught me by surprise. I didn't know what to say. She no longer believed I was just a burnt-out trader looking for a new lifestyle. Maybe the corporation counsel had told her the truth.

"Did something traumatic happen to you?" she asked. "Were you in the Trade Center? Were you caught up in the collapse?"

I'd already gone over this ground with her. I had been working in the World Financial Center across the street from the Trade Center, and jogged back to my apartment along the West Side Highway. But she seemed to suspect I was leaving something out.

"Nothing traumatic," I said. "I left after the first plane hit. I saw the whole thing on TV, like everyone else."

"Did you have close friends who died?"

"I knew a couple guys at Cantor. I talked to them on the phone a lot, but we only met a few times. I knew three or four other people. But I wouldn't call them friends."

"Something must have affected you if you gave up your trading career a few weeks later."

"Yes, that's right," I said. "Something must have affected me." I was acknowledging what I hadn't quite figured out for myself. In some respects the collapse of my career was indirectly related to the collapse of the Trade Center. But I couldn't draw a direct line between the two events.

I wanted to tell her the truth, but I couldn't find the right words to say it.

"We moved across the river a week later," I began. "To Exchange Place, New Jersey. I really hated it there. Everything was all screwed up. The computers didn't work. The war in Afghanistan was starting. Everybody was going nuts. I was having constant fights with this guy who sat next to me."

I couldn't go on. I couldn't lie to her. But I couldn't tell her the truth.

"Things just fell apart for me after that," I said. "That's all I can tell you."

There was a long period of silence. We were alone, surrounded by the things I didn't know about her, and the things she didn't know about me. Then she drifted off to sleep. I marked it as another first for us, falling asleep together.

I woke up on the couch a couple hours later and went to bed.

Chapter 9

When I arrived the next morning, Susanna had Tim Scott's folder opened in front of her, and copies of his trading records spread around her in neat piles. At her feet was a big leather bag packed for her weekend trip, a stylish affair, mimicking a gym bag, but made from strips of multicolored leather.

"Stu was the wrong guy," she said. Her eyes were focused on the screen and she was typing in quick bursts. "But we still have Tim."

Her investigative fury was a bit intimidating. She was manually going through the data of every trade Tim was involved in during the past four weeks, comparing how much he was supposed to make with his actual trading profits. I had worked from summaries of the profitability reports for a much longer period, but hadn't bothered to go into each deal. I grabbed my own cup of coffee and started looking at the deals myself.

Something was off in a lot of them. Tim's equity-option deals were packages of different options, which were designed to bring in a particular profit. Susanna had the right metaphor earlier in the week. It was as if you were a baker who had sold someone a special birthday cake. You calculated how much it would cost you, based on the price of eggs, flour and sugar, but when you went to buy the ingredients, you found the price had gone up, so you made less money on your cake.

Each trade was a different story, a different set of numbers to investigate, but no pattern was emerging. Sometimes the price of the options rose dramatically one way and the bank lost money. But you could find plenty of examples where the market moved the other way, and the bank ended up making more money than it expected.

I focused on the trades where the price spikes were particularly dramatic. I set up a spreadsheet and sorted the deals by asset class: currencies, equities, bonds. No pattern. The process was deeply fascinating and frustrating at the same time, but I was quickly losing my perspective, finding fleeting patterns in the data where none really existed.

My obsession with finding a trading pattern was merging with my sexual obsession, refueled by the previous night's moondance. We had arranged our chairs at opposite ends of the conference table, with the bulky monitors giving us a modicum of privacy. But I discovered that if I pushed my chair back a few inches, I could stare at her with abandon. Before looking in my direction she'd have to swivel on her chair a bit, giving me a critical millisecond to avert my gaze and begin checking the ceiling for cobwebs.

She wore a lemon yellow knit suit as protection against the air conditioning, the only burst of color in the room, and I will always associate that suit with her glamour look: perfectly coifed, sitting ramrod straight, a brunette career-girl Barbie without the boobs.

Between spreadsheets, I began assembling a collection of mental snapshots of her at work. In most of them, she is captured in mundane gestures of concentration: biting her lower lip, tapping the bridge of her nose, grabbing her hair behind her neck as if she were about to give it a big yank. It was during these moments, when she was completely distracted, that the impossible burden of glamour fell from her shoulders, and with it, some of her power over me. I was eager to turn her back into just another woman, an auditor, so I could free myself from my absurd lust.

I was waiting for the right moment to tell her what I couldn't tell her the night before. "*By the way, I had a trading problem of my own a few months ago...*" Or: "*You asked me why I quit my trading job. Well...*"

I'd have to do this away from the office. Maybe when she came back Sunday night. Maybe this time in bed instead of the couch?

At lunchtime, she disappeared for half an hour and came back with a yogurt and an apple, which she ate as she flipped through the back pages of *Vogue*. Then she got behind her computer and stared intently at her screen. Soon after, I heard a familiar series of cascading bleeps.

"Is that Alien Attack?" I said, getting up so I could look over her shoulder.

She had set the action as fast as it would go and was nailing the aliens a half dozen at a time, before they got halfway down the screen. She was terrific at positioning her cursor to anticipate the next swarm.

"I told you I have three older brothers," she said. "You ought to see me in a video arcade."

At 2:30 p.m., I realized I had skipped lunch. The search for a pattern in the data was driving me nuts. The profitability of certain deals was ruined because at the last minute somebody else in the market bid up the prices. Instead of focusing on finding a pattern in the trades, I decided to focus on finding a pattern in the price spikes. What happened to prices of the options in the period directly before the bank purchased them? And instead of looking only for big price spikes, I looked at every spike — even the smallest blip was suspect.

I looked at one deal in particular, to focus my thinking. A client in St. Louis wanted to buy a basket of eight chemical stocks in the S&P 500 Index: Dow Chemical, Air Products, Rohm, Celanese and four others. The order came through at 11:21 and the trade was completed at 11:45. I looked at the prices of those eight chemical companies during that 24-minute period versus all the prices of all the other stocks in the S&P 500 Index. Some option prices went up, some went down, but those eight chemical stocks all went up. Interesting, but maybe it was just chance. Then I looked at the detailed price history of those eight options.

My breath stopped for a few seconds while I checked and rechecked the numbers. At 11:39, some option trader somewhere in the anonymous trading universe had made aggressive bids on those eight options, driving the price up one or two percent. That was no coincidence. He knew which eight options the bank needed. Then, over the course of the next few minutes, he sold them back to the bank for a small profit. $40,000. Not big enough to attract attention. But a little slice taken out of the profitability of the deal.

"Tim Scott!" I yelled. "You cocksucker!"

Susanna looked up, distracted by something on her screen.

"Come here," I said.

"Let me finish this."

"Get over here quick!" I demanded. She gave me a nasty look, but complied.

I pointed at the trade order on my screen. "At 11:21, a client in St. Louis buys a basket of options on eight chemical stocks. The bank charges him a price, based on an estimate of what it would cost it to assemble the pieces of the basket. But when the bank goes into the market to buy those options, the price on all eight is a little higher than predicted. Why?" I pointed to my spreadsheet and pounded my fingers into the paper. "Because somebody came six minutes before and bid up the price."

"By how much?" she asked.

"About one or two percent. Not dramatically higher, but enough to slash the bank's profit to smithereens."

"Did you find this pattern in more than one trade?"

We flipped through a few more trades in horrified concentration. The scenario was the same in trade after trade. The trade was booked, Tim found out exactly what options the bank needed to buy, then his accomplice bought them and sold them back to the bank for an instant profit.

It took a minute to really sink in. Somebody somewhere was making a killing at the bank's expense!

This was the fraud we'd been hired to find.

Susanna went to the bulletin board in a trance and took down the original handwritten tradeflow diagram. Now the damn thing made sense. It was clear now that the upward arrow was pointing to Tim's partner.

Whoever he was. Wherever he was.

She copied the diagram onto the whiteboard. We sat across the table from each other, each in our own world, savoring our success.

"He might go to jail for this," she said. "You know what this means for us?"

"For us?" I asked.

"For our careers in the bank."

"Right." When it came to bank politics, she was always a step ahead of me.

"We can try to set ourselves up as a special audit team," she said. "For trading fraud cases. You could get a permanent job out of this."

"But who was Tim's partner?" I asked.

That was tomorrow's mystery. It was time to tell Ed Lewis the news.

Ed picked up his phone on the fifth ring.

"We want to come by and talk to you," said Susanna, putting him on speakerphone. "Right now."

"I'm busy with something else. Can it wait till Monday?"

"You've got to see us now. We found it. David did."

"You found what?"

"We discovered the fraud. No question about it. It involves one of Markowitz's traders. A guy named Tim Scott. He and somebody else are siphoning off bank profits from the derivatives desk."

There was a long pause. Then we heard him mumble something to somebody else in his office. Then another long pause.

"Well... Tim Scott isn't going to be working here anymore," he said.

"He's been fired?"

"I said Tim isn't going to be working here anymore. Come up at 4:30. I'll tell you the whole story."

Susanna put down the phone and stared at the handset for a while. Then she took her silver pen and clicked it open and shut a few times.

Her face fell apart in a way I'd never seen before, distorted with disappointment and grief.

"Then he gave himself up," she said.

Possibly, I thought. But not necessarily.

"'Tim's not working here any more' could mean a lot of things," I said.

"They're going to slap him on the wrist."

A dream shattered. She had already locked him up. Now they were letting him go.

I didn't share her disappointment. Any way you looked at it, Tim was history. Through a combination of luck, skill and perseverance, we had stopped a big financial fraud in its tracks. The idea of Tim negotiating a deal didn't strike me as appalling. In fact, it seemed the only reasonable thing to do. A few months before, I had done the same thing myself, with the help of a securities lawyer, and a legal fee of $25,000.

"We found him," I said. "We completed the assignment. It's our kill. They can't take that away from us."

"The fix is in," she said, shaking her head.

The door to the corporation counsel's office was wide open when we walked in. Lewis was on the phone and pointed us back into the hallway. He even got up to close the door behind him.

He beckoned us back a couple minutes later. My chair was still warm from its previous occupant, and the room had the close smell that comes when guys spend an hour or two together in a small room. Maybe Tim's lawyer was one of these tough defense lawyers that don't give an inch.

The office was pretty much the same as the day I was hired. Miss Liberty was still looking forlorn out in the harbor. The mini-blinds on the easternmost shade were closed to shut out Ground Zero. And Lewis' son was still glaring at us menacingly from his suburban karate studio. The only difference was the wastebaskets. Now he had three: a black one for trash, a blue one for white recycled paper, and another black one with a handwritten label marked "SHRED."

"Before we do anything else, I want to commend you guys for doing a great job," he said.

Although Lewis didn't look like he was in a particularly good mood, he gave us this praise genuinely, and with some enthusiasm.

"I got a nasty call from Rick Markowitz yesterday, but I figured you guys had to rattle a few cages to do your research. I guess he hasn't been really cooperative."

"Rick's okay," Susanna said diplomatically. "He's just a little defensive. That's natural."

"Let me just take care of some logistics," he said, glancing at a printout of an e-mail from his desk. "Susanna, you're being sent back to the audit group and reassigned to investigate the mortgage-backed securities desk. Markowitz says there are some shenanigans going on there, so why not? And Dave, I'm hiring you to help her. I'm doubling your salary to $10,000 a month. If the next couple of jobs work out, the head of audit says he'll find a place for you in his budget."

We started grinning at each other like fools. I wanted to reach over and give her hand a squeeze, but I didn't dare.

"Okay, let me tell you the news about Tim Scott," he said. "I'm afraid you're going to have to stop smiling. Tim Scott died sometime last night in his apartment. From a drug overdose."

The air got thicker all of a sudden. More viscous, harder to breathe. I was aware of the sound of my breath. Something I ignored all day long. In and out.

Lewis took a yellow document from a folder on his desk. It looked like the second copy of some multipart handwritten form. Then he put on his reading glasses and squinted at the handwriting.

"It was administered by injection by somebody else. Some kind of gay S&M thing. It couldn't have been self-administered, because his hands were bound."

I heard high heels clicking down the hallway outside. A secretary in a hurry. Then my stomach decided it didn't like all the coffee I'd drunk that afternoon and started to churn.

"I just spent an hour chatting with a detective from the First Precinct, who gave me a little crash course in gay S&M," said Lewis. "Apparently, a lot of these guys are into sexual practices which take you pretty close to death. It's supposed to heighten the experience. Then on top of that they take drugs I've never heard of. PNP. Ketamine. I guess they went a little too far."

I glanced at Susanna. She was staring at the ground, mumbling something. I suspected it was a prayer.

"But Tim wasn't gay," I said. "At least I don't think he was gay."

"There have been four or five deaths in the last year or so associated with this particular kind of sexual technique," he said. "It seems to fit some kind of pattern they're investigating."

"Did you tell the cops we were investigating him?" I asked.

"I told them that some people happened to be conducting an audit of his trading desk and that the results weren't in."

"But we found something!" I said. "That's what we're here to discuss. He was running an equity-options scam."

"What kind of scam?"

I turned to Susanna to let her explain, but she was pinching her mouth with her fingers. It seemed to be a way of suppressing speech or nausea.

"He was operating with an accomplice," I said. "They were front-running the bank's options purchases and bidding up the price. He and his partner stole at least two million dollars since 9/11."

Lewis looked at Susanna for corroboration.

"Oh, God," she said, covering her face with her hands and letting our report drop to the floor.

I grabbed it and gave to Lewis.

"Read this thing," I told him. "Now!"

He took the report reluctantly, as if it were dusted with some kind of poison. Then he started turning the pages by the corners.

I don't know how long it took him to skim through the pages. My mind was skipping every which way, but my body was stricken with enormous fatigue. I took another look at Lewis' desk and spotted two business cards. They were hard to read because they were upside down and on a diagonal, but they had an official symbol of some kind. They must have been the cops he had just spoken to.

Susanna opened the fingers covering her face as if she were playing peek-a-boo. She was not crying. She was still in shock.

"This doesn't change anything," Lewis said, skimming through the appendix. "I told the police that the desk was under investigation, and that was the truth."

Then the phone rang. He picked up the call and listened for half a minute.

"I can't talk," he said. "They're in my office right now." Then he hung up and ushered us to the door.

"We can discuss this more next week," he said, practically pushing us out of his office. "On Monday morning, you should both report to Jeffrey Ialeggio, the head of audit. He'll work out the details of your new assignment. This investigation is over."

"But it wasn't an S&M thing!" Susanna said, suddenly finding her voice. "We told him we were onto him. His death was our fault!"

"If you can find a way to charge a dead man with a violation of the banking code, please let me know," Lewis snapped.

Then he closed the door in our face.

Chapter 10

The elevator down to our office was crowded with the 5 p.m. rush, but Susanna refused to move from her position in the center of the car, and let people arrange themselves around her.

"It was our fault," she said grimly, as she shut our conference room door. She had reached that conclusion on her own but she wanted me to confirm it.

"We did nothing wrong," I said angrily. "Tim was the criminal. He stole from the bank. We were just doing our job."

"If we hadn't launched our investigation, Tim would be alive today."

"If he hadn't stolen the goddamn money, he wouldn't have gotten himself killed."

She shook her head. I simply didn't understand. She grabbed her big leather bag and threw her raincoat coat over her arm. What I admired about her, her self-assured moral certainty, now felt like moral superiority, and it made me angry.

"Where are you going?" I asked. "To the airport?"

"To New Jersey. A car service is picking me up downstairs in five minutes."

"Can I come along for the ride? I want to talk about this."

"This was not some accidental drug overdose, that's pretty obvious."

"I'm coming with you in the car."

She didn't object, so I followed her downstairs and sat beside her as the car crept through the uptown traffic to the Holland Tunnel.

I hadn't liked Tim and couldn't will myself to like him now that he was dead. Somehow, the fact that he was gay was as shocking as the fact that he had been murdered. For the second time this year, somebody had managed to fool me like that.

I thought about Steve, my former trading buddy who died of AIDS, and about the life he had to keep secret from me and everybody else. What was real and what wasn't? My mind jumped back to one particular Friday, just after the close. The receptionist announced that a woman was waiting for Steve in the 17th floor lobby. He wouldn't tell us who she was, but we assumed it was Jeanne, his much-discussed fiancée. We followed him out to the lobby for a look, but he ran ahead of us and hustled her down to the elevator as we saluted the descending couple with wolf-whistles. Was that an event staged for our benefit? Or was he just meeting a friend after work?

How could Steve go into the office — day after day, week after week — and chatter away so convincingly about his drunken weekends with Jeanne and her job at Ann Taylor and her yellow Miata? Turning his life into something acceptable to his colleagues was a staggering act of creativity.

As our car entered the Holland Tunnel, I tried to remember bits and pieces about the gay people I knew. Wendell, a guy on the fringes of my college clique, led a quietly gay life in my college dorm, then settled down with another guy soon after graduation. He made no secret of his sexual identity as he climbed the partner track at a Wall Street law firm. He had a certain way of speaking that might identify him as gay, but it didn't leap out at you. In the late '90s, he and his lover and their two dogs moved to New Jersey, and invited the gang over for a mini-reunion. A lot of things about their life were true to type — the racks of musical theater CDs, the '50s furniture and knick-knacks — but they were otherwise indistinguishable from their yuppie neighbors. Seven years later, Wendell and his partner were the most stable couple I knew.

Our car stopped suddenly, and a police officer strolled past us on the catwalk, holding a police radio to his ear. Then we heard an ambulance siren approaching us in the opposite lane. It whizzed by, its siren lowered an interval by the Doppler Effect. What was inside that ambulance that would make them close one lane of the tunnel?

"I'm not eager to be your psychoanalyst," I said at last. "But you seem to be looking for ways to assume the guilt of his death. You can't. The guilt belongs to the person who killed him."

"Plural," she said.

"Huh?"

"The people who killed him. He was killed by the Anne Street Group. They made it look like he was gay. He was going to spill the beans on their scam, so they killed him."

I took a deep breath. Okay, she had already done her initial sort through the evidence and had reached her conclusion. Maybe it was a reasonable theory. But at the moment, it was only a collection of assumptions.

"We don't know that," I said.

"Don't know what?"

"That he wasn't gay. Tim was killed by his accomplice. Or one of his accomplices. But we don't know anything more than that."

Our convoy sped up briefly and then stopped just as suddenly. A pickup truck with a flashing yellow light came by in the opposite direction. A worker was walking behind it, methodically picking up the plastic pylons in the center of the lane and tossing them to some other guys, who stacked them neatly in the truck bed.

"He was not gay," she insisted. "It's obvious. He was playing that British teen porn thing. And we read all his e-mails about his weekends."

"He could have been fooling everybody. We know very little about how he was killed. How much do you know about gay sex?"

"Absolutely nothing."

"I don't know a whole lot, either. But I do know that you can strangle yourself, you bring yourself close to death, and that heightens a certain sexual effect. You get somebody to tie you up and then you do various things to postpone and heighten your orgasm. Leather hoods and chains and whips."

I'd gone a bit too far on the details. She closed her eyes in disgust.

"That culture is sick," she said suddenly.

"And just what culture are you referring to?" I asked.

"Gay culture," she said. "S&M. It's sick."

There was nothing I could say that was going to change her mind, but I felt I had to try anyway.

"The two are not synonymous," I explained as calmly as I could. "I think you're focusing on the tiny little slice of gay culture that you've just heard about. But there's much more to it than that." I tried to explain that gay life, as I understood it, was not just about people shooting up and having sex. It was about regular people just trying to get through life, with jobs and partners and rent and everything else. There were a lot of sleazy things about gay culture, but they didn't have the lock on S&M. There were a lot of sleazy things about straight culture, too.

We emerged from the tunnel and sped down a northbound artery. The road was lined with lube shops, malls and franchise food outlets. The elegant residential neighborhoods that supported this roadside sprawl were hidden just a few blocks away.

"S&M is not fun," she said. "It's sick."

"If both people want to do it, I don't see any reason..."

"It's not a matter of personal *choice*!" she said, just short of a scream. "It's clearly wrong. Gay culture, S&M culture, whatever you want to call it, it's the same thing. It's sick. They have sex without thinking about it. One partner after another. There's no spiritual dimension, no context, no center, so the focus is getting more material things: more sex, more clothes, because that's all there is."

In another time and context, I could have accepted all that as a reasonably astute critique of some aspects of gay life. But I thought the materialist bit was pretty hypocritical coming from somebody wearing a yellow knit ensemble that must have cost a few hundred bucks.

"And you don't care about material things?" I asked.

"Of course I do," she snapped. "I'm an auditor at an investment bank. I make $122,000 a year, two years out of college. But that's not all I think about. There has to be something more than what you want to do this minute, or want to buy or what you want to eat. Driver, don't get on the turnpike. Take the second right."

She took a tissue out of her bag and wiped some sweat off her forehead. Sometimes she was the woman I wanted to spend the rest of my life with. And other times, she was an alien. Not a science fiction alien, but an immigrant alien, like the Haitian guy I used to buy bagels from. We could chat about the weather every morning, but then we'd go back to our different worlds, knowing somehow that it was all for the best.

The car turned off the highway and headed toward the green band of suburbs to the west. Susanna began checking her hair and makeup. The party, or whatever it was, didn't appear to be a dressy affair. She was wearing flats, and her yellow suit. Maybe she kept heels and a little black dress in her bag.

The house was a cross between a large New Jersey Victorian and a small prewar mansion, built on a double lot at the end of a cul-de-sac. Dormer windows on the third story, and a big back yard for the kids to play in. Good schools. The kind of place a wealthy trader would buy to raise his family in. A van delivering flowers was parked in the circular driveway but no other cars. Maybe she was early.

Susanna walked to the front door, her back straight, like she was Queen of the Manor. The smile on her face was pasted on. A skinny teenage boy met her halfway to the door and took her bag and she disappeared into the house.

I stayed in the car and told the driver I'd pay for the trip back to the office. Watching her walk away, without so much as a wave, left me with a sexual ache. The lemon-colored suit with its Jackie Kennedy buttons would not come off in my presence. A suit in a very small size. I'd never taken women five feet tall seriously as sexual objects. They were just a curiosity. But now I'd had a taste. The simple pressure of her body against mine was good enough. Bad sex was always better than no sex. Any fool knew that.

As the car drove back through the Holland Tunnel, I was left with the essential fact: My actions had led directly to Tim's death. I wasn't responsible for actually killing him, of course. But I had precipitated his murder. Although Tim and I had committed similar crimes, his was considerably worse. I had committed a crime of passion. His was a premeditated fraud.

When he was alive, Susanna and I were both determined to uncover this fraud and see him punished. But unlike Susanna, I didn't believe he deserved to spend time in jail. He should have been punished as I was: banished from the society of traders and a given a stiff fine that robbed him of his wealth. He certainly didn't deserve to die.

And what about Steve, my protégé, dead of AIDS at 25? I couldn't stop myself from doing some guilty arithmetic. He probably started his sexual career in the '90s, when everybody knew about safe sex. He must have skipped some precautions that got him infected. But he didn't deserve to die, either.

I couldn't mourn Tim's death with any real feeling because I barely knew him, but I found myself mourning Steve's. There was more than enough mourning to go around. The guys at Cantor Fitzgerald were just ghosts on the phone, but Steve had been my apprentice. He had chosen my trading style over Ray's, and was beginning to make some decent money at it. In the midst of all the Wall Street nonsense, he remained an Army brat who never stopped being amazed about his leap into investment banking. I had been so caught up in my own problems that I never really thought about how I missed him.

Tim was a more of a cipher. All that energy spent impersonating a heterosexual. He was living the same double life as Steve. But on top of that, he was living a third life, as a criminal who was running a clever multimillion-dollar scam.

The driver let me off at the police sawhorses in front of the World Financial Center just as the sun was setting across the Hudson. Out on the sidewalk, I saw a sight that made me laugh. A bunch of big-hitters in suits were huddled around a surly taxi dispatcher with a walkie-talkie. In the old days, a long line of idling black sedans waited to take the masters of the universe home to the suburbs. Now, because of security precautions, they gave the dispatcher their car number, and waited meekly while the cars drove up from a parking lot around the corner.

I walked past them and up the long escalator to the third floor. At the huge slab of marble that served as a reception desk, a single guard stared dully as I approached. Friday night at an investment bank. The traders had left at sharply 4:15, their gym bags in tow, and most everybody else soon afterwards. Upstairs, a few M&A types, their lawyers and interns were racing to meet the 8:45 FedEx deadline. And perhaps a few others working late before a Friday night date.

Then somewhere in Chelsea, a couple cops were probably tramping through the bars, spending whatever time they'd budgeted, investigating an accidental drug overdose. How much effort would they think it deserved? Not much, I guessed. That was okay. For my money, the answer was hidden in some computer file somewhere in this building. And I was the guy to find it.

The technical question that confronted me was simple: How did Tim get a message out to his accomplice without anybody knowing about it? He could have done it with a phone call, but everyone knew the trading desk lines were recorded. We had already tracked his e-mails and what Web sites he visited and found nothing.

But if he were signaling by some physical means — perhaps by leaving his desk to speak to somebody who then forwarded the signal to somebody else — we'd pick up his movements on one of the eight security cameras that kept a watchful eye on things from discreet mountings in the ceiling.

It took me more than three hours to eliminate that remote possibility. A series of cryptic help screens guided me to the surveillance camera database and to the key 24 minutes of February 2. The images were jerky and froze every few seconds, but they were good enough for my purposes. Tim was clearly visible at the right edge of camera four, just above the time stamp. I could even zoom in on him by clicking on a little control panel, and play everything back to pick up details I might have missed.

It was a strange thing to watch. From my bird's eye view, it looked like a normal scene at midday. People made phone calls, typed e-mails, talked to each other, wrote notes, watched their screens, left their desks to go to the bathroom. At 11:32 a secretary took lunch orders for a half dozen people. A couple other people left to get their own. Shortly afterwards, a trader directly beside Tim began making weird hand gestures. What was that all about? After a few replays, and an extreme closeup, the mystery was solved: He was wearing a wind-up Rolex. I was going crazy. Every scratch, every gesture became a potential clue.

And what was Tim doing during those 24 minutes? Essentially nothing. He placed a few small trades for his own account, and ran his fingers through his hair a few times. At 11:26, he raised his hand over his head and swiveled it, but that couldn't be a signal. Whatever form it took, the signal would have to convey a lot of details: what trades, how many, what date. After staring at the footage half a dozen times, I gave up. Maybe it was time to run all 2,000 of his trades through the supercomputer again to see if there were any patterns I'd missed the first time.

I had to ask a security guard to escort me to the sub-basement. The computer people had left for the weekend, and the hallways were darkened, but the air-conditioning system continued to pump fierce blasts from the vents in the ceiling. The glass door to the area I wanted was locked. I could see Shivakumar sitting at a table, bent over his programming manual, waiting for his weekend Monte Carlo run to finish. He smiled when he saw me and let me in.

"I'll be done in 10 minutes," he said, checking his watch. "Twenty minutes at most."

"That's great," I said. "This run won't take much time."

His face turned solemn. "I suppose you heard about Tim."

I nodded.

"There was an e-mail sent to everybody in capital markets at 5:30," he said. "It was very sad. He was very clever man."

"I didn't know him that well," I said. "He seemed like he added a little fun to the trading desk."

Shivakumar shook his head sadly. "I wouldn't know," he said. "I'm only the risk cop for the derivatives traders. I can't be their friend. I don't look like them or talk like them or dress like them. I'm a mathematician. If I had my druthers, I'd be teaching advanced trigonometry to grad students. But I have a large family to support. And I happen to find options interesting."

"So do I," I said.

"You're a mathematician too?" he asked.

"A failed one," I said. "It was my undergraduate major, but I never really wanted to teach."

"Options are very peculiar mathematically," he said. "An option trade is the most devious instrument in finance. A trade is not just a trade. A trade can be a probe. Testing what the market thinks of this or that price. A trade can be a signal. For somebody who understands the numbers, a signal of future intentions. You never know what it really is. If you all spend your time examining options trades, as I do, you'll often find yourself on the brink of madness."

"That just about describes where I am now," I said.

"You see? We have the same job in the same bank but we work for different departments. I try not to get emotionally involved. If I find irregularities, I report them. If I discover that this or that trader is playing a little trick to pump up his bonus. I submit my reports, then I wait for somebody to take action. If the people I work for don't take any action, that's not my affair. There are many business issues that I'm not privy to. I don't have to concern myself with them. Maybe just my presence here keeps them honest. That's what I tell myself when I'm here all alone at night. Or at least more honest than if I wasn't here. Do you understand what I'm talking about?"

"I think so," I said.

"Last week you said you wanted to scare a trader shitless. Did you succeed?"

"That's a good question."

I hesitated. An awkward meeting of the eyes.

"Was the trader Stu Lister?" he asked. "Or Tim Scott?"

"I'm sorry, but I can't tell you," I said. "We work for different departments."

He shrugged his shoulders.

"I heard you discovered that Stu was pushing his volatility numbers. You and Susanna did all the work by yourselves, re-creating everything I did. I could have saved you a lot of trouble."

"I know," I said. "But no hard feelings, okay?" I turned to leave.

"You don't want to wait for your turn?"

"No thanks. I don't need it any more."

I practically ran back to my office. Shivakumar, my insightful comrade in arms, had given me a golden clue.

A trade can be a signal. To somebody who understands the numbers on his screen, a signal of somebody's future intentions.

I had that exhausted exultant feeling you get in college, working late in the library stacks on a term paper that's finally coming together.

Just a little bit more, Dave. Keep pushing.

I went back to February 2, the date Tim purchased the basket of options on chemical stocks. I sorted through the trade database and looked at all the trades he placed between 11:21, the time he would have learned about the bank's impending trade and 11:45, the time it happened.

During that 24-minute time period, Tim had bought a few very cheap long-dated options, worth about $55 apiece. I had ignored them before because they were small change, but this time I drilled down to get the actual names. Dow Chemical. Air Products. Rohm. Celanese and four more. I blinked a couple times, then looked again. They were very familiar. He had bought the same collection of options on chemical stocks the bank would be buying a few minutes later — but for the wrong date.

What the hell was he doing? My momentary elation was tempered with confusion: The bank needed to buy options that ended in December 2002, but Tim was buying options that ended in December 2004.

It didn't make sense. If you wanted to make money based on your inside knowledge of what the bank was going to do, you'd buy 2002 options, not 2004 options. Hardly anybody cared about 2004 options. They cost $55 while 2002 options cost thousands. I checked my monitor. The December 2002 screen listed hundreds of people who had bought options dated December 2002. The December 2004 screen was practically empty.

Then the fog cleared. And my jaw fell a couple inches.

You can signal with a trade.

I was dumbstruck by the sheer audacity and simplicity of the plan. Tim finds out what 2002 options the bank needed to buy. Then he buys a few of the same options, but dated 2004 instead of 2002.

Meanwhile, his accomplice is sitting in front of a market screen somewhere. He waits for somebody to buy a series of 2004 options in a certain pattern. When he sees the signal, he buys the same options for 2002. A few minutes later the bank comes into the market, desperate to buy the options. He sells them at a nice profit, and stuffs the money in his pocket.

When Tim bought those obscure 2004 options, he was broadcasting an anonymous signal visible to anybody in the financial world who knew where to look. His accomplice could be down the street or across the world. You could see the accomplice's trades on the screen, but you couldn't identify who he was or where he worked. He was protected by the anonymity of the market.

What a perfect way to scam the bank!

I wanted to go back to Shivakumar and give him a bear hug. Buy him a beer at his favorite bar. A gift card to Amazon. Or some toys for his kids.

Tim had come up with an almost foolproof way to quietly skim a few thousand bucks a day from the bank. At various times, over beers with various trading buddies, we had all tried to invent scams of our own, more for amusement than anything else. Our bimonthly paychecks always seemed pathetically small compared to the millions we were making for our employer. But most of the schemes we had concocted required the trader inside the bank to lose money — drawing attention and endangering his career — while the accomplice outside the bank picked up the money he lost.

Tim's scam was perfect. Nobody was at fault. Prices were just a little higher than expected. And you'd never have discovered it if you weren't alerted that something funny was going on. The real beauty of the plan was its size. A nickel here, a dime there. Big scams were easy to catch. But who would notice a few thousand bucks missing from a bid/offer spread?

A lopsided grin planted itself on my face and refused to leave.

There were a lot more questions to be answered. How much did these guys actually make? Did the pattern appear in other trades Tim did? Were other traders on the desk involved in similar scams? And most important: How could this lead to Tim's accomplice?

With a giddy smile, I waved goodbye to the somnolent security guards and wished them a good weekend. I bought a gyro from the guy on the corner, just as he was folding up his cart. I called Susanna, and got a chirpy cell phone message. I didn't care.

Tim and I were both traders who had gone astray. He was another guy in my fraternity. Whether I liked him or not, he was my brother. The police would be chasing leads up and down Chelsea, but I was the guy who was going to figure out who killed him.

I grabbed a few hours sleep and returned to my office at 7 a.m. on Saturday. I spent the morning in a fever, checking other traders who might have been able to pull off a similar scam. Nothing. I rechecked the security cameras, the e-mails, the Web site visits. Nothing. I rechecked our spreadsheets of trades with disappointing profits. Ditto. As far as I could tell, Tim and his partner were the only guys in the game.

Susanna finally called me back at 8 p.m. Saturday night, just as I was settling down in front of a Bulls game with a bottle of Canadian Mist.

"I think I know what happened," she said. "I've been thinking about this all weekend." She was trying to talk over some conversation in the background. And music. A single instrument, perhaps a guitar.

"No, you don't," I said, interrupting her. "I found the signal. It's obvious. It's undeniable."

"What?"

"He signaled with a trade."

"Wait," she said. "Let me go to my room."

I heard her stomp up the stairs two at a time. When she got to the top, she put her mouth to the phone again, breathing hard. I told her the story piece by piece. The tip from Shivakumar. The option trades two years out. The way the signal worked. By the end, her breathing had stopped.

"Oh, my God," she said. "That's it."

For a few moments we said nothing, separated by the Hudson River and a few miles of suburbia.

"I'll be back very late Sunday night," she said. "You're brilliant. I can't wait to get started. Come by my place at 7 a.m. and we'll walk to work."

I hung up and looked down at my pants in disbelief. I had an erection.

Chapter 11

When I came by her apartment the next morning, I found the door open a half inch.

"Come in," she called from inside.

What was the smell this time? Not a smell exactly. Steam from her morning shower. And a bit of perfume from the shampoo. The living room windows still dark this early in April, but lights on in her bedroom.

She stood in front of a full-length mirror, in gray slacks and a tight camisole, brushing her hair. A black cashmere turtleneck and a heavier dark green cardigan lay folded on her bed.

Her bedroom at last. Like the rest of the apartment, spare and off-white. A big down duvet stretching across the bed, puffy as a cloud.

She was staring at her hair skeptically, tilting her head this way and that to see how it slid across her shoulders. It looked perfect to me, but it required another dozen brushstrokes on either side to teach it who was boss.

"Take one of those to work," she said, nodding to two large Adidas gym bags. One black, one gray.

"What for?" I asked.

"Our files are still in our old office," she said. "I'm sure the custodians haven't moved them yet, but they might do it first thing in the morning. We should leave soon."

She was right. When we arrived at 7:45, our office key still worked and our files were in the same piles we'd left them Friday afternoon. I couldn't take all of them, so it was a matter of triage, grabbing the important ones and stuffing them into the two gym bags. Meanwhile, Susanna moved the key computer files onto a memory stick.

"Where are we going to put these things?" I asked.

"We're going to take them home tonight," she said, zipping one shut with a loud rip.

I hefted the bags. Twenty pounds of paper each.

"I suppose this is breaking the law," I said.

"The bank is breaking the law, not us," she snapped.

We got to our offices on the auditing floor before 8 a.m. Susanna hid the bags under her desk, then took me to meet Jeffrey Ialeggio, the head of audit — Susanna's boss and now mine as well.

He was one of the firm's alpha accountants, a spare little man who kept only one file at a time on his desk, open and perfectly centered. A year ago, he probably had a serious comb-over. Now he sported a shaved head.

"My new options trader!" he exclaimed when he saw me, giving my hand a nervous pump. "They aren't all as big as you, are they? Ed Lewis said you did a bang-up job on that derivatives project."

"Thanks," I said.

"Ed wants to keep you guys together as a separate trading fraud unit, funded from corporate. Which is great for me, because I'll have you two on my headcount but not my budget. So I can hire somebody to replace Susanna."

"Great," I said.

"You'll continue as a consultant until the third quarter at your current rate. Then we'll give you a little raise. Is that okay?"

"Fine."

I figured Ialeggio was the kind of guy who spent his days going through mental checklists. Just answer him quickly and let him do his thing.

"I've been paying these thieves at Ernst & Young a fortune for the use of their trading specialist. I'd love to do that in-house." Then he gave me a full-body stare that asked: "Can somebody built like a truck be smart?" He quickly decided yes. "Ed told me the derivatives thing is all wrapped up and you're ready to start work today. Is that right?"

"That's right," Susanna answered, even though Ialeggio was looking at me.

"I want you two to spend a week getting acquainted with the mortgage-backed securities market. Read some trade magazines. Talk to some people here. Go out and buy some books. Whatever you need. Then next week we'll send you out to Connecticut. Where do you guys live?"

"We both live downtown," I said.

"There's a company van that leaves from here for the Connecticut office at 7:40 every morning. It's quite comfortable." Then he looked at his watch. "I'm late for an 8:00 conference call. Just find an empty cubicle and get going. My assistant, Sharda, will help you set up."

Then he grabbed a folder and disappeared down the hall.

A few minutes later, I was set up in a cubicle of my own. It was only a few feet away from Susanna's, but we wouldn't be able to talk to each other without being overheard. We had to use a conference room nearby, which was not the best place to meet, because anyone passing by could glance over our shoulder.

"We have this room for half an hour," Susanna said, opening one of the duffel bags.

"Ialeggio is not as bad as I thought," I said.

"He's a sexist pig," she said. "He thinks you did all the work. I couldn't possibly understand derivatives."

"Yeah, but at least you're finally out of the audit group," I said. "We're his new crack trading fraud team. He likes me, and you're going to benefit."

"We're his *Connecticut* trading fraud team," she corrected. "Where are the trade confirms for the chemical stocks?"

I sighed. This was a new thing: Susanna in a bad mood.

She was clutching a kid's school notebook with a marbled cover, filled with handwriting. "I did a lot of thinking about this case over the weekend," she said. "Late at night. I think I've gone through all the possibilities. But I want you to walk me through everything you've found, piece by piece."

We went through the spreadsheet I had compiled, taking pains to match each of Tim's trades with the individual trade confirmations she had in her files. She highlighted the relevant evidence with a turquoise highlighter, made her own notes on the back side, and organized them by date, adding notes to her notebook.

"It was a beautiful concept," I said, after we'd compiled a small stack of trades. "You have to admire his handiwork."

"What are you talking about?" she said, scowling. "It's wire fraud and grand larceny."

"I know, but purely objectively, you have to admit he found a very elegant way to make money at the bank's expense."

"A crime is a crime," she said. "There's nothing beautiful about it."

It was time to go back to our cubicles and bone up on mortgage-backed trading. Once I got acclimated to my cubicle, I found myself quite happy browsing through mortgage-backed trading sites. This was the start of my new professional life: David Ackerman, forensic auditor. In Ialeggio's eyes, I was clearly the dominant player on the team — and Susanna didn't like that at all. I spent some time plumbing the intricacies of mortgage-backed securities models, thankful that I had a job where my skills were appreciated.

At one point, I struck up a conversation with my neighbor, who was reading the sports pages of the Post and who turned out to be a Mets fan. I introduced myself as a White Sox fan, and we had an amiable discussion about the joys and sorrows of supporting lost causes. When he found out I was a former trader, he asked if I could help him understand an options trade he was working on. A few minutes later, he asked if he could bring his two team members into the discussion, and before long, I had four people sitting in chairs, listening to my improvised graduate seminar on trading practice.

I dropped by Susanna's cubicle an hour later to see if her mood had changed.

"She left a moment ago," said her neighbor, pointing towards the doorway.

I caught her figure walking down the hall. I don't know what possessed me at that moment. I didn't want to run after her, so I decided to follow her and catch up to her when she entered the cafeteria. I found it all very erotic. She had very narrow hips, and the bottom of her cardigan swung back and forth in rhythm with her hair. I said a little prayer: Maybe tonight.

I held back a little as she turned the corner. She walked past the cafeteria and entered the vestibule beside it that had two sets of glass doors. One led to a stairway, the other to the offices of the company's travel agency.

I sauntered past half a dozen travel agents staring into computer screens. No Susanna. I was about to turn around when the receptionist stopped me.

"Can I help you?"

"I was trying to buy some tickets to Chicago."

"We don't take orders on the phone or in person anymore. You'll have to fill out a requisition online," she said, handing me a Xerox with instructions.

I walked through the stairway, which was the only other place she could have gone. It functioned as a kind of fire exit, but a very wide one, built to handle the evacuation of a large building. It had big platforms at every flight, lit by large windows and graced with the same marble that lined the building's other public areas.

Then I heard a man singing or chanting in the stairway above me. As I walked up a flight I recognized what it was: Someone was going through the Orthodox Jewish prayer service, singing a few lines of Hebrew and then mumbling a paragraph or two at high speed. Other practiced voices joined him. I walked up as quietly as I could, stopping a flight below the singing, and then inched up a few steps at a time until I was just below their line of sight.

A dozen pairs of pants and shoes were pointing east. I took another couple steps and saw the backs of a dozen guys in business casual, mumbling into prayer books, most wearing little knit yarmulkes attached with bobby pins. One man with a big beard stood off to the side, wearing a dark suit with no tie. He was clearly the rabbi. Then I caught the dark green legs of Susanna's pants standing on the beginning of the next flight, two or three steps above everyone else. I'd heard of similar services before, but they usually met in conference rooms.

Susanna was standing beside him, leading a short singsong prayer. Apparently performing the number two role in the service.

I beat a silent retreat back down the stairs and out the glass doors.

I had a message from Ed Lewis waiting for on my voicemail.

"I've been trying to reach you for 15 minutes," he said, when I called back. "I want you guys to come by my office right away."

"Susanna's at lunch. She'll be back in a few minutes. Anything important?"

"Just come up as soon as you can."

When we got to Lewis' office, we found Markowitz sitting at the smudged glass table, looking mean and downcast. To his right was somebody who clearly wasn't from the bank: a dark, sharp-eyed guy in his late 40s with an unassuming jacket and tie. He was staring at the same yellow sheet that Ed used to tell us details of Tim's death. Lewis pointed us to the only empty seats.

"This is Detective Nardulli, from the First Precinct," he said with a polite smile. "And this is Susanna Cassuto, and David Ackerman, who are auditors assigned to investigate irregularities on our trading desk. I guess you guys are in the same business, more or less."

Nardulli nodded hello and released a tiny grimace. He didn't like being compared to an auditor.

"On Friday I told Detective Nardulli about your investigation of Tim Scott's trading irregularities," Ed continued. "But I explained that they were of a very technical nature and were unrelated to his investigation of Tim's death. He's come back this morning to talk with Tim's boss and get some more information from you."

The subtext was obvious: Zip your lip.

I saw our report open in front of Nardulli on the desk. He wrote down our names in a little notebook and flipped through it.

"Mr. Lewis tells me you were studying some problems on the trading desk where Tim worked," he said. "I don't know much about option trading. Could you tell me a little about what Mr. Scott was doing?"

He had a thick Bronx accent and heavily-lidded eyes that suggested somebody who was either bored by his work or cultivating a careful nonchalance.

"Tim was involved in a multimillion-dollar trading scam," Susanna announced. "We pieced the scam together over the course of a few weeks and submitted a report to Mr. Lewis on Friday afternoon. We concluded that Tim had been murdered by his accomplice. Or one of his accomplices."

Her interpretation of the facts gave Nardulli a little start. Markowitz looked at the ceiling and Lewis followed his gaze.

"You know who killed him?" Nardulli asked.

"It's obvious," Susanna said. "We told Tim that we were investigating his trading records. His partners killed him to shut him up."

A general silence settled over the room while Nardulli ingested the information. Lewis and Markowitz were throwing flames in Susanna's general direction. She clearly liked the splash she was making, but I thought it was the wrong tack to take with Nardulli. I didn't think he liked people telling him how to do his job.

"Okay, let's start from the beginning," said Nardulli, regaining his deadpan. "I want to ask you a few questions about Tim and the people he associated with on the trading desk."

"His accomplice did not work on the trading desk," Susanna snapped. "That's not going to get you anywhere."

I could see Nardulli putting Susanna in a box: hysterical female. And I could see where he was going. He was determined to find some other gay person in the bank who might lead him to the guy Tim had sex with the night he died. Susanna, for her part, was desperate to explain Tim's scam so the detective would understand why he was following the wrong lead. It was an unstoppable force meeting an immovable object.

"Did you know Tim very well?" he asked. "Are you friendly with the people on the trading floor?"

"Pretty much the opposite," she said. "As an auditor, you're in an adversarial relationship with the people you investigate."

"Were you investigating just Tim or did you interview other people as well?"

"We investigated a number of people, but we narrowed it down to him."

"So as far as these trading irregularities go, Tim wasn't working with anybody else in the bank."

"We don't know. Tim bought certain options as signals to his accomplice, who was working outside the bank, and who bid up the prices of other options the bank needed to buy."

Nardulli nodded his head, but looked completely confused.

"How did this investigation start?" he asked. When Susanna didn't answer, he turned to Markowitz and finally to Lewis.

"It was a result of our regular risk management practices," Lewis explained hesitantly. "A few deals that raised a red flag. Nothing more than that."

Lewis picked up our report and turned his attention to Markowitz.

"You're the head derivatives trader. Do you agree with Ms. Cassuto's assessment? That it was related to a fraud that occurred on your trading desk?"

Markowitz folded his hands and stared at them. "As I explained before they arrived, I wasn't aware that Tim was doing anything wrong. All I know is what I read in their report."

"But is the report plausible to you?"

"It's quite convincing. I was aware that some of Tim's trades weren't as profitable as I'd hoped, but you can say that about almost everybody's work. His scam was very subtle. Very clever."

"I don't quite understand why you think his trades were illegal," Nardulli said.

"They weren't illegal in themselves," Susanna said, interrupting. "They were a signal to his accomplice, who made money on the other side of the trade."

Nardulli reluctantly turned his gaze to Susanna.

"But Tim wasn't allowed to make these trades?"

"He was. He bought and sold options all the time. That was his job."

"So what did he do wrong?"

"The trades in themselves weren't the crime. The bank lost money as a result of the trades his partner did. The partner was the one who made the money."

"How could the bank lose money on trades somebody else did?"

"The bank needs to do certain trades for its clients. But it ended up paying too much, because Tim bought certain options."

"But didn't you just say that was Tim's job? To make money buying and selling options?"

"Tim wasn't supposed to make money at the bank's expense!" she said, losing her patience at Nardulli's ignorance. "He was front-running. That was the scam!"

I shot a quick glance at Lewis, who was trying to suppress a smile. Nardulli clearly didn't understand the first thing about options trading, and Susanna's tone was only making things worse.

"Let me see if I can take a stab at this," I said. "The option purchases were not the crime in themselves. The purchases were a signal to his accomplice. It was sort of like insider trading, but instead of telling somebody a piece of inside information, Tim would buy certain options as a signal that told his accomplice what the bank was about to buy. Then the accomplice bid up the prices before the bank's purchase."

I'm not sure Nardulli followed me, but he nodded appreciatively. "Do you think Tim was in a sexual relationship with this accomplice?"

"Tim wasn't gay, if that's what you're asking," said Susanna. "He was killed by his accomplice, who wanted to make it look like he was gay. They're trying to fool you, and they're obviously succeeding."

Nardulli locked his jaw and raised his chin in an obvious attempt to control his anger. "Okay," he said. "So who do you think is fooling me?"

"We don't know. Whoever was on the other side of the trade. I actually suspect it could be a group of people."

"Do you have any evidence to support your idea?"

She was frozen for a moment in disbelief. "What more evidence do you need?" she cried. "Our whole report is the evidence. Can't you see how obvious it is?"

He had stopped taking notes long ago. He had given up on her completely, and she knew it. She pushed her chair back an inch or two, trying to preserve whatever shred of credibility she had left.

Nardulli stretched his legs and turned to me. He would try to get the information he needed from the more reasonable half of the investigative team.

"Mr. Ackerman, did you know Tim very well?"

"No."

"Was he particularly friendly with other people? Other people who might be gay?"

"I don't think so. There aren't a lot of people on trading floors who admit they're gay."

"How many is a lot?"

"I was a trader for 9 years. I didn't know a single trader who admitted to being gay. There are a lot of guys who aren't married, who claim to have girlfriends. The news about Tim came as a surprise to me. I'm sure it was a complete surprise to everybody on his trading desk."

Nardulli turned to us and folded his hands, as a preface to an announcement. He started to say something, thought better of it and began again.

"We're looking for a white gay male, thin, young, about five-feet-nine, about 150 pounds," he said. "Does anybody you know fit that description?"

Lewis and Markowitz looked at each other and shook their heads in disbelief.

"There are several hundred white males on the trading desk," said Lewis. "Several dozen would fit that description."

"What about you?" he asked Markowitz. "Do you have any people on your team that you think are worth investigating?"

Markowitz hesitated. He spun his wedding band around a few times and grimaced.

"We talked about all this in the morning meeting," he said. "I had no idea that Tim was gay. Nobody on the derivatives desk was aware that he was gay. And if there are any other people in my group who were gay, they certainly didn't announce it."

"You don't know a single trader who's gay?"

Markowitz shook his head solemnly. "Let me tell you how Wall Street trading floors work. They're like high school locker rooms. A couple hundred guys sitting a few feet away from each other. Everybody's looking for some stupid thing to throw in your face. Your nickname. Your fat ass. If you let it out that you were gay, the shit would never stop. The teasing would be merciless. And it would hurt your career. If I were gay, I wouldn't let anybody know about it. I'd keep it a secret, too."

Nardulli stared at the row of Lucite deal plaques arrayed near Lewis' window and we all followed his gaze out the window to the Circle Line tourist boat floating by in the Hudson below. The light was changing off the river, brightening by a couple degrees. Just five people in a room, talking about a dead guy. We could hear jackhammers outside from the Trade Center, always just beyond consciousness those days.

"He was a first-class equity options trader," Markowitz said into the silence. "And now I've got to find somebody to replace him."

That seemed to exhaust Nardulli's interest in the discussion. He'd come to find some other gay traders, and he had to leave empty-handed. He put the copy of our report in his briefcase, got our contact phone numbers and thanked us politely for our time.

We all stared at his closed door until Nardulli was safely out of earshot, then Lewis turned abruptly to Susanna.

"Are you *nuts*?" he asked, striding across the room as he tried to contain his fury.

Susanna had prepared herself, assuming her miniature Buddha posture, back perfectly straight, her gray flats just grazing the floor.

"Do you actually *want* to have the cops crawling around here? You want to let them in the *door*? Do you have any *inkling* of what that would be like?"

"That was a little too close for comfort," said Markowitz, glaring at her and pulling on his collar.

"He didn't have a clue about what happened," said Susanna, shaking her head in disbelief. "He was completely ignorant!"

"Well, of course! He's a detective!" said Ed. "Why would he know anything about institutional finance?"

"But he's simply wrong. Tim's death was not a coincidence. It was directly related to the fraud we were investigating. You can see that, can't you?" Susanna asked.

Markowitz picked up our report and scanned a few a pages. "I've read this thing very carefully," he said. "It's brilliant. You found evidence that the market moved against Tim's trades in several instances. There certainly appears to be something wrong. But it's really just a theory. It explains the data. But you never actually caught him communicating with somebody outside the bank."

"He was signaling via *specific* trades," I said. "We have records of those trades. It's not a theory. It's a fact."

Markowitz and Lewis looked at each other.

"I didn't see that in your report," Lewis said.

"We just figured it out," I said.

"Since Friday afternoon? When I told you to drop it?"

"Yes," Susanna and I said in unison.

Lewis closed his eyes and pinched the bridge of this nose. He began to speak but Markowitz interrupted him.

"I know you're not supposed to speak ill of the dead," Markowitz said. "But it's no secret that I hated the guy. He was a real asshole. And most of the people on the desk — except for his little clique — would agree. It doesn't really matter either way at this point."

"Tim Scott was scamming the bank out of two million bucks a year," Lewis said, picking up the yellow crime sheet and putting it into a folder. "The scam is over. And I'm sure whoever he was working with is going to become pretty scarce."

"But we're not talking about an accidental drug death!" Susanna shouted. "We're talking about a murder!"

"He's dead. That's as far as I need to go," said Lewis. "I know that you want to get to the bottom of this, but so do the cops. That's their job, not ours. There is no reason for you to talk to them. Tim Scott no longer works at this bank, and you are no longer investigating his scam."

Then he looked at me and gave me a dark stare. "That applies to you too, Dave. You did a great job on your first assignment. Against my own better judgment, I'm actually beginning to trust you. You've got a great career at this bank if you keep your nose clean. So don't blow it. Am I being clear?"

"Yes," I said. "Very clear."

"You have any more questions?"

"No," I said.

We walked back to our office and headed straight for the conference room, but it was crammed with half a dozen auditors working against some awful deadline. The only other place to talk was the coffee room, which had a tiny table for two and a gizmo that dispensed a dozen different types of coffee from foil packets. We sat facing the door so we'd have advance warning if anyone approached. I threw some reports on mortgage-backed securities on the table to make things look legit.

"I really blew it, didn't I?" Susanna said, extracting her cup of French roast. She was apologetic, but I picked up a trace of self-righteousness too.

"You certainly did," I said. "You completely alienated the cop. He thinks you're a complete flake."

"It wasn't all my fault," she said. "I explained it as simply as I could, but he didn't understand a word."

"He's not an idiot. He just doesn't know much about Wall Street."

As we stared at our coffee, a couple of admins came in and grabbed Snapples from the refrigerator. Then a middle-aged guy who knew Susanna from a previous assignment stopped to regale us with the joys of his summer bungalow in the Catskills. When he left, we gazed glumly at the table, trying to figure out what to do next.

"Did you notice Ed lied about how the investigation started?" she asked. "He's protecting somebody on the board of directors."

"He doesn't want cops hanging around the trading floor looking for gay traders," I said. "And he doesn't want them calling up his board members, asking embarrassing questions about a gay S&M death. That doesn't mean the board member was part of some group that planned the fraud. Or that he had a hand in the murder."

"But the board member might have some more information. He had suspicions about one particular desk. The derivatives desk. And instead of a regular audit, the job is given to two people who report to the bank's corporation counsel. That's just weird."

"We don't know anything about the director's motivation," I said. "Maybe it's some political thing we're not aware of. Maybe Markowitz pissed off one of his corporate rivals, and the rival gets one of his director buddies to dig up some dirt on him."

"But if we knew who the board member was, we'd have a better idea of what he'd wanted us to look for."

"We're not going to get anywhere making guesses about the board member. If we had his resume and his shoe size and his favorite brand of golf clubs we still wouldn't know a damn thing," I said. "I want to talk to him as much as you, but we can't. So let's drop it."

That, of course, only inspired her to pursue it.

As we got ready to walk home, she handed me a copy of the bios of the 17 corporate board members that had been posted on the bank's Web site along with additional material on each of them. There were no surprises. A collection of CEOs of other financial companies, most between 50 and 70, with several double chins, and enough interlocking board memberships to keep a conspiracy theorist happy for months.

"What does this prove?" I asked, flipping through the pages. "Do you think the board member that assigned us to this project is part of some conspiracy to defraud the bank? That makes even less sense. If he was part of an organized fraud, he wouldn't hire us to investigate it."

"I don't know what's going on here and neither do you. But there's a pattern of fraud that involves several people buried in these documents."

"How do you know several people were involved?" I asked, throwing my hands up in the air in sheer exasperation. "That's what your guess is. But we don't know if it's true. It's an assumption we have yet to test!"

I sounded like my dad, arguing with my mom about whether to buy the El Dorado or the Olds 88. They shared the same uncertainty, but they staked out opposite positions just for the hell of it.

The most powerful truth remained unstated between us. We knew Tim had committed a crime and we knew how he did it. But we were no closer to identifying who he was working with. Or who killed him. On Monday, we'd start commuting to Greenwich, which would effectively put an end to our research. And at some point the cops would decide to move on to the next accidental gay S&M death. Time was becoming a scarce commodity.

We were both exhausted, beat up by the day. On the walk home, I suggested going to the health club together to unwind. She said she wanted to make some phone calls. Maybe I could stop by around eight.

When I got home, I called my friend Doug, who had some degree of expertise when it came to religious women.

"So how's your love life?" he asked. "Did you ever make it with that chick who spoke Hebrew?"

"Well, sort of. That's why I'm calling. It turns out she's Orthodox."

"Oh, boy. How Orthodox? Orthodox Orthodox?"

"I don't know. She goes to a prayer service at lunch. I'm just trying to get a little perspective on what's going on with us."

"So what happened?"

"Sexually?"

"Yeah."

"We're on the couch, the blouse stays on, she gets off rubbing against my leg..."

"...and you get a hand finish."

"Yeah."

"Par for the course. What date are we talking about?"

"We've never really been out on a date. We work together. You might call it the third date."

"That's pretty good. What are you complaining about?"

"I'm not complaining. I'm trying to understand what I've got here. I've never dated somebody Orthodox."

"Orthodox women have their own set of religious responsibilities that are completely different from men. Their families pound it into them. They're supposed to run the household. They're supposed to be practical."

"What about sex?"

"It's all over the map. Some of them sleep around. Some of them are virgins until marriage. Some of them sleep with their college boyfriends and then marry them."

"They get married right after college?"

"No. Before they graduate. After they have sex for the first time."

"Wow."

"They're under tremendous pressure to get married. If they're not married by the end of college, they're regarded as something of a stray."

"Susanna's got a job as an auditor in an investment bank. She has some sexual experience. She mentioned a boyfriend who was a securities lawyer, but she said they broke up."

"Do you want to convert? That might help things along."

"I'm already Jewish."

"No, I mean, do you want to move to Orthodox? Because if you do, I can put you in touch with a rabbi."

"I don't care about Judaism. I care about her."

"You're how old? Thirty?"

"Thirty-one."

"It's time you settled down. Maybe this girl will do it. I'll tell you one thing. Some of the Orthodox girls were attracted to me because they thought I was more sexually experienced. But others thought I was too dangerous. Not to be trusted. I never really clicked with them anyway. I married somebody like me, who moved up to orthodoxy."

"So you're saying we might spend a lot of time in our pajamas."

"You might. You might not. All I can tell you is that I never had any really interesting sex with Orthodox girls... Except one woman. And she was on her way out."

"She was moving from Orthodox to Reformed?"

"No, she was going out the door. From Orthodox to eating lobster on Yom Kippur. Like a fallen Catholic. If that's what you've got, you're in for a wild ride."

I managed to fix myself dinner in spite of the dense fog of erotic anticipation that filled my apartment. She opened her door in an oversized dress shirt, half-buttoned and worn over a very tight pair of jeans. The jeans were low slung, the better to show off her diminutive innie, and carefully torn at the knee by a Chinese sweatshop worker, following the instructions of some Seventh Avenue fashion twit. Great looking, I thought, but they'd be hell to take off. In no time flat we were on the couch, hitting the limitations of what two half-buttoned and zipped bodies could do with each other.

I was able to nibble at her neck and pull back the top of her shirt to get at her shoulders, but I could only go so far without strangling her. The top button would have to be undone. At the very least. Railroads were built across the wilderness in the name of progress. Rockets were sent to the moon. I couldn't see why one or two buttons couldn't be separated from their buttonholes.

I pulled off my sweatshirt in the wild hope that it would inspire her to do the same. She lay there on the couch, her thumbs tucked into the top of her waistband, smiling.

She clearly wanted me to unbutton it for her.

No. I was not going to do it. Not without some active encouragement. I wanted to see a lustful nod: "Yes." Or even a few lustful nods in a row: "Yes, yes, yes!"

I fashioned my two fingers into a little creature that started walking across her shoulder, took a left at her collarbone and walked down the v-neck to the top button. It circled the button for a while and then drummed impatiently. Then it stopped, awaiting a signal.

My lust was gaining on my patience. I had seen my share of slow serial seductions, where it took several dates to progress from couch kisses to bedroom intercourse. That was par for the course. What was driving me nuts was the crazy, nightly pace of this romance, the unending, unconsummated tease.

I remember that button quite distinctly. It was made of brown plastic that was supposed to simulate wood grain. I wriggled it back and forth in my fingers, then pulled, as if testing the strength of the thread. Then I moved my eyes from the button to her eyes. We stared at each other a while. She gave me a sheepish smile, pushed my hand away and unbuttoned it.

I was ready to bite the rest off her blouse and spit them out like watermelon seeds. But being the guy I was, I unbuttoned them slowly and deliberately, with pecks that ran down her sternum to mark each victory.

Our first body-on-body contact felt like a dive down a well, or a wave of water rushing across a dry plain. After years of chasing women with mountainous breasts, I was surprised by the sheer flatness of the new landscape.

I was also practically smothered in hair. We flipped over so she could sit up and straighten it. In this particular position, it was a two-step process. The first step was to bend her head down so her hair fell in front of her face. Step two was to gather it into a ball.

Her hair was dumped on my chest in a formidable curtain. It weighed a ton. As she started to gather it together, I grabbed her arms, pushing her back to her previous position so her hair fell across my chest. She took up the idea and pulled it back the other way, then started swishing it this way and that.

She was proud of her hair, and getting into it: bracing herself above me so the bottom tips grazed like a silk broom across my nipples and my chest hair.

It became clear the jeans were meant to stay on. In fact, they seemed to be chosen specifically for that purpose, with buttons instead of a zipper. The kind you'd have to take off with needlenose pliers.

Then she shifted position and draped her hair across her chest, Lady Godiva style. I pushed away her handiwork and lowered myself onto her, careful to distribute most of my weight onto my knees.

More than a decade ago, at my first corporate Christmas party at my first job, I stumbled onto a drunken clique of women complaining about male sexual performance. "They always go straight for the tits," said one, and others nodded in agreement. After that, I resolved to take my time. I devoted quite a bit of attention to her shoulders, particularly the parts that adjoined her upper back, which I could probe with my upper teeth. At the same time, I tried slipping my hands down her jeans, but only got as far as the downy small of her back. They were impenetrable, more nylon than denim.

In the middle of all of this, she remembered something. She stopped the action, sat up, and reached across me awkwardly to flick off the ringer on the phone beside the couch.

Then we continued, in our fashion.

In a certain way, it wasn't that different from seducing a client into buying a particular Treasury bond. The structure of seduction was always the same. The more you know about the client's needs, the more likely you are to succeed. At some point, in sex and in business, you know them so well that you can do whatever the hell you want.

But first you need information, and I wasn't getting any. I didn't mind silence. Silence can be a virtue. If somebody is grabbing your dick, sticking their tongue in you ear, and digging their teeth into your shoulders, you can assume that things are going pretty well.

But Susanna was simply uncommunicative. I had run into a couple women like her in my time. They wanted you to lead the dance, but they also expected you to rent the room and direct the band. I was left begging for clues on how to proceed, for what worked and what didn't, for the very confirmation that what we were doing was consensual.

I tried mumbling "Mmm?" as a question, but got no response. Occasionally, when I needed reassurance, I would look up and see her Mona Lisa smile, and return to my labors.

After a certain point, I decided it was time for bold action. I grabbed both of her wrists, and moved them so they were slightly above her head. I don't think you could call it "pinning her to the bed," but it was pretty close. Then, I planted my tongue in a flat motionless kind of way over her nipple, just claiming the real estate as my own.

I felt a little twitch in her arms, which could be interpreted as either as an involuntary response or an attempt to wriggle out from under my grasp. I was about to let go when she drew her breath in sharply. I decided to take that as a positive sign. I continued in slow motion, waiting for a response. "Yeah?" I asked. "Hmmm?"

I felt periodic movements in her arms and hips now and then, but by that time I was caught up in my own pleasure. I knew I was going out on a limb, but all she had to say was, "No" and I would have released her in a millisecond. She didn't. I couldn't see her face from my position, but I could feel her clenched fists through her wrists. At least it was information.

At some point I decided to reposition myself for an extended stay in the neighborhood: I grabbed one of the couch pillows and threw it to the ground, giving us another six inches of room. Then I planted my elbows on both sides of her chest, gave her a peck on her sternum and then moved right. I circled around one nipple, which tightened a bit, then pushed my tongue into a point and pressed hard, as if ringing a doorbell.

Ding-dong! Anybody home?

"Um," she mumbled.

I didn't quite know what to make of it.

Did she mean: "Um, no?"

Then it came again. "Um."

Neutral. One word, intoned in a single musical pitch and delivered without force. A throwaway syllable, as in: "I'd like a coffee light with, um, a bran muffin."

As I kept going, a thought came fluttering in from the edge of my consciousness: Was this the first time she had felt a tongue there? I decided I was flattering myself, or else building up some kind of virgin fantasy about her. But I wasn't sure.

Then I heard her say something else, a whole phrase, or the beginning of a sentence, but it was coming from far off. It sounded like a recording, or some chatter in the hallway, or a bit of conversation you might hear through a bathroom ventilation shaft.

"Shit," she said.

I realized it was her answering machine. She had turned off the ringer on the phone, but not the volume switch on the answering machine in her bedroom, which was now advising people to please leave a message after the tone.

She tensed up like she was about to make a sprint for it.

"Ignore it," I said, letting go of her wrists.

She hesitated a minute, and then sat up on the couch.

An older woman's voice came on. "Shoshanna, here's the information on that boy I told you about the other day," the machine said with motherly intimacy.

Shoshanna?

She started racing to the phone, her shirt abandoned on the arm of the couch. "His name is Adam Elias," the voice continued. "He's about 29 and he's a real estate lawyer and the only one in the family who didn't go into the restaurant business. Bob Elias is his older brother. Dad and I met him..."

"Sorry, Mom," she said, picking up the phone in the bedroom. "What's up?"

I put on my shirt and walked into the kitchen. She appeared in the open doorway of the bedroom, zipping up a white Columbia sweatshirt. "I was coming back from the laundry," she said, exaggerating her breathlessness. "I had to fight for a dryer."

I smiled because it was the first time I'd heard her tell an outright lie. She caught my expression and started jabbing her finger at a laundry basket at her feet that was filled with newly folded clothes, as if that made it true.

Her mother launched into an extended monologue, apparently about the guy she wanted her to meet.

I made a quick inspection of the kitchen. A picture of her family was attached to the refrigerator in a little magnet frame. Taken when she was in college, it was a studio photograph with the abstract paint-spattered backdrop fashionable in the mid-'90s. The family displayed two genetic strands that never united: Mom, Susanna and her younger brother were all small and rail thin. Dad and the two older brothers were normal-looking Jewish guys, tending toward the pudgy.

I grabbed one of her premium beers from the refrigerator and started pawing through the drawers for an opener. She put her finger to her mouth. I was making too much noise.

"Actually, Mom, I have *several* guys over here now," she said. "They're lounging around, reading magazines and smoking crack. We're going to have an orgy pretty soon, but we're waiting for a couple more people to show up."

My beer spurted through my nose onto the floor of the kitchen.

"Mom, I've got to hang up my blouses before they get wrinkled. Let's talk in a few minutes."

She stood in the doorway of her bedroom, shaking her head in a way that indicated she was beginning the long, meticulous version of her hair-straightening ritual.

"That was interesting," I said.

She magically produced a hair band from one of the very back pockets that I had found impenetrable. "It was my mom," she said.

"Yes, I figured that one out myself," I said.

"She's trying to fix me up with this guy," she said, bending forward and whipping her hair back over her shoulder.

"I figured that one out, too."

"He's a lawyer. His family is from France. They run a couple of restaurants that my parents go to all the time."

"Kosher restaurants."

This took her by surprise.

"How did you know that? Do you know Adam Elias?"

"I know that you're Orthodox. That's your little secret."

"How did you find out?"

She was distressed at this. Instinctively she checked her hair in the bedroom mirror once more. Had it betrayed her? What had she done wrong?

"How could you tell?" she demanded.

"You go to a prayer group at lunch every day."

Another long pause.

"How did you know that?"

"I have my spies."

"You know somebody in my group?"

"I can't reveal my sources. How long have you been Orthodox?"

"My whole life."

"Does your father wear black hats and long coats?"

"No, that's Hassidic. But my family was pretty religious."

"They're not anymore?"

"They're still religious."

"And you?"

"Not as much," she said, eager to change the subject. "What about your family?"

"Not at all religious. Not even Yom Kippur or Passover. My dad likes eggs and bacon on Sunday morning. He calls it his cholesterol blowout."

A sardonic smile lit her face. "And your mom is the same way. Lobster. Ham and cheese sandwiches."

"My parents think ham is over the line. But they eat shrimp in restaurants."

She was leaning on her elbow, her head supported by her palm. There was lots of cogitation going on up there, but I couldn't tell whether she found my background appalling or deliciously risqué.

I suspected it was a little of both. I had spent my life as a math geek in a football player's body. Maybe I was her version of James Dean. I was surprised in my own way. I had originally tagged her as a party girl. I suppose that's what I really wanted her to be. But now it appeared she was something quite different.

"Are you ashamed of being Orthodox?" I asked.

"No, of course not."

"Then why didn't you tell me? Why didn't you say, 'I go to prayer meetings on my lunch hour.' "

"It's called *mincha*. I don't tell anybody at work. How did you find out?"

"I saw you leaving the cafeteria. Then I followed you."

"Like a spy?"

"Yeah."

She thought about that a minute, as if she were deciding whether or not to get mad. "Why did you do that?"

"Because I'm crazy about you."

"Oh," she said. "I mean oh-oh."

"I'm not supposed to be crazy about you?"

"Don't you think this is kind of nuts? We spend all day working together. And then we live in the same building. And then we..."

"Yeah, but it's a nice kind of nuts," I said.

I grabbed an apple from a little basket near the sink, along with a Plexiglas cutting board and a paring knife, and brought them to the dining room table. She sat down and watched absentmindedly as I peeled off the skin in a single strand, then sliced the apple into eight pieces and arranged them with exaggerated care on the cutting board. Then I ate half of them, one by one, accompanied by sips of beer.

"My mom knew you were here," she said. "She has extra-sensory perception for anything that involves my personal life."

"Oh," I said.

"I haven't told her about you yet," she said.

"I gathered that," I said. I looked out the window toward New Jersey, as if I was trying to see her mother across the river. "Is that a problem?"

"You don't want to know about my family," she said.

"Yes, I do."

"No, you don't," she said, shaking her head vigorously. A brief storm of emotion passed over her face and subsided a second later. She saw my surprise, and tried to defuse it.

"I'll tell you all you need to know about my mother," she began. "My mother is a very nice Orthodox Jewish lady who is very concerned about her daughter. She doesn't like the fact that I live down here. She'd much prefer that I worked in my dad's office near Penn Station, where he and my three brothers can keep track of me. She doesn't understand why I don't want to live at home and why I'd want to have a regular life and why I haven't found a husband at 25. My brothers are equally concerned about me. This is the favorite family topic. They fight about everything else, but this alone brings them together."

We both looked out the window, instinctively.

"My parents ought to write a book," she said, after a pause. " 'How to Drive Your Daughter Crazy.' By Azriel and Sheila Cassuto. The world's leading experts."

I got up to put the cutting board in the sink. "So I wouldn't pass," I said.

"You might as well be a Mormon as far as they're concerned," she blurted out. "I mean you eat pork, don't you? You don't go to synagogue. You're just a big..."

She stopped and bit her lip.

"A big what?" I asked.

"A big...sexy...smart...nice...guy. And that's all they need to know."

My soul shot upwards into heaven! She loved me! Or she liked me. Or at the very least she found me "big" and "sexy" and "smart" and "nice." She had her finger on the zipper of her sweatshirt and was moving it up and down, slowly and absentmindedly, unaware of how her simple action was making me breathless.

"Does this have anything to do with the house in New Jersey?" I asked.

"That was a retreat."

"A religious thing?"

"It's a group I belong to," she said, brushing the hair out of her eyes. "It's very casual. We pray, we eat, we have discussions. It's a way to get away from the world on the weekends. To get a perspective on things. It's for people who want to become Orthodox."

"But you're already Orthodox."

"Yeah, but I like it. I'm sort of a tutor. It's a nice mix of people."

I didn't like the sound of it. On the weekends meant every weekend. Or certainly a lot of them. I had no desire to spend my weekends praying and having discussions, even if Susanna was leading them. I'm not particularly prone to jealousy. But I also didn't like the fact that "a nice mix of people" would inevitably include "a nice mix of guys." Or maybe one guy.

"Your mother called you Shoshanna," I said. "Is that your nickname?"

"It's my Hebrew name."

"What name is on your birth certificate?"

"Shoshanna."

"When did you start calling yourself Susanna?"

She was losing patience with me. "How many more questions do I have to answer?"

"I'm almost done."

"I became Susanna on March 2, 2001," she said. "The day I got hired by the bank." She sighed and her eyes darted to all four corners of the ceiling. "Shoshanna is the name I grew up with. And Susanna is the name I use at work."

I gave her a bewildered smile.

"You don't understand at all, do you?"

"I guess not. What don't I understand?"

"I'm trying to pass, okay?"

"To pass?"

"I just want to be *normal*, like everyone else. I want to have normal friends... and normal relationships. And a regular job. Sometimes I feel like I'm from another country. And I am. I'm an immigrant. It's a new world I'm entering. The whole sex thing... some of it I've done. But some of it... is very new to me."

She zipped her sweatshirt all the way up to her throat and folded back the flap. The evening was over as far as she was concerned.

"I'm going to start calling you Shoshanna," I said. "Is that all right?"

Then the phone rang.

"You told your mother you'd talk in a few minutes," I said. "Why don't you let the machine pick up?"

She considered this bit of mad advice for a few seconds. Two more rings. Then she bolted for the bedroom.

"I've got to take this," she said.

"That's okay," I said, standing up. "I've got to go."

Chapter 12

Our attempt to examine the trading records on other desks was interrupted the next morning by the sudden arrival of the risk manager of the Connecticut trading desk, who got wind of our impending special audit of the mortgage-backed trading desk and dropped by in order to limit whatever damage our investigation might do to his career.

He felt that this required sequestering us in a conference room so he could deliver two PowerPoint presentations: The first was a high school-level introduction to the mortgage market, which explained the mortgage loan process with the help of dorky illustrations of citizens, bankers and construction workers passing wheelbarrows of cash back and forth. The second was an hour-long 80-slide monstrosity that described the models risk managers in the mortgage-backed market used to calculate when American mortgage holders would be inspired to refinance their mortgages.

All through the presentations, I struggled to recast the woman whose ankles casually brushed up against mine beneath the table. Two weeks ago, she was Susanna, the wealthy Jewish or Italian party girl. And last night she became Shoshanna, the lapsed daughter of orthodoxy, whose father and three brothers wore yarmulkes and who still felt a need to pray on her lunch hour. I couldn't go back to thinking of her as Susanna. I was not going to be fooled like the rest of them. By turning her into Shoshanna, I was in on her secret, and that made me smile.

It took us all morning and a desultory lunch to get rid of our visitor from Connecticut. When we finally returned to our desks, we found a funeral notice in our e-mails, sent by Rick Markowitz to everybody on the trading desk, with us in the BCC box. The listing was copied from that morning's *New York Times*.

Scott, Timothy W. On April 12. Beloved son of Randall and Helene Scott, brother of Susan Scott Thomas and Sally Scott Ridge, beloved uncle of Sean and Jessica Thomas. A memorial service is scheduled for Tuesday, April 16 at 7 p.m. at the Ardmore Chapel, 280 Madison Avenue, New York.

"I know where this is," I said. "It's a tony place uptown where they had services for Jackie and JFK Jr."

We looked into each other's eyes. There was no question of not going. But what were we expecting to find? How would it advance our cause?

The Ardmore Chapel was a converted mansion on Madison and 79th Street with a private alley in back for the hearses. Tim's service was scheduled for 7:00, but the previous service was running late, so we found a small line of people on the sidewalk waiting to get in. We took a seat by the front window of the wine bar next door, so we could stare at people discreetly as they entered the chapel.

Just before 7:00, two cabs disgorged seven guys from the trading floor, led by Markowitz himself. A minute later, another cab arrived with three female admins. Somebody had gone out and bought identical black silk ties, which made the men look like members of some secret society. They all stood around awkwardly, as if they were huddled together for protection.

"I don't care about the guys from the trading floor," I said. "I want to see his personal friends."

A little while later, a limousine arrived. The funeral home doorman lifted a collapsible wheelchair out of the trunk, and positioned it outside the passenger door. An older woman with wavy blond hair emerged. She stood up, and supported herself against the car door as two younger women, obviously her daughters, emerged from the limousine.

The daughters were in their early 30s. All three women looked wealthy and imposing, with black dresses that set off their masses of curly blond hair.

"I see my calling," said Shoshanna, getting up and giving her own hair a tuneup. "It's time to make some new friends."

I followed her up the stairs to the second floor at a discreet interval.

The chapel could have held a hundred people, but there were only a couple dozen sitting in the pews when I arrived. The white walls were barren of religious ornament, other than a wooden figure of Christ that I guessed was designed to work with both Catholic and Protestant services. A pulpit stood on a little stage, a raised platform held the closed casket, and an organist, off to the side, was playing a medley of somber warm-up tunes.

Shoshanna sat up front in a pew directly behind the mother and daughters. Markowitz's contingent was in the middle right. I wanted to sit near one of Tim's friends, but nobody looked obviously gay.

I decided to take a chance with a guy about my age sitting by himself in the last row. He had a black suit, the kind people wore in place of a tux. Then another shorter guy in a black turtleneck came in and took a seat a few feet away from us. The two caught each other's eye and nodded. The short guy had brown hair, with red highlights at the tips. A good sign, I thought.

Somebody handed me a program, which listed six hymns, to be followed by remarks from Reverend Paul Smith, deacon of the Lexington Avenue Methodist Church. There would be no trip to the cemetery, since Tim's body was to be cremated, but there would be a reception following the service.

We sat through two hymns — "Shall We Gather at the River" and "How Can We Name a Love" — that were made even more somber by the modest audience participation. Then the organist appeared to have some kind of technical trouble and left abruptly.

The guy in the black suit signaled to the short guy and put his fingers to his lips: Time for a smoke? They both got up and headed for the exit. They didn't look particularly sinister. I followed them down the stairs and out the front door at a discreet distance.

The only logical place to smoke was in the little driveway where they parked the hearse. I showed up just as the two of them were lighting up. The guy in the black suit introduced himself as Todd, the other guy as Ross. I rubbed my fingers together, indicating that I wanted a smoke, too. Ross threw me one. It was way off, but I caught it in a quick lunge.

"Nice save," he said, with a coy smile.

I saluted him with my cigarette and snapped the pack of matches out of the air with equal panache.

"You know Tim from work?" he asked Todd.

"From Stanford. Let's just say we're friends of Dorothy's," Todd said.

They smiled. It was some kind of ironic joke I didn't understand.

"What about you?" Ross asked.

"Oh, yeah," I said, trying to adopt the same wry smile. "Dorothy and Tim and I go way back."

"I forgot that he went to Stanford," said Ross.

"He got his B.A. from University of Texas," I corrected, calling up his resume from a back corner of my mind. "Then he went to Stanford for his MBA."

A moment of meditation as we cycled through our first puffs. Ross looked like an aging cherub, with a flagrant gay accent. Todd was slightly taller, with little rectangular glasses, but he could have passed as a hetero in a minute. The hearse driver was standing just inside the back door, talking with a guy from the funeral home. Ross peered inside the empty hearse and shook his head.

"A damn shame," he said. "Completely stupid and unnecessary."

"Puerto Rican hookers," said Todd bitterly. "One of his great weaknesses."

"One of his many," said Ross.

"The teenagers are the absolute worst," said Todd. "They want you to get as wasted as possible, so they can split and go home."

Upstairs, we heard the minister start his speech, but the words didn't carry.

"Not a lot of people up there," I said.

They both nodded.

"I saw his mom and his sisters, but I didn't see his dad," I said.

"His dad died two years ago," Ross said. "He was some kind of oil executive. They had a farm an hour or so from Houston. Did Tim ever tell you the stories about growing up out there?"

Nobody said anything. It seemed like an appropriate enough time to reminisce about Tim's life.

"It was a real redneck little town," Ross said. "His Dad had a nice-sized ranch, but there were all sorts of poor kids living in trailers nearby. Tim told me that when he was 14, all the boys used to go to the woods after school and fuck each other in the ass. It was just a normal thing you did because you were horny. Then, of course, you were supposed to grow up and go after cheerleaders."

"Happens all the time," Todd said. "Group amnesia."

"Exactly," said Ross. "A couple years later, when they were 16, Tim would ask them: 'Hey, don't you guys remember what we did in the woods?' "

"Did he ever tell you that story about his dad and the drive from the airport?" Todd asked, tossing his cigarette beneath the tire of the hearse.

"Sure," Ross said.

"I never heard that one," I said.

"I think this was his sophomore year in college, right after he came out," Todd said. "The whole gay thing threw his Mom for a loop, but she accepted it eventually. His dad just refused. He was a very strict sort of guy. I think he was a deacon in his church. Anyway, so his dad is picking him up from the airport. They're driving down this county highway at night in the middle of nowhere. And Tim asks his dad:

" 'You remember my friend Tom and my friend Phil? You remember those boys?'

"And his dad says, 'Yeah, they were nice boys.'

" 'And you remember my friends Chuck and Howie?'

"And his dad says, 'Yeah.'

" 'So what are they up to?' Tim asks.

"His dad tells him. One's selling insurance and has two kids, another's an oil broker and has four kids, and another's running a farm, whatever.

"Then Tim says: 'When we were in eighth grade, we all used to go out in the woods and fuck each other in the ass.'

"His dad stops the car right there and tells him to get out. It was 10 o'clock in the middle of nowhere, a state highway between two towns, and it was 20 degrees. But he tells him to get out and find his own way home.

"So Tim starts walking until he finds the next farmhouse and calls his mom, who drives out from home to pick him up. But instead of going home, he asks to be taken back to the airport. And he gets on a flight back to school, and spends Christmas eating SpaghettiOs in his dorm."

A trio of French tourists with maps walked up to us, trying to find their way to the Metropolitan Museum. We waited as Ross pointed them back to Fifth Avenue.

"Did you get a call from this cop?" Ross asked me. "A guy named Nardulli?"

"I talked to him," I said. "He was looking for gay traders Tim might have slept with. I work on Tim's trading floor."

"Are you a trader?" Ross asked.

"I used to be. I didn't know him that long."

"What did you tell the cop?" Ross asked.

"I told him that there are no gay traders on Wall Street," I said with a smile. "Ain't no such thing."

"You can be a securities analyst," Todd said, nodding in agreement. "You can be a securities lawyer. But you can't be a securities trader."

"So what do they think you are?" Ross asked, giving me a once-over.

"I guess the people think I just never found the right girl," I said, smiling. "Why? Did Nardulli contact you, too?"

"I live in Tim's building," he said. "The detective was going door to door in case somebody heard anything, but I live on the fourth floor and Tim was on the first. Then he asked me if I'd ever slept with Tim. I told him: 'Yes, many times, in my dreams.' Tim was quite particular. You had to have a certain kind of body. You had to be big and hairy. And be a top. So I was out on all counts."

"Did you discover the body?" Todd asked.

"Somebody else in the building did," Ross said. "I don't know who. When I went to work there was a cop standing outside his apartment, but you could peek inside. They had him on one of those rolling hospital stretchers with a sheet over him. The ambulance guy said his hands had been tied to the bedpost with rubber hospital gloves. And urine, you could smell a lot of urine, I don't know exactly why."

We heard the organ play the introduction to "Amazing Grace." Then it was joined by a spare chorus of voices. We participated by listening silently, our own little funeral service.

"He picked up the wrong trick," Todd said when the singing concluded. He ground his second cigarette under his heel. "We ought to get back upstairs."

We all walked back toward the entrance but I saw Nardulli standing in front of the entrance, his notebook in hand. He was talking to one of the guys from the trading desk. Ross hesitated going up the steps.

"I don't want to go back up there," he said. "That place gives me the creeps."

"Same here," I agreed.

"I feel like walking downtown," he said. "Are you going that way?"

"Sure," I said. "I live in Battery Park City."

We headed south on Madison Avenue and got into a very conventional discussion about why I moved to Battery Park City and the kind of work I did. Once he heard a little about me, he was eager to tell me about his career as a corporate librarian, first at Lehman Brothers, then at Pfizer. He had a tiny fourth-floor studio in the same town-house as Tim, on whom he had a long-term unrequited crush.

"Tim and I were closer 10 years ago, when he moved into the building," he said. "He had just graduated from business school and he hadn't lost his Texas accent. When the guy living in the basement apartment died of AIDS, Tim took over the lease and got the landlord to put in a stairway connecting the two floors. That's the last time I was in his apartment."

"He was a very clever guy," I said. "He knew a lot about options."

"I was too queeny for him," Ross said bitterly. "And too short. And too old."

We made it down to Chelsea in about 45 minutes. I was eager to see the building where Tim was murdered, but when we got to the townhouse, it was something of a disappointment. One of a series of brownstones, built at the same time. A row of recycling cans chained to the fence. Nothing to indicate anyone had died there. As if reading my thoughts, Ross pointed out the police notice papered over the entrance to the basement apartment. "There's another notice like that over Tim's front door."

Neither of us seemed eager to end the conversation.

"It's a great block," he said. "Dark Star is on the corner. On Saturday nights, they have crowds of people hanging around trying to get in."

"I've never been there," I said.

"You're kidding?" he said. "I'll buy you a drink."

If I'd seen Dark Star empty, I'd have guessed it was a popular neighborhood bar, with five taps, a pool table and satellite TVs over the bar. But this one was packed with a hundred or so guys dressed to kill.

We grabbed a table in the corner and Ross went to get us some beers. A dozen eyes checked me out and then turned away. It didn't seem like rejection; I was merely being inspected. The blackboard had a long list of names waiting to play pool, but people seemed to care more about how they looked than how they played. Some guys had sets of keys dangling from the right or left sides of their belts, which I guessed was some kind of code. The physicality was more explicit than in a hetero bar. Squeezing biceps or touching arms and legs was normal in the course of conversation, and two or three couples were sucking face by the entrance to the women's bathroom.

Ross and I spent an amiable hour or so talking about two of Ross's obsessions: Burmese cats and Japanese woodblock prints.

"Did you ever hear Tim talk about another trader?" I asked when the conversation began to wind down. "I think he was working on some big business deal when he died."

"I wouldn't know," he said. "He'd never tell me anything personal. 'Hi, Ross, how you doing? Beautiful day, isn't it?' That sort of thing."

"So what do you think of Nardulli's theory?" I asked. "That it was an S&M thing with some guy he picked up."

He shrugged. "Everybody's done a little S&M. And he liked to pay for sex. Not that he had to. He was in good shape, he dressed well. But if that's how you want to spend your money, who am I to say it's wrong?" His eyes followed a little drama happening at the table beside us.

A burly guy in a light tan leather jacket was having a wordless discussion with a younger guy at the bar 20 feet away. They appeared to be using their eyes to negotiate and sign a contract for the rest of the evening, with details to follow. The semiotics were way beyond me. The younger guy gave off hooker vibes. The other was in his early 30s. But they suddenly left their respective seats and started putting on their coats, as if they were a suburban couple on the way to the mall. It struck me as odd because in hetero prostitution, the hooker and the john often met across different social classes. These two guys seemed like birds of a feather. Other guys were pairing off all around us without exchanging money. So why did one of them want to pay for something he could get for free?

"Tim wasn't hitting the bars every night, but he had a thing for teenage Hispanics, 18 or under," he said. "I remember one January, after his bonus, he was bringing home a new boy every night. You traders have too much disposable income. I told him he was going to get in trouble some day."

Somebody started screaming with delight at meeting an acquaintance at the bar. I was aware of a couple guys trying to drill a hole into me with their eyes. One of them smiled and nodded when he caught my eye.

"I haven't been here in years," Ross said, picking a young kid out of the crowd for closer inspection. "I'm like an old married person, but without a marriage. If my boyfriend doesn't commit soon, I'm going to say 'Adios, Amigo.' "

We put on our coats and got up to leave.

"I'm in a new relationship right now myself," I said. "I'm completely in love, but I'm not sure it's mutual."

"Best of luck," he said, patting the back of my hand. "Hold on to the dream."

The phone was ringing when I arrived home. Shoshanna had stayed for the reception after the service, chatting with people from the bank. Then she got up the nerve to approach one of Tim's sisters. "Her name was Connie," she said. "She was drinking rum and cokes and was almost hysterical. I said I knew Tim from work and told her I thought he was handsome. That was the right thing to say. After that, she grabbed my arm and wouldn't let go. She told me all about the girlfriend he had in high school, who was small just like me. Their two families went to the same church. She showed me a picture. She thought her parent's big mistake was sending him to the University of Texas at Austin, where there were a lot of gay people. If Tim had gone to Texas A&M, where she'd gone, she was sure he would have married Connie. She said she kept praying to restore his soul to harmony, but that Jesus took him back instead of answering her prayers."

Her voice was shaky, on the verge of tears.

"Are you all right?" I asked.

"Sort of," she said, letting out a huge breath. "It's so sad. So sad. I keep thinking about Tim as this criminal. But he was also her older brother, and she loved him. The picture was from Tim's high school prom, with this girl, who was the class valedictorian. A little blond thing. They seemed so happy."

I waited to give her time to collect herself.

"We have to do something," she said suddenly. A completely different voice: Faster, determined and a little frightened. "We're going nowhere by ourselves. We have to go back and talk to the cops."

I did not like the way she put it. It was not something to be discussed. It was a demand.

"We have to go back to Nardulli and tell him everything we didn't tell him before," she said. "Everything."

I wasn't ready to do it just yet, but I tried to keep my voice neutral. "Hold on a minute here," I said. "Let's discuss this together. We have to think this thing through."

"The report we gave him didn't say anything about the Anne Street e-mail or bigdick99," she said. "Or about the board member. And he should know about that. It might convince him that he's wrong."

She stopped and waited for me to agree.

"Let's think about things from his perspective," I said. "Nardulli believes this is a gay sex crime, so he's trying to find out who was Tim's sexual partner that night. We tried to tell him that it was a financial crime, but he didn't get it. And he doesn't want to get it. He's given up on that angle."

"It was a gay sex crime *and* a financial crime," she said. "He knows a lot more than we know about the murder. He has all the evidence. Maybe the e-mail or the board member involvement is the piece he needs to pull this whole thing together."

I spent the next few seconds in hapless indecision. Going back to the cops was probably the right thing to do. I would agree in a minute if the corporation counsel hadn't made it very clear he wanted us to do just the opposite. I was not eager to disobey him. I had spent months trying to find a way back into Wall Street. This was my lucky break, my meal ticket to a better life. They liked me, and were even willing to overlook the fact that I'd committed a $112 million bank fraud just a few months before. If I blew this job, I might as well leave town.

"So you want to go back to Nardulli and tell him everything," I said.

"Absolutely."

"Even though we might get fired."

"Of course! How can you ask that question?"

"Well, frankly, I like this job. And I'm not really eager to lose it."

"You can get another job! You're an experienced trader. You're in high demand."

I had no good answer to that. I wasn't in high demand, but I couldn't convince her otherwise unless I told her about my personal familiarity with securities fraud.

"Let's consider this," I said. "Right now, we're employees of the bank, and we have access to a lot of information that might lead us to the accomplice. If we get fired, we're going to lose that access."

She knew me too well.

"You care more about your job than finding out what happened," she said, raising her voice sharply. "We're twiddling our thumbs while the trail goes cold."

"Can we talk about this tomorrow?"

"I can't believe we're even *having* this discussion. This is not just bank fraud. Somebody was *murdered*! He was bound with hospital gloves in his own bed. We can't let a murderer go free. It's as simple as that. I'm going to meet Nardulli tomorrow. If you don't want to join me, I'll go myself."

Chapter 13

The room Nardulli brought us to didn't look anything like the ones in the cop shows. During the day, it functioned as an office where three clerks sat processing reports of one kind or another. Each desk had a computer, a stack of files and a set of family photos taped to the wall, along with cheap plastic fans in various states of repair. Nardulli sat behind one of the desks in the corner and took out his notebook.

"Let's reiterate what we said on the phone," Shoshanna said, as we sat down. "We're meeting with you on the condition that this is completely confidential. We were told not to talk to you anymore, so our jobs are on the line."

"I appreciate that," said Nardulli. All was forgiven, he seemed to say. Let's make a fresh start.

"I'm afraid we weren't being completely truthful with you the other day," she said. "You asked us if we had any other evidence to support our theory. We have two important pieces of evidence we didn't tell you about."

"Okay," he said, slouching back in his chair. "Let's hear what you've got."

"The first is the whole origin of this investigation," she said. "It began in a very strange way. We didn't find out about the fraud in the course of our regular audits. A member of the bank's board of directors told the bank attorney to look for some fraudulent activity on the derivatives trading desk. He gave him a handwritten diagram that sketched out a possible crime, but didn't give any other details. That led to my assignment and to David being hired as a consultant."

"Okay," he said. He took the sheet of paper with the trade-flow diagram and stared at it. "So...?"

"So it's obvious that this board member clearly knew something about the fraud. And we feel he might know something more about Tim's death."

"This is not evidence," he said, putting the paper aside. "I wouldn't even call it a lead. What else have you got?"

"About five weeks before he died, Tim received an e-mail from somebody that indicates other people might be involved in his scam. It was from something called 'The Anne Street Group' that met on weekday evenings at 22 Anne Street. We think they get together at a Thai restaurant downstairs."

"You went over there yourself and looked around?" he asked skeptically.

"Yes," she said. "That's the only likely place in that building."

"Did you ask the manager of the restaurant if he knew anything about this group?"

"No," she said.

"And how do you know this group was gay?"

"We didn't think it was gay until after Tim died. The e-mail was from bigdick99@aol.com."

Nardulli shifted in his chair.

"Bigdick99?" he asked slowly, writing it down in his notebook. "Who else in this group received e-mails?"

Shoshanna gave him a copy of the email. "It was sent to a group list," she said. "He was the only one visible on the e-mail."

Nardulli's interest seemed to wane. He flipped back a page in his notebook and shook his head.

"What about the board member who knew something about the fraud?" he said. "The guy who wrote the diagram. Was he gay? What's his name?"

Shoshanna looked at me and hesitated.

"We don't know who he is," I said. "They never told us."

Nardulli put his pen back in his pocket and closed the cover of his notebook. He took a slow look at Shoshanna, as if trying to reassess his previous opinion of her.

"So now you believe Tim was gay," he said.

"Yes," she said.

"But the other day you told me you were certain he wasn't," he said.

"I was wrong about him not being gay," she admitted. "But Tim was involved in a fraud that involved more people. We were closing in on him. It couldn't have been an accident. The timing was too close."

"I'm looking for a gay trader. What about Markowitz?" he asked.

"Markowitz?" I asked.

"Yeah. Are you sure he's straight?"

We looked at each other, but with different expressions. Mine was simple astonishment. Hers was a withering grimace.

"Look, guys," he said. "I appreciate all your efforts, but I don't buy it." He dug our report out of his briefcase and flipped through it. "I read this thing four times. I asked a friend who works on Wall Street about this. It still doesn't add up. Tell me if I've got it right: The client wants to buy options to protect himself in case its stocks go down."

"Right," I said, nodding furiously as encouragement.

"So Tim found out what options the client needed to buy and bid them up before the client. That's called front-running and my friend says it happens all the time. Banks ripping off their clients."

"Not quite," I said. "You're missing an important step. The bank wasn't just acting as a broker, buying options for its clients. It was acting as a dealer. It sells the client protection, and then it's got to buy options for its own account. So Tim wasn't ripping off the client, he was ripping off the bank. And he did it through an outside partner."

Nardulli gave me a cloudy look, as if he was on the verge of figuring it out. Then the moment passed.

"You're saying banks don't front-run their clients?" he asked.

"Yes, they do. They rip them off all the time. But in this case, the bank was the one losing the money. Tim was ripping off the bank."

"That's larceny," he said. "That's not homicide."

"But the larceny is related to the homicide!" Shoshanna pleaded. "Please try to understand this. It's as plain as day!"

Nardulli paused to summon the last of his patience. We were well-meaning citizens, eager to help him solve a crime, but we were getting to be a pain in the ass.

"I have no idea whether Tim was ripping off his clients or ripping off the bank," he said. "I'm not the Securities and Exchange Commission. It doesn't matter much to me either way. All I know is that I've got a white male who died of an overdose while tied up and wearing gay S&M paraphernalia. And I've got a lot of other evidence I can't tell you. Do you want to know the typical setup for this situation? A Wall Street guy picks up a trick and brings him back to his apartment. They shoot up, they do whatever they do. Then they go a little too far and the rich guy dies. There are variations. Sometimes both of them die. Sometimes it's not a trick, but just somebody the Wall Street guy picks up in a bar. Sometimes it's an accident. If the sexual partner was a known associate, you've got a better chance of finding out what happened. But otherwise, it's a complete crapshoot."

It was time for one more try.

"We believe the S&M paraphernalia was there to make it look accidental," I said as slowly and calmly as I could. "I'm not an expert, but it seems that crime should be fairly easy to fake."

"You guys don't know the first thing about how he died," said Nardulli.

"Shoshanna and I know a little bit," I said. "We know he was tied to the bed with rubber gloves and there was a lot of urine everywhere."

"Who's Shoshanna?" he asked.

"I meant Susanna."

"Then why did you call her Shoshanna?"

"It's my nickname," Shoshanna said.

"And why do you think he was tied to the bed with rubber gloves?"

"A guy named Ross told me," I said.

"Tim's upstairs neighbor," Nardulli said. "I've already talked to him. And how did you meet him?"

"At Tim's funeral," I said.

He nodded sullenly and his breathing became quicker. "You went to the funeral. To pursue your own investigation. Because you thought I was barking up the wrong tree."

"I also met a guy named Todd, a trader who was friends with Tim. They both said that Tim had a thing for teenage hookers."

"And you met Todd at the funeral, too."

"Right."

Nardulli gave me a long look.

"We're not complete lunatics," I said. "We have some evidence to support what we believe. We have the fraud, the e-mails, the board member's involvement."

"You have shit," he said. "The thing with the board member doesn't prove anything. I'd be very surprised if the e-mail Scott got from that group turns out to be worth anything. It could be a bunch of people getting together for some event, a charity event, or to play cards. It doesn't prove a murder."

"What about the fraud?"

"He was ripping people off at work. You guys on Wall Street are always ripping each other off. It seems to go with the territory."

"Why are you so sure the S&M thing wasn't a setup?" I asked.

He paused a moment, as if deciding in advance how far he would go.

"He was wearing a leather halter when he died and he had S&M paraphernalia in his closet," he said, enumerating the evidence with his fingers. "He had a postcard flier for an S&M event in his mailbox. He was recognized by bartenders at Leather City and Manhole, two 10th Avenue S&M bars that are crawling with tricks. His hands were tied with a certain brand of rubber gloves that may link this to other things we're working on. Or they may not. Plus at 1 a.m. Friday morning, a young male, possibly gay, about 5-8, 150 pounds, was seen stumbling out of Tim's apartment building and walking in an inebriated manner toward Sixth Avenue where he probably grabbed a cab. And there's other stuff I can't talk about."

Shoshanna and I looked at each other. It was time to give up.

"Look, guys," he said, nodding to the door. "I appreciate your concern about this case, but you're going to have to let me do my job. I've been covering homicide in the Village and Chelsea for four years. I get most of the gay-related deaths. Before this, I worked for eight years in burglary and robbery in Bed Stuy. I've got a B.A. in criminal justice from John Jay. I know what I'm doing. You're just going to have to trust me."

"Why don't you first show us that you're worthy of trust?" asked Shoshanna. "You're not the least bit interested in understanding an important part of this case!"

"Why don't you two go back to protecting the people who rip off your clients? Isn't that what you do for a living?" asked Nardulli.

Shoshanna stood up and said, "I'm going to write a letter to the police commissioner."

"Here's my badge number," he said taking out his wallet and pointing to a number engraved below the department seal. "You want a pen to write it down?"

He was holding the badge a few inches from our faces so we could get a good look at the seal of the New York City Police Department. An odd engraving: Underneath the eagle and the scales of justice was a cowboy with a rope challenging an Indian with a bow and arrow. I guess the cops were supposed to be the cowboys.

Shoshanna gave a little snort and made a beeline for the hall. I stayed behind to give Nardulli a silent apologetic handshake.

I caught up with Shoshanna as she stood on the corner outside the First Precinct.

"Completely ridiculous," she said. "I can't believe the murderer is going to go free because this idiot is handling the case. That's not right."

The precinct house was in a strange part of town, facing something called Ericsson Square, which could have been a magnificent park if it weren't filled with the spaghetti exit ramps from the Holland Tunnel. We stood at a stoplight beside a stalled line of cars. The drivers, still revved up from their quick trip through the Holland Tunnel, were faced off against a jaywalking stream of pedestrians from the nearby Citibank building heading to the Seventh Avenue subway. In spite of all that, developers were carving million-dollar lofts out of old printing-industry warehouses for people who wanted a view of the fumes.

Fumes might have been coming out of Shoshanna's ears as well. She stood there, snapping and unsnapping the narrow outside pocket of her leather bag that was designed to sheathe her cell phone.

"We learned something in there," I said. "We learned that Tim had a genuine interest in S&M. It wasn't completely faked."

"The whole thing was a fake," she said. "They wanted to make it look like an accidental drug death. So they faked what he was wearing. They put stuff in his closet and his mail. They hired somebody to walk out of his apartment building drunk."

"But his picture was recognized by the bartender in that S&M bar."

"You're not going to argue that it was an accident, are you?"

There was no answer to that.

It was a solemn 15-minute walk back to our place through Tribeca. Along the way, we passed one fancy eatery after another, brimming with lights and conversation. As we passed the Odeon Cafe, I asked: "Do you only eat in kosher restaurants?"

She stopped and stared in the window. She looked inside and gazed at the bar, already crowded with people. "I've heard of this place," she said. "And I'm starving." The combination of longing and fear was painful to watch.

"You could order some fish," I suggested.

The maitre d' saw us hesitating and opened the door for us.

But she couldn't do it. Her feet were frozen.

"Why don't we cook something at your place?" I suggested, putting her out of her misery.

"That's a great idea," she said, smiling and taking my arm.

The menu at Chez Cassuto that evening was sautéed chicken breast with spinach and rice. She refused to let me cook and sent me into the living room to watch TV with a glass of kosher Cabernet and a bowl of peanuts.

Gradually, the sounds of 10 giants stomping around a basketball court melded together with the hot oil and chicken in the frying pan and the clink of plates and cutlery being set on a glass-topped dining room table. We had worried enough about Tim Scott for one day. It was time to get on with the business of life.

I found something very erotically charged about our little dinner. Stage one of our relationship was behind us. We were now managing the passage into stage two, when you hang out and try married life on for size. This is all good, I told myself. Don't worry about the sex. Soon enough, your patience will be rewarded.

It was a nasty game, with the Knicks hopelessly overrun by the Lakers offense. By the fourth quarter it became an abusive ego-destroying massacre. At one point, Shoshanna drifted over to the TV while she was waiting for the rice to finish.

"They're showing no mercy," she said.

"That's right," I said. "How much do you know about basketball?"

"Quite a lot," she said proudly.

"Oh, yeah?" I asked. She was not the first woman I knew who had made this claim.

"Every Sunday afternoon my dad and my brothers watched basketball in the den," she said. "I would usually join then."

"Okay," I said. "Name the five positions on a basketball team."

"Center, point guard, shooting guard, small forward and power forward."

My mouth was agape. She stood beside the TV, her tiny hips cocked to one side.

"Okay. What does team does Shaq play on?"

"Come on," she said. "Ask me something harder than that."

"All right. Where did he play before the Lakers?"

"Orlando."

"Where did he play in college?"

"Somewhere in the South. Louisiana State?"

"Very good. Excellent. Describe the principal offensive strategy of the Chicago Bulls."

She smiled and took a deep breath. "The Bulls use a triangle offense where the 'two' position is the swing man or the shooting guard. Jordan was a 'two.' "

"Excellent. Who designed this strategy?"

"There's some debate about that. It was a very old strategy that had fallen by the wayside, but somehow Jordan gave it new life. My brother Nathan believes Phil Jackson should get the credit, but my dad thinks it was really Tex Winter."

I wanted to rip her clothes off, but I restrained myself.

"Where did Phil Jackson play and what were his key career statistics?" I asked.

"That's ancient history," she said. "I only watched basketball in the '90s."

"The correct answer: Phil Jackson played for the Knicks, where he averaged 12.4 points per game with 4.7 rebounds. His free-throw percentage was .683. But he averaged almost 15 points a game when he played at Temple."

Then I pounced on her, grabbing her by the waist and carried her caveman-style to her bedroom, where I did a little pantomime of male sexual madness, careful all the while, not to throw my entire weight on top of her. Then I started unbuttoning her blouse accompanied by grunts of caveman impatience.

"Red light," she said.

"Yeah?" I said. Surely this was just a feint. I began nibbling her earlobe.

"We have to talk," she insisted.

I had heard women say that phrase many times and found that it never led to a conversation you'd characterize as fun. The best thing to do was ignore it and hope for the best. I went from nibbling her earlobe to sucking it gently, but she had a thin gold earring which was getting in the way.

"I talked to my rabbi about you," she said, quite seriously.

"Don't worry, I'll convert. I'll get circumcised again. Anything he wants." I moved from her earlobe to licking the back of her ears.

"He says we shouldn't have sex if we're not sure it'll lead to marriage."

"Okay, let's get married."

"David, I'm being serious."

"I'm serious! Fine. Let's get married." I pulled back the collar of her blouse and bit into the back of her shoulder.

"We're just going to have to discuss this while we eat dinner," she said, straightening her hair and walking back into the living room.

We sat at opposite ends of the dining room table. In spite of my fears, she turned out to be a quite accomplished cook. The chicken was neatly plated and seasoned with a confident toss of rosemary. She dug into it with relish, then began unfolding a piece of paper from her jeans.

"The rabbi gave me a list of questions to ask you," she said.

"You're shitting me," I said, pouring her some wine.

"No, I'm serious. This is an important decision we're making here. I don't want it to be clouded by sex."

"Can you tell me a little about this rabbi?"

"Sure. He's in his mid-30s and has a bushy beard."

"Par for the course."

"Yeah, but he's very worldly. He knows a lot about the business world. When people talk about their jobs, he asks very intelligent questions."

"Okay, so he reads the *New York Times*. What else?"

"He lives in New Jersey in a big house that's connected with some foundation that introduces secular Jews to the modern Orthodox movement. He runs a retreat every weekend and a couple lunchtime prayer sessions downtown."

"The one you go to at lunch?"

"Yes. He's eager to meet you. I'm taking you out there this weekend. And tomorrow night we're going to visit my friend Gigi. They've invited us for dinner. Is that okay?"

She didn't give me much time to respond.

"Then it's settled," she said.

Her first questions were about my family. I explained that my father had sold his car leasing business four years ago and was now busy organizing chess tournaments for seniors on the North Shore of Chicago. My Mom had spent most of the last 20 years working as a volunteer with dyslexic kids. I told her about my sister and her husband who had bought a home a block away from my parent's house so they could take advantage of the free babysitting.

As I seemed to be racking up points with this depiction of close-knit family life, I waxed poetic about the place my parents bought in Florida and how my sister and her kids spent their winter and spring vacations there. I didn't tell her what really went on during those vacations, but, to my credit, I did not say anything that was patently false.

Then she asked me a series of questions about my personality. I told her that I generally tried to avoid confrontation and preserve harmonious fellowship whenever I could, but that I did not shy away from an argument if somebody pissed me off — and I had a reasonable chance of winning it. It was a personality trait I associated with being big enough to beat the shit out of almost anybody. I'd never been physically violent, but I did break somebody's ankle in a high school wrestling tournament because I was careless and wanted to win.

I was ruthlessly analytic at work, but I could be quite impulsive in my personal life. I did not spend a lot of time making decisions, or worrying about them after I made them. I generally tried to maintain a positive attitude toward life. I was even-tempered and slow to anger. Although I had my periodic funks, I didn't get into extended depressions. I had smoked dope in my youth, and could be garrulous when drunk, but I did not have a drinking or a drug problem. I had a talent for making people feel comfortable, particularly people who were not in my socioeconomic class. I was a middle-of-the-road Democrat, and tried not to commit massive fraud on my income taxes. The only thing really weird about me was my obsession with numbers, but that found a socially acceptable outlet in sports statistics. I was in very good physical condition, and reasonably handsome.

"In conclusion," I said, "you can tell your rabbi that my sperm contains superior genetic characteristics. I would make an excellent husband."

As we talked, she parked her heel on my chair, between my legs, and massaged my pants with her toes to keep my erection going. She seemed to enjoy having that power over me.

Other women, of course, had made their own investigations of my character. I found that women first wanted to know if I was good enough in bed or had any unattractive personal habits. Inevitably, however, the focus of their investigation moved to whether I would make a good husband. Shoshanna was simply making this process explicit.

"Have you ever done anything morally reprehensible?" she asked.

"That's an unfair question."

"Why?"

"Everybody's done something morally reprehensible at some point in their lives."

"Okay, we'll leave that issue for another discussion."

"You mean there will be more of these?"

"Yes. Several more."

I mulled this over a bit and decided not to get angry.

"I don't know yet. It's going to take a while," she said, getting up from the dining room table. She rearranged her hair around one shoulder and then pulled it down across her chest like a thick rope.

"How long is a while?" I asked. "Two days? Two weeks?"

"I can't tell you yet. I can't believe you know all those statistics."

"I am the king of sports statistics."

"My Dad's going to fall instantly in love with you."

"Until he finds out I eat BLTs."

"No, he's not."

"You're not going to tell him?"

"No, you're going to have to stop eating that stuff. From this point on. Okay?"

It was a sobering thought. A big, big life change.

"Not another BLT?"

"No."

"No more clam chowder?"

"Nothing. That's it. Lips that touch *trayf* will not touch mine. Is it a deal?"

"I'll have to think about it."

She gave me a deep French kiss and a quick pat on my crotch just to make sure I was still interested. Then she sent me to sleep in my own bed.

Chapter 14

Shoshanna's friends, the Steins, lived in a big prewar building on Columbus Avenue overlooking the Natural History Museum. She gave me a quick briefing on the elevator ride up: Gigi was her best friend from both high school and college, and was doing an internship in genetic disease counseling at Mount Sinai. Ken was SVP of operations at the Bank of New York, and looked just like Steven Seagal. They had two boys, 3 and 5, named Morry and Izzy, and a cat named Felix, which hid in the closet when visitors were around.

As the elevator door opened we heard a child's voice around the corner: "Dad, they're here!" followed by some whispers.

"I think I hear a robot," Shoshanna said fearfully.

Then around a corner came Ken, walking with robotic stiffness, one boy hanging onto his back and a smaller one riding on his shoulders. All six arms were waving wildly and the older boy was repeating, "I AM A ROBOT, I AM A ROBOT," at the low end of his vocal range.

"Oh, no!" Shoshanna shrieked, and began running away in tiny steps.

"Wait," I said, holding her protectively. "It might be a friendly robot. Are you friendly?"

"Yes," said the younger boy.

"No," said the older one.

"Hey, man," said Ken, putting out a beefy hand. He was a big guy, not as tall as me, but heavy enough to make me feel comfortable. He did look a lot like Steven Seagal, and even wore his hair in the same slick, long-haired, tough-guy manner.

We shook all of the robot's hands, and a couple feet as well, and followed it down the hall.

Gigi met us at the door with two huge goblets of red wine and directed us to the big leather couch, which was the only toy-free zone in the living room. She was taller and curvier than Shoshanna, but she had graduated from the same school of hair care, with shoulder-length tresses that swung in and out of perfectly matched crescent curls. She sat down between us on the couch and gave me a head-to-toe physical inspection, patting me on the side of my arm as if I were a quarter of beef.

"I approve," she said to Shoshanna with a thumbs-up. "But I've got to attend to the lamb for a few minutes. You guys chat with Kenneth."

The apartment fought for a modicum of elegance beneath a blizzard of toys, kids' books and advanced audiovisual equipment. A small dining room appeared as an oasis of adulthood behind French doors, with the table set for four.

"She's pulling out all the stops if she's serving rack of lamb," Ken said, settling into what was clearly Dad's armchair. "It's her signature dish."

"I bet you can't find us, doo-doo," the younger boy said, peeping around the corner.

"Are you calling me a doo-doo?" Ken shouted, in mock anger. "Dave, we've got to teach these little punks a lesson. Shoshanna can keep Gigi company."

The boy's room had a bunk bed and a big futon on the floor which served as a gymnastics mat. An electronic keyboard sitting on top of a changing table was missing one key, but the older kid had set it to play a circus melody.

"Say it, Dad," the younger one insisted. "Say it!"

Ken cupped his hands into a megaphone: "Ladies and gentlemen, Introducing two of the world's greatest young acrobatic talents, from New York City... Morry and Izzy Stein!" The boys then treated us to a frenetic display of somersaults and half cartwheels.

When that was over, we played "Overboard," which involved grabbing their legs and flipping them backwards on the futon. Then Ken and I invented "Pillow Bombardment," where we threw pillows at the kids in three distinct spin styles: horizontal, vertical and ceiling bounce.

In the middle of all this, we managed a polite version of the Wall Street chest-thumping ritual in which the males try to: (a) inflate the importance of their careers while appearing to denigrate them; (b) display their knowledge of each other's specialty and say nice things about each other's firm; (c) try to figure out how much money the other guy makes.

Judging by his apartment and his description of his job, Ken was making about as much as I had at my peak. On September 10, he had transferred to a new job in securities processing because it allowed him to get home at 5:30. Then he spent the next two months working 16-hour days, trying, as he put it, "to support the illusion that normal trading could be conducted in the U.S. bond market."

I, of course, had nothing to brag about. I explained that I was consulting to Shoshanna's audit group, a job that was clearly a few rungs below my previous job in status and compensation.

"Why did you quit trading?" he asked.

"I had a bad experience after 9/11," I said, which ended the discussion pretty quickly. Maybe it would become my new excuse.

Gigi had the meal perfectly scheduled. The boys, who had been fed earlier, were whisked off to bed five minutes before the lamb was scheduled to come out of the oven.

The whole thing was quite impressive. The lamb was rare but had been perfectly charred by their new high-tech oven, and was accompanied by grilled vegetables and a fancy California Shiraz from a kosher vineyard.

"I understand you two met at work," said Ken. "You're part of some trading-fraud SWAT team?"

"Something like that," said Shoshanna. "Dave's the former trader. I make sure all the procedures are followed."

"She's the audit cop," I said. "I just point out some technical things she might miss."

"Shoshanna's very tough when she needs to be," Gigi said. "But very sweet inside."

"I certainly agree with the first part," Ken said.

"So you're a *former* trader," Gigi said. "Why did you quit trading?"

I hesitated a moment. Which lie this time?

"It was a 9/11 thing," said Ken, coming to my aid.

"He was standing outside the World Financial Center when the first plane hit," said Shoshanna. "He ran halfway uptown before the second tower was hit. He thought the whole thing was a helicopter accident."

After that, everybody had to tell their own 9/11 stories. Shoshanna managed to get on a bus to Brooklyn just before the first tower fell, then walked back across the Brooklyn Bridge and across Manhattan to her brother's house on the Upper West Side. Gigi was at Mount Sinai, and ran across the park to pick up her kids. Ken was at the Bank of New York headquarters downtown, but got out early and was able to leave a message before the cell phones went down. Then he went back downtown the next morning under police escort to bring the bank's backup tapes to their temporary headquarters in Tribeca.

I was eager to change the subject.

"So how did you two meet?" I asked.

Gigi looked at her husband, who reluctantly gave her permission to tell the story.

"My friend Judy invited me to go slumming at B'nai Jeshurun," she said. "It's a very trendy Conservative synagogue at 84th and West End, and she said a lot of hunky secular guys would be hanging around afterwards on the steps outside. She was right."

"There she was, my blushing bride," Ken said. "Flirting with two or three guys at once. So I waited my turn and asked her out the next night."

"Were you a member of the synagogue?" I asked Ken.

Both women laughed. "Kenneth is about as religious as our cat," said Gigi.

"Let's just say I'm spiritually challenged," he said.

"Ken only prays during Jets games," explained Shoshanna.

"We had a pre-wedding meeting with the rabbi to discuss how we'd keep a kosher home," Gigi explained. "My future husband asked him if there was any way he could watch college basketball on Saturdays."

"What did the rabbi say?" I asked.

"Well, after arguing about it for half an hour, Ken convinced him that since our TV had an energy-saver button, it was never really off. So he wasn't really turning it on to watch the game."

"Plus, I was honoring the Sabbath by relaxing and enjoying myself," he said.

"While I go to *shul*," Gigi said.

"That's right," he said. "Somebody's got to pray for our souls. Somebody's got to watch the game."

"It sounds like a good division of labor to me," I said.

"Did you know that this woman knows a lot about basketball?" he asked, jabbing an appreciative finger at Shoshanna as he cut another serving of lamb chops. "You ought to marry her."

"So I've been told," I said. "Did you think Ken was religious when you met him?" I asked.

"I had no idea how completely ignorant secular guys could be," Gigi said. "He faked it pretty well the first night. I found out later."

Things got a little more raucous after the presentation of the chocolate mousse cake, which was served with champagne. Because it was a meat meal, Gigi was trying out a new recipe substituting dark chocolate for milk chocolate and margarine for butter. This led to a discussion about the absurdities of keeping kosher as their families practiced it. I knew that Orthodox Jews ate only kosher meat and didn't eat milk with meat in the same meal, but the rules were much more elaborate than I ever imagined.

Instead of simply rejecting the traditions she grew up with, Gigi seemed to be engaged in a creative reinterpretation. She bought kosher meat from a butcher on Broadway, but didn't bother counting the hours between milk and meat meals. She kept four sets of dishes: two everyday sets for milk and meat, one good set for meat, and a single plastic set at her summer share, because "the rules don't apply on Fire Island."

Neither she nor Ken worked on Saturdays, but they turned on lights when they wanted to and did anything that was in the spirit of relaxation. If they had to run to the store to buy diapers, they would. As a gentle slap at her parents, she served young swordfish in caper sauce at a pre-wedding reception. Every fish had been approved by a rabbi, who certified that their scales had been intact before cooking.

"It was easier to bend the rules after I ate fish in a non-kosher restaurant," said Gigi. "Kenneth made me eat there on our second date."

A new bottle of white wine joined the empty Shiraz and the champagne. Ken and I watched as our two women told stories about crocheting yarmulkes for boyfriends and hiding combs and lipstick in the synagogue ladies room. The challenge they shared in high school was to find creative ways around the rules, while still remaining faithful to the theory behind the practice. They were still doing it now, but the struggle had evolved from finding an excuse to watch a videotape of "Dirty Dancing" to adapting chocolate mousse cake recipes from the *New York Times*.

"Did you know Shoshanna was a feminist revolutionary?" asked Gigi.

"No, I missed that one," I said.

"We wore uniforms which were these dull navy blue jackets with pleated skirts, and you were supposed to wear them with white knee socks. So one day, Shoshanna showed up with white bobby socks. And the next day everybody in our class was wearing bobby socks. And the day after that, the whole school was wearing bobby socks. So Rabbi Mendel had to print out a new version of the rules that strictly forbade socks that did not cover the entire leg below the knee. That sealed her reputation as a troublemaker."

"But I was always a good student," Shoshanna said. "You were considered a wild child because you rolled up your skirt on the bus."

"Wait," Ken said. "I never heard this one."

"It was ridiculous," Gigi said. "It was an all-girl bus, but there was Zvi, the Israeli bus driver, who was very handsome."

"I can't believe you thought he was handsome," Shoshanna said. "He was huge."

"Excuse me," I interjected. "Can I say something in defense of big guys?"

"He wasn't like you," Shoshanna said. "He was all fat. You're all meat."

"Look at the way she talks now," said Gigi. "She used to be a nice Jewish girl from Ridgewood."

"It's obvious David is corrupting her," said Ken.

"Did you know that Shoshanna is also a great inventor? She invented the *frum* dresser."

They both started giggling hysterically, and Ken took it as an opportunity to pour some more wine.

"*Frum* means religious or observant," explained Gigi. "At Stern, you could wear almost anything. But you had to dress nicely when you went home for the weekend. So Shoshanna bought a second dresser where she put her frum clothes. And everybody copied her."

"Wait," I said. "I thought you went to Columbia."

"I went to Stern for the first two years and then transferred."

"To be closer to a certain unmentionable person," Gigi said.

"Stern is like Barnard," Shoshanna said. "It's the women's counterpart to Yeshiva, but it's on 34th Street, a hundred blocks south, and you don't attend classes together."

"People always thought of me as the wild one and Shoshanna as the good girl," said Gigi. "But she turned out just as bad as me. She refused to work at her family's accounting firm. Then, instead of living with her family in Ridgewood and taking the bus to the city every day, she got her own apartment, and it wasn't even on the Upper West Side! That's at least two strikes."

"Plus I'm 25 and not married," added Shoshanna.

"There you go," said Gigi. "That's worth three strikes all by itself."

"You should talk," said Shoshanna.

"True!" said Gigi, pressing her arm across her forehead with mock theatrics. "I was three months pregnant when I was married. The *shonde*!"

"The scandal!" Shoshanna translated.

"I may be wrong about this," said Ken, "but I think Shoshanna's drunk."

"I am not drunk," she said, as Ken poured the last of the wine into her champagne flute. "I'm merely inebriated."

The rest of the evening passed by in a happy blur: We heard about the public health nurse brought in from Trenton to teach their state-mandated sex education classes, the rabbi who insisted that there was a kosher equivalent for every taste, including seafood, and the Israeli paratroopers they flirted with on their summer vacations in Israel. I tried to keep up with the blizzard of details about her life, including passing references to her former boyfriend and her fights with her family. Gigi, who was sitting on my right, kept patting my arm to make it clear she liked me. Meanwhile, Ken and I turned the rack of lamb into a pile of bones. I was drunk and completely in love.

At 10:30, I stood up and patted my stomach. "Thanks for dinner," I said. "It's a long way to Battery Park City."

"Stay right where you are," said Gigi. "You guys aren't taking a cab home tonight."

I must have looked a little confused.

"The couch turns into a hide-a-bed," Shoshanna said. "Do you mind if we stay here?"

"No, not at all," I said.

"I slept on it for three months after 9/11 while my apartment building was closed. It's very comfortable."

"She was supposed to stay with her brother," Gigi said, who started clearing away the dessert dishes. "But they had a... what should we call it?"

"We're not going to talk about it," said Shoshanna.

"It was a slight disagreement over some issues," Gigi said. "Have you met any of her brothers yet?"

"No," I said. "I think I'm still a state secret."

"Jeremy, the younger one, is okay," Gigi said, "but the two older ones are very protective. No guy could possibly be good enough." Then she yawned. "Ken is setting you up with blankets."

Shoshanna disappeared into the bathroom while Ken and I pulled out the hide-a-bed and fitted it with the sheets.

"Hey, Ken," I began as we stuffed the pillows into pillowcases. "Can I ask you a very personal question?"

"Sure."

"Did you really score on the first night?"

"Not quite." He smiled at the recollection. "But we did go back to her dorm room afterwards. She had a single."

We sat there on the bed for a while in quiet drunken fellowship, two big secular Jewish guys in love with our semi-Orthodox women. I tried to send him a telepathic summary of my sexual experiences with Shoshanna, in hopes of getting some advice.

He seemed to receive it.

"It took a while," he said, shaking his head. "First they've got to be sure you want to marry them. Then they've got to be sure they want to marry you. But once that's settled, you're in. How long have you two been going out?"

I had to stop and think, since we didn't actually "go out." "A couple weeks."

"That's all?" he asked, looking at the open bed. "I think you're doing pretty well."

"Can I ask you another question?"

"Sure," he said.

"Did you have any problems with her parents?"

Another pause as he scanned through some memories he didn't want to share. "That took a while, too," he said. "But after you give them a couple of grandchildren, they cut you some slack."

We heard muffled chatter behind the bedroom door.

"Those two will talk all night if you let them," he said. "Come on, Gigi. It's time to go to sleep."

"Are you going to New Jersey this weekend?" I asked.

He rolled his eyes. "One weekend was more than enough," he said. "It's a strange scene out there. Very serious people, looking for something new. Guitar playing. She and the rabbi and another couple guys give these informal lectures. But there's a sexy thing in the air, too. Frankly, I think he's using her as bait."

"Bait?"

"Showing everybody that being Orthodox can be cool. Orthodox girls can be hot. That kind of thing. I think he has his eye on her myself."

"The rabbi?"

"He's divorced, with two kids. She's the glamour queen in that crowd. The guys want to sleep with her. The women want to sleep with her. Or else claw her to pieces. That's just a word to the wise."

Shoshanna emerged from the bedroom in a pair of Gigi's pajamas with the sleeves and pant legs rolled up. She gave me a new toothbrush and sat on the bed and brushed her hair with a domestic casualness that surprised me.

"The 3-year-old comes through here every night to sleep with his parents," she said, glancing at the bed. Then she grabbed my earlobe and pinched it.

She fell into a drunken slumber almost immediately, but I was buzzing with excitement. We were sleeping together on a bed instead of a couch, but that was only a small part of the thrill. The evening had been one of those magical times when you discover a new group of friends and the world flips itself around in a new way. I'd found a new club — the Gigi and Ken and Shoshanna and the kids club, and I wanted to join it with my own kids and with Shoshanna, and live more or less like they did.

I wanted the complete package. I wanted a futon on the floor of the kids' room and a dining room and dinners with good wine. I wanted to watch football games on Saturdays with Ken and sleep next to Shoshanna in bed every night, even if she drove me crazy, as I'm sure she would. My single life, with all its supposed freedom, felt stale and tasteless.

I had spent most of my adult life chasing unconventional women, and now I was in love with somebody who honored, in her own way, a particularly well-described set of conventions. The conventions were part of the attraction, something she was bringing to the marriage. They were not something I wanted to follow very seriously, but I liked the idea of having them around, to lend contrast and insight to my own life. I hoped that her own habitual struggle and compromise with them would somehow keep me straight.

Her friends were rooting for me. They wanted Shoshanna to join the marriage club with them. But that kind of approval could only go so far. Most women I had been involved with were capable of acting like they were in love as a kind of romantic courtesy. Shoshanna's refusal to play that game was a reflection of her basic honesty. She was interested in me, and in lust with me, but she was still trying me on for size. I had momentum on my side, and lust, but there was still a long way to go.

Then there was the matter of my final trading episode in November. At some point, I'd have to tell her the truth.

The hide-a-bed mattress was awful. I tried a number of positions before imitating Shoshanna, who slept on her back, her mouth open like a corpse.

I woke up a few minutes before dawn and found her sitting on the side of the bed, sifting through her split ends. The living room looked out on the southern lawn of the Museum of Natural History, where a couple of joggers were stretching before their run in the park. The light from the window put her in silhouette.

"I don't want you to get the idea that I hate everything that's Orthodox," she said. Her voice was still husky with sleep, but I thought it betrayed a certain sadness as well. "I may hate individual members of my family sometimes, but we had a wonderful time growing up."

Looking for split ends had put her in a deep trance. She talked as if she was continuing a conversation that had gone on all night.

"Shabbat was really something special," she said. "After dinner, you couldn't turn on the lights in your bedroom, so you'd hang around downstairs with the family. You couldn't watch TV, so we'd all play board games, or look through my Mom's old photo albums, or just sit around and tease each other. On Saturday night, there was a special service for the ending of Shabbat and you lighted these big spiral candles, and my Dad would tell me to hold the candle as high as I wanted my future husband to be tall."

That sent her way back into memory-land. She played with her hair while I looked out the window absentmindedly at a streetside mini-drama: an SUV trying to wedge itself into a parking space that would have challenged a subcompact.

"So why did you move to Battery Park City?" I asked.

"My boyfriend and I broke up last year," she said, beginning a new search on the next clump of hair. "My family considered it some kind of tragedy because we'd been going out for a long time. My parents and his parents really got along. He and my brother Nathan became very close. Everybody was mad at me for breaking up something that was considered a done deal. I had an apartment on 92nd Street. Nathan lived with his wife and kids two blocks away, and my other two brothers were nearby."

She moved closer to the window to get more light.

"My brothers would try to fix me up with their dorky friends, or their friend's cousin's friend. There are only a half a dozen kosher restaurants on the Upper West Side, so all my dates were on public display. Afterwards they'd ask me: 'How did it go? What was wrong with *him*?' Everybody knew I was *kallah moed*, which is Yiddish for 'on the prowl.' Gigi was busy with her family, and all my friends from Stern and Columbia were already married. I was getting this reputation as an ultra picky bitch who would never find a husband."

She gave one hair a slow tug and watched it separate into a half dozen wispy strands. "Wow, look at that!"

"Very impressive," I said, as she turned it this way and that in the light.

"Then one day I woke up and decided to break my lease and move downtown," she said. "That was two months before 9/11."

I wanted to bring the conversation back to us. "So you liked living in Battery Park."

"I *loved* it," she corrected. "Nobody knew who I was. I was just another yuppie. I could do what I wanted and nobody would know. I took a yoga class at the health club, with the chanting and everything. I made friends with gentile girls for the first time. I even have a friend from Pakistan. When I couldn't get into my apartment after 9/11, I stayed in Nathan's apartment because he had an extra bedroom. But we had a big fight and I spent the next three months sleeping on Gigi's couch. That was when I started spending weekends leading the women's classes at Rabbi Zimmerman's place in New Jersey."

"Can I ask you a personal question?"

"Sure," she said. "About what?"

"Sex."

"Oh," she said. "That."

She tugged at her shoulder straps, then looked down at her chest to make sure her camisole was in place.

"When you're a girl, your parents tell you all these things you can't do, so what's forbidden becomes exciting," she said. "You want to see what you're missing. What's it like to eat crab? So you buy some imitation crab at a Korean salad bar just to try it out. It's nothing special, but always you wonder if real crab tastes better. You've been reading about sex in Cosmo for years. What would it really feel like to do this or that? So you try a few things with your boyfriend and then stop doing them. Then you wait to get married. It's a perfect way to drive two people nuts. And apart."

She puffed up her cheeks and then let the air out all at once. To indicate a little explosion.

"After we broke up, I moved out here. All these thoughts keep running through your head. Everybody's hitting on you. At work. Shopping for groceries. Why not him? Why not pick up some guy, some guy you barely know, and take him back to your apartment?"

A big proud smile, halfway to a laugh. Then she shook her head. "I can't believe I really did that with you."

"And what about us?" I asked.

Her smile collapsed as quickly as it formed. "I don't know what I'm going to do about you."

"You could marry me," I said. "In a minute."

"Yeah, I know. But you're trouble."

"*A boy like that.... wants one thing only,*'" I sang in my best Puerto Rican accent.

"*One of your own kind, stick to your own kind,*" she sang, picking up the second half of the chorus.

"Did your parents let you watch 'West Side Story'?"

"No," she said. "It's Gigi's favorite musical. We've rented it a million times."

Chapter 15

We spent a long day at work, cramming for next week's assignment in Connecticut. I half considered joining her at her lunchtime prayer service as a gesture of goodwill, but thought that might come off as desperate and insincere. Instead, I kept my distance.

In between preparations for next week, Shoshanna had been working on a grand compilation of all the evidence we had gathered thus far. I had done just about all I could do for that effort. But something Nardulli mentioned in passing was beginning to bug me: *I'm looking for a gay trader. What about Markowitz?*

I didn't think he was gay, and I didn't think a guy making four or five million a year was likely to try to risk everything in a fraud in order to make another couple million. But I wanted to see what made the guy tick. How did somebody a little older than me climb to the top of the heap so quickly? A quick troll through his e-mails made some sense.

He usually answered them in two marathon sessions. The early session occurred after he came out of his 8 a.m. staff meeting. These were fired off wholesale, sometimes two or three a minute, with little concern for typos, and with the singular goal of getting things off his desk. The messages were usually blunt and scatological, and not beyond flattery, which he used to good effect with both superiors and employees: "Please take care of this asshole's absurd request with all of your inimitable skill." Or: "Is this the same dickhead that fucked us by doing that tax trade with Morgan Stanley? If so, please tell him he can't expect us to clean the shit out of his stable until we see more business."

The 6 p.m. e-mails, which sometimes took an hour or more to complete, were more reflective and analytic. What strategies can we come up with to capture more business? How can we implement the strategies in the most effective way possible? He would dream up a new product and write a business plan off-the-cuff, complete with the necessary risk management, recruiting and technology challenges and how he proposed to solve them. He understood it all: budgets, regulatory capital issues, market data, order routing, trading system design, accounting. I was awed. He had all my trading skills and something else: directness, efficiency and a global grasp of the business of finance.

After spending an hour shadowing his thoughts, I began to understand his operational ethic: The people on his team were treated with respect. Everybody else was either a complete fool or somebody who had to be deferred to. I was clearly a complete fool, one of the legions of bank clerks, accountants and other pests who existed only to prevent him from making money. But I had to sympathize with his arrogance. From all the information he'd been given, his only logical conclusion was that I was an ignorant quant unworthy of judging his work.

After lunch, when my neighbor invited me to join a meeting with his boss and some guys from the Frankfurt office, I accepted. His boss had already gotten a rave review about me from somebody else the day before, and asked if I could join his group full-time when the job in Connecticut ended. I told them it wasn't my decision to make, but I had no personal objection to the idea. Then, flattered by their attention, I gave them a very astute introduction to key episodes of equity-market trading volatility before and after the advent of the euro.

I was leaning back in my chair lecturing like an economics professor when Shoshanna knocked on the glass window of the conference room. I felt a little guilty, as if she had caught me cheating on her in some way.

"Ed wants to see us in his office," she said.

Lewis was talking on the phone as we approached his open door, but motioned us toward two seats. I noticed two envelopes on his desk with our names typed on the outside, just out of reach. He was listening to somebody who allowed him to add "Sure" and "Okay" from time to time. Every few seconds he looked at his watch, as if that would encourage his caller to hurry up. Then he said a final okay and turned his attention to us.

"I got a lovely call earlier this morning from Detective Nardulli," he said.

Out of the corner of my eye, I saw Shoshanna grab her purse and place it protectively in her lap.

"He asked me if any of our board members were gay. He seems to think one of our board members may have been having an affair with Tim Scott before he died. I told him I thought that was extremely unlikely. He said that he'd heard that a board member had ordered an investigation of Tim's fraud. I asked him how he'd found out about that."

Lewis stood up suddenly and took a peek through the slats of his mini-blinds at Ground Zero. It seemed to be a nervous tick he had developed.

"He said you two told him. You made an after-hours visit yesterday to the First Precinct. Against my specific instructions."

He sat down and scrutinized us one by one, as if he were an insurance salesman trying to sell us a big life policy with all the trimmings.

"Tim Scott is dead," he said. "He defrauded the bank out of a couple million. We're never going to get our money back. The scam is over. We can't prosecute a dead man. The best thing I can do — the only thing I can do — is to control the damage to the bank."

Then he stood up and fixed his gaze in the general location of the senior executive offices on the west side of the building.

"I told everybody down the hall that I had this thing under control. But you know what Nardulli wants me to do now?" he asked, his voice climbing higher. "He wants me to give him the contact names and addresses of all of our board members. Human resources is furious. Legal is furious. My boss, the chief operating officer, is furious. Can you imagine what might happen? Can you imagine our board members getting visits in their offices from a New York City detective asking them if they've ever engaged in any homosexual behavior?"

He closed his eyes and squeezed his temples theatrically. He took the two envelopes and pushed them a few inches towards us. Then he picked up a phone and buzzed his secretary. It seemed to be some sort of cue.

"I tried to treat you two honestly and fairly," he said. "I told you very explicitly what I wanted. I told you to end your investigation. I told you not to go back to the police. I made that very clear."

Then he nodded to the envelopes, indicating that he was waiting for us to open them.

Mine contained a check for $5,000 and a letter making it clear that the bank no longer needed my services. Shoshanna's was three pages long, and took her quite some time to read.

When I looked up, I saw a security guard opening the door of the office. He was an older black guy with a full head of bushy gray hair. He asked for our identity cards very politely, attached them to his clipboard, and told us that any personal effects left in our desk would be sent to us by UPS the next day. Then he escorted us down the stairs and out of the bank.

We stood around outside the entrance to the building for a while, staring at the river. It was another bright cold April day. Across the river, about a mile away, I could see Exchange Place, where a security guard had escorted me out of another building on November 12. I seemed to be having problems staying employed at buildings situated on the Hudson River.

I don't get depressed very often, but when I do, I fall pretty hard. A few minutes ago, I had a new job, a new career. Now...

And at some point, I knew I would get angry at Tim Scott for dragging me into his messy life and his even messier death. And now he had cost me my best shot at a new life.

At some point I would also get angry at Shoshanna for insisting that we go back to the cops. She would find another job in a minute. But I was being been thrown back headfirst into unemployment hell, and she didn't even know it.

"We didn't do anything wrong," she said, digging through her purse for her sunglasses.

The sun was bright, but I thought she might be using the glasses to cover up tears. Then I realized she was on the other side of the emotional spectrum. She wasn't upset. She was happy she'd lost her job. She was a modern-day Joan of Arc, a female warrior, proud of her achievement.

"We were cooperating with a murder investigation," she said. "Ed Lewis was interfering with it. He was breaking the law, not us."

Once I knew she wasn't upset, I found her presence unsettling. "Great," I said. "I'm happy that we've joined the ranks of all the other unemployed people in this town."

There was nowhere else to go, so we walked through the construction maze at the building entrance and south to Battery Park City.

Our office tower was still the only fully occupied building in the Financial Center, and it was still surrounded by construction equipment from the crews restoring the glass-enclosed Winter Garden nearby. The upscale harbor had been turned into a temporary ferry landing for people commuting to New Jersey. The weather was a little chilly, but we sat down on some benches, bundled against the wind. You could see the office buildings of Exchange Place across the river. It was the perfect time to tell Shoshanna how I'd lost my job.

"You know what?" she asked.

"What?"

"If we find the killer, we can sue the bank."

"For what?"

"For firing us unlawfully. We were doing our job as auditors and we were cooperating with the authorities in a murder case. They had no right to fire us for doing the right thing. That's definitely a legitimate lawsuit. Or a big out-of-court settlement."

She was on a righteous indignation high, and I was closing in on lows I hadn't hit since adolescence. What the hell was I supposed to do with my life?

"The rabbis tell you not to worry," she said. "If you do the right thing, good things will come to you. You're not supposed to be depressed."

"I'm not depressed," I said. "I'm devastated."

"Why? You're very employable. I'm very employable. We'll get other jobs."

It was time to tell her. Now. I tried to think of how to begin. I would confess that I had lied about a few things. I had committed securities fraud, a felony, just like Tim. I could have been put in jail, but the bank swept it under the rug. It was now or never.

"You see those buildings over there?" I asked, pointing across the river. "That's where I worked on November 12, the day I left trading."

"Stop thinking about it," she said, interrupting me. "You'll find something else."

Her plan was to call some recruiters, then meet later that afternoon to organize our files. At three o'clock or so, we would take her car to her rabbi's place in New Jersey.

Spending the weekend with young people eager to explore their Jewish roots did not fill me with excitement. I tried to keep an open mind about it in the vague hope I would have some dramatic life-altering experience, but I wasn't expecting much.

As I made myself a rejuvenating pot of coffee, I found myself struggling with a mathematical story problem: If Dave had a $5,000 check and another few thousand in the bank, and he was working as a temp at wages of a few hundred dollars a week, how long could he afford to live in Battery Park City?

The answer: not very long.

When I went to work that morning, I was a consultant to a bank auditing team, about to begin a challenging new assignment in Connecticut. Now I was back to my default status: unemployable. My three weeks of experience as a forensic auditor didn't matter. If I listed it on my resume, employers would call Ed Lewis to check me out, and I could imagine all the wonderful things he'd say about me. Wasn't there anything I could do to make a living?

I buckled down and spent a couple of grueling hours dropping in on a few chat rooms inhabited by other out-of-work Wall Streeters. We were all former MBAs from top schools who earned in the low and middle six figures. Now we were sitting around in our pajamas, bitching about whatever did us in. If it wasn't the tech crash, it was the JP Morgan/Chase merger. If it wasn't that, it was 9/11. If it wasn't 9/11, it was the economic malaise that followed.

Some of my out-of-work colleagues, fired in the post-9/11 bloodbaths, had tried to start their own hedge funds, but found it impossible to get investors. There was no money to be made. I wondered abstractly: Where did all the money come from? Where did it go?

I was glad when Shoshanna interrupted me a little while later. She'd finished a draft of her resume and was going to the gym. I told her I'd meet her downstairs.

She was waiting for me by the elevator bank in her sweatsuit, peeking out the glass entrance of the building at a car parked on the street 50 feet away.

"What's wrong?"

"That car. I think I saw it at the funeral. And it was here yesterday too."

It looked like a normal car service sedan to me. It was a late-model Ford Crown Victoria with tinted windows, the kind you'd find idling outside corporate headquarters all over Manhattan. But dark blue instead of black.

"I don't understand. Did something happen?"

"I don't know," she said, her voice bordering on hysteria. She was clutching her apartment keys to her face. "Maybe. I'm not sure. When I went outside to look for you, it was parked across the street, then started to drive towards me, so I ran towards the promenade. Then it sped up, like it was trying to get to the end of the sidewalk to cut me off."

She ran her fingers through her hair, then zipped and unzipped the top of her sweatshirt.

"What did you do?"

"I just sprinted back to the lobby. I just kept running."

"Then what did the car do?"

"It's still there."

"So what do you think it is?"

"Maybe somebody followed me back from the funeral the other night."

"You mean Tim's partner?"

"I don't know who, exactly," she said. "I don't think it's likely, but it's a possibility."

"Are you sure this is the same car you saw at the funeral?" I asked. "Was it dark blue?"

"Yes," she said, giving it a closer look. "Or maybe. I'm not really sure." She took a few steps to the side, to get a different angle.

"Come with me," she said, pushing open a heavy metal door that led to the basement garage.

We walked past a row of cars to another fire door that opened onto a narrow sidewalk on the side of the building. She pointed me out the door: "Why don't you walk by and take a look?"

The sidewalk ran along the east end of the building to the circular driveway where the car was parked. Now it was gone. A dry-cleaning van was idling a few feet away. Nothing suspicious. It was about noon on a Friday, an ordinary overcast day and most people were at work.

When I went back into the garage, I saw Shoshanna standing beside a silver Acura Legend, unlocking the passenger door.

"Let's get out of here," she said, tossing me the keys.

"Where are we going?"

"To New Jersey."

"But we haven't packed."

"I want to get out of here. Now!"

I got into the driver's seat, pushed the seat all the way back and started adjusting the mirror.

"Don't worry about that," she demanded. "Just go!"

I zipped out as soon as the garage door opened. A little strange, but who knows? I ran a stop sign on the way to the West Side Highway, while Shoshanna slumped down in her seat, silently scanning the road for dark blue car-service sedans. We hit the usual congestion at the entrance to the Holland Tunnel, exacerbated by a security check for a convoy of fuel trucks, and were funneled into a single lane, sandwiched between a Port Authority tow truck and an off-duty ambulance from a New Jersey hospital.

The protection of the two vehicles seemed to reassure her. She sat up in her seat and gave her hair a nervous once-over.

"Maybe the driver wanted to talk to you for some reason," I said. "Maybe he was rolling down his window."

"Sure," she said. "Maybe he wanted to chat about the weather."

It was just past noon when we turned off the commercial artery and drove west into the green confines of New Jersey. The neighborhood seemed to be catching its breath before the Friday afternoon assault from school buses and commuter trains.

We parked in the driveway, behind a Subaru and a white Ford Econoline that had been converted into something like an airport shuttle bus. A sign on the side of the van said: "New Horizons, Ridgewood NJ."

I felt as if I had traveled hundreds of miles from New York. We'd hit a little rain coming out of the tunnel but now it was no more than a mist. As we got out of the car, we both stood silent, soaking up the new sounds: water dripping off leaves, a bird here and there, the muffled sound of trucks on the arterial street a few blocks to the east.

The same skinny teenager came out to greet us. He shook Shoshanna's hand familiarly, and asked about our bags in a thick Russian accent. When we told him we didn't have any, he led us inside.

The furnishings were upscale New Jersey, but a bit frayed around the edges by institutional use. An aluminum coat rack by the entryway held two dozen empty hangers, and a sign by the wall telephone said: "NJ, NY, CT calls only." Off to the right was a living room with some couches arranged in a semicircle and throw pillows on the floor to seat a dozen or so more.

Dmitri told us the rabbi was on his way back from the city and would arrive in a few minutes. Shoshanna said we'd wait for him in his study, and walked up the staircase as if she owned the place.

The second floor was obviously a residential enclave for the rabbi's family, but there was no sign of any family. We passed two kids' bedrooms, one decorated with crossed hockey sticks and New Jersey Devils pennants, the other with Britney Spears posters. The master bedroom had been converted into a study, with the rabbi's desk in a deep bay window overlooking the backyard. There was a stack of long, thin leather-bound books in Hebrew on one side of his desk, bristling with paper bookmarks, as well as a laptop with a bright green cable that snaked across the floorboard to a blinking cable modem. Opposite the desk were two leather armchairs that seemed to be made specifically for discussing weighty spiritual matters.

Other than traffic directions, Shoshanna and I hadn't said a word to each other since we emerged from the tunnel. She grabbed a book from one of the bookshelves and sunk into an armchair as a way of continuing the silence.

I walked back down the hall to peek into the son's bedroom. It could have been my bedroom, circa 1986, if you removed the iMac and changed the featured sport from hockey to wrestling. An assortment of jeans, soccer balls, dirty socks and sports magazines leaked out of the closet. Martin Brodeur, the Devil's star goalie, had signed one of the hockey sticks with some words of advice: "Keep your skates sharp!" I even spotted my high-school calculus textbook on his desk, now published with diagrams in full color.

After a while, I drifted back to the rabbi's study and noticed a drum set in a little room that might have once served as a walk-in closet. It was lollypop red and came complete with a microphone stand and an amplifier.

"Who plays drums?" I asked Shoshanna.

"His daughter," she said, without looking up from her book. "She's 6."

I heard the rabbi's car pull into the driveway downstairs. I settled into the second armchair and waited for him to arrive.

At first glance he looked like an old-fashioned type of rabbi, small of stature, with a dark, bushy beard and a slight stoop. At second glance, he looked a bit younger: He was at some indeterminate point in his mid-30s. He wore a dark-gray suit with no tie and his beard ended at mid-chest in a carefully trimmed point, but it seemed a bit studied, as if he were trying for some kind of self-conscious effect.

Then I stared at his wrist. He was wearing a Rolex Oyster, or a damn good copy.

He nodded hello to both of us, straightened his papers and reflexively checked his e-mail. We were still dressed for the gym, Shoshanna in her matching designer outfit and I in my mismatched sweatshirt ensemble.

"I wasn't expecting you to come so early," he said checking his watch. "How are you two doing?"

"We're okay," said Shoshanna. "Rabbi Zimmerman, this is David Ackerman."

"She's told me about you," he said, looking at both of us in turn. "You both look pretty awful."

"Well, we had a busy morning," she said.

She told the rabbi about what had happened in front of our building, then brought him up to speed about the events of the past few days. He seemed to be aware of the general nature of our fraud investigation and Tim's murder. Shoshanna explained our visit to the funeral home, our session with Nardulli at the police station, and how we lost our jobs.

Her delivery of all that information was too fast to be completely comprehensible. The rabbi focused on the nature of the threat posed by the car service sedan, and he appeared to be confused about what the evidence really meant.

"How can you be sure somebody was trying to hurt you?" he asked. "Do you think there's some other explanation?"

Shoshanna told him she thought somebody had followed her home from the funeral, and was trying to harm her in some way. My silence made it clear I wasn't convinced.

"Was it the same car you saw the first time?" he asked.

"I'm not sure," she said. "It was dark blue. They're usually black. But it's hard to tell."

Then he stopped and paused for a few moments to consider all the facts.

"Somebody could have been trying to intimidate you," he concluded. "Or maybe they wanted to harm you in some way. Or maybe it was nothing. We don't really know. In any case, I think you need to get away for a while."

He took another look at her, as if trying to assess her mental state.

"Rabbi Schulman is running a weeklong retreat for teenagers at the Circle Lodge in the Catskills, starting tonight." He checked his watch and reached for the phone. "A dozen girls from one of the religious middle schools around here. I'm sure they could use an extra set of hands."

"That would be great!" she said, suddenly brightening at the idea. "I'd love to get away for a while."

He left a message on the rabbi's answering machine and then turned to us with a bemused smile.

"You both lost your jobs this morning, but you don't seem too concerned about it," he observed.

"I'll go see some recruiters next week," said Shoshanna. "I've already written my resume."

"What about you?" he asked, focusing his laser eyes on me.

He was taking my measure in a practiced sort of way. I shrugged, and let myself be open to his gaze. What could he possibly tell about a guy in black sweatpants and a gray sweatshirt?

"You're not worried?" he asked.

"It's not a great time to be pushing resumes," I admitted.

"Shoshanna tells me you're quite a successful trader. You should be in high demand."

"I'm a former trader," I said. "I've been working as a consultant on forensic audits, examining problems on trading desks. At least that's what I was doing this morning when I came to work."

"And why did you stop trading?" he asked, leaning forward and forming a little dome with the tips of his fingers.

My boilerplate answer was ready and waiting. But this time I let the question hang in the silence.

"It was a post-9/11 reaction," said Shoshanna, filling in the awkward pause.

"No, that's not quite true," I said. "Actually it's completely false."

Shoshanna whipped her head around and gave me a wild stare: What are you talking about? I cleared my throat once or twice, as if the truth was caught somewhere in the phlegm. I didn't know what was happening to me. My standard answer was ready to go, but I couldn't do it. I could not lie to this guy in the beard.

"On November 12 of last year, I had a fight with the guy who sat next to me at work," I said. "So I did a few stupid trades that lost a lot of money. Then I compounded it by losing more money. Then I committed securities fraud by trying to cover it all up.

Then I lost my job."

"How much did you lose?" the rabbi asked.

"$112,884,221." I said. I don't think I had ever told anybody exactly how much.

Shoshanna looked ashen. I thought I saw something in her face shut down. What the hell, I told myself. At least the relationship was ending in a blaze of truth.

"Did you repay it?" the rabbi asked.

"Did I repay what?" I replied.

"The $112 million."

"I paid $612,000 to the bank in a settlement, but I lost my license to trade securities," I said. "That's why I took a job as an auditor's assistant."

"Are you going to try to pay back the rest?"

"No," I said, a bit shocked by his whole line of questioning. "I don't have a job and I don't have many prospects other than working as a temp. I'm unemployable as a trader. I have less than $10,000 in my bank account."

The rabbi's eyes ping-ponged between Shoshanna and me a few times, trying to read what was going on. Then the phone rang. It was Rabbi Schulman. He would love to have Shoshanna help out on the retreat. Shoshanna should drive to the synagogue parking lot immediately and meet him before the bus left.

"Bring your cell phone in case I have to call you," I said.

She looked at me briefly, as if I were some homeless guy who had accosted her in the subway. Then she swung her bag over her shoulder and walked down the hall. We listened to her quick steps move down the stairs, past the front door, and across the gravel to her car. Her exit from the driveway was fast and noisy.

I didn't feel anything at that moment. I stared out his window at the backyard, which was a modest narrow area, bordered with evergreens. On the obligatory deck, the redwood furniture was getting wet in the rain, along with some sodden leaves from last fall that didn't have the courtesy to decompose.

"I know all about big guys like you," the rabbi said quietly. "You're the most fragile of them all."

The shock was beginning to sink in.

He saw right through me, saw the whole relationship unravel with a few glances. I didn't mind. In fact, I was glad to be here. He didn't seem like much of a threat. He wasn't much older than me, but I trusted him, and understood why he was Shoshanna's guru.

"I want to talk to you some more," he said, "but I've got to deal with something downstairs for half an hour. You can wait here. Feel free to browse the library."

After a few minutes perusing some inscrutable titles in Hebrew I walked down the hall and stood in the doorway of his son's room, a perfectly preserved museum of my late adolescence. I ran my eyes lovingly over the hockey team notices taped to the wall. They trained four afternoons a week, 4 to 6. One-hour warm-up, one hour on the ice. If they won the next two games, they'd make it to the regionals.

The closet doors held back an explosion of sports equipment: inline skates, tennis racquets, baseball gloves, along with a well-used set of Spaulding Pro golf clubs in a leather bag. A gift from somebody in the family who played serious golf. The chaos of the bedroom was in direct contrast to the perfectly-made bed, evidence of a cleaning lady's weekly visit.

I leaned against the door frame, closed my eyes and took a "Twilight Zone" trip back to 1986, when I lived in a bedroom very much like this in suburban Chicago. My dad was watching TV in the den. My mom was in the kitchen, opening three cans of Hungry Man soup for our dinner. My sister was in college. I was exhausted from wrestling practice. I would take a quick nap and then go downstairs to dinner. After that, I would dig up a NoDoz from the stash in my desk drawer and speed my way through my AP physics textbook, preparing for the midterms I knew I would ace.

I loved high school. I was going to finish in the top 10 in my class. My SATs were in the 99th percentile. I was destined for greatness. I was not going to be just another rich guy like my dad. In the year 2000, I would be 30, unimaginably old, established in my profession and living in a huge house with a garage filled with futuristic cars.

And true love? Somehow that was the easy part. In those days, I imagined her as a teenage version of Jennifer Curtis, a Playboy centerfold I'd seen the previous summer. My future wife was out there somewhere, in her room, doing her homework. And somewhere out there was a high school student who would eventually win the Fields Medal in math. Maybe it would be me.

But, as it turned out, becoming just an average rich guy was a lot harder than I thought. And true love? That was harder still.

I walked back to the rabbi's office and sank deep into the leather chair. I hoped the rabbi's son made it to the regionals.

"David?"

Rabbi Zimmerman touched my shoulder. His voice, coming from above me, seemed miles away.

"Oh yeah," I said, with a crick in my neck. "Just a minute."

It was very dark outside. Maybe the rain had returned.

"You slept for two hours," the rabbi said, looking at his watch. "I didn't want to wake you."

I was groggy and vulnerable. A set of horrible dreams lay just outside my consciousness, as if I had already slipped into a terrible depression, but my waking mind wasn't aware of it.

I made no attempt to disguise all this as I sat in the armchair opposite his desk. I was a soul in trouble, and he was the rabbi with the comforting eyes who could find out what was ailing me.

"So you never told Shoshanna that you committed a multi-million dollar fraud," he said.

"Well, I tried to a couple of times but..."

"Incredible," he said. "The two of you are supposed to be looking for fraudulent traders, but she had no clue that she was working with one! And you expected a real relationship, a real marriage to be based upon such shaky foundations?"

"There's a lot of stuff she didn't tell me," I said.

"We're not talking about her," he snapped. "We're talking about you. The trading genius. Who doesn't know the first thing about honesty."

I could have stood up and left, but I didn't. This wasn't my turf. It was Shoshanna's. But I didn't have anywhere else to go.

"What was your logic?" he asked. "Did you think you could keep it a secret forever? What was going through your brain?"

I assumed he meant it as a rhetorical question, but I was wrong.

"You've got to tell me," he said, bending forward. "What were you thinking? Did you believe that if you lied, she'd fall in love with you. And then, after you told her the truth, she'd still be in love? Was that the strategy?"

"Something like that," I admitted. "It was a deception."

"It's not deception," said. "It was active trickery. You caused somebody to believe what was not true. And this obviously wasn't your first brush with dishonesty. You're a recidivist. What inspired you to steal the hundred million dollars? Why did you do it?"

"I didn't steal it. I lost it," I pointed out emphatically.

"Okay, so what happened?"

"I already told you," I said. "I did a very stupid option trade that went bad. Then I did another trade that lost even more money. Then I tried to cover the whole thing up."

"I didn't want to know *how* you did it, I want to know *why* you did it."

I was still groggy from my long nap. I had to pull the details from the back of my mind, but they were coming out at half speed.

"The guy who sat next to me on the trading desk was a real jerk," I began. "He kept making life terrible for me, getting under my skin. I wanted to get back at him, to show him I was as good as he was."

"You're still not telling me why. Why did you allow him to drive you crazy? I know lots of people that work with jerks. Horrible people. Day in and day out. But they don't let them destroy their livelihood."

"I don't know why," I said, after thinking about it for a while. "I thought I knew, but I'm not sure any more."

"My guess is that it has something to do with the environment you worked in," he said. "Everybody on Wall Street is busy making money. There's nothing wrong with making money. We've all got to eat. But maybe you wanted to make more than this other guy. And something snapped."

"It was only peripherally about money," I said. "It was really about something else."

"Okay," he said, warming up to the inquiry. "Now we're getting somewhere. So what did this guy have that you didn't have? Was there some girl involved?"

I shook my head. I knew the answer, but I didn't want to admit it.

"Was he younger? Better-looking?"

"He was more talented than me," I blurted out. "He was a superstar trader. He did it all effortlessly. And he let me know it."

The rabbi seemed amused. He smiled and ran his fingers along the edges of his beard.

"How much were you making? Five hundred thousand a year?"

"More."

"$700,000?"

"Yeah."

"So here's David Ackerman, a big-shot trader, making $700,000 a year. And here's some other schmuck sitting beside him. You're both at the top of your profession. You have more money than 99 percent of the world's population. But that's not enough for you. You want more. Is that what you're telling me?"

I sighed the deepest sigh of my life. It was pretty much what I expected to hear from a rabbi.

"So nobody can be better than you?" he asked. "That's some kind of crime?"

"You asked me why I did it," I said. "I told you why."

"Just think about these ghetto kids," he said, pointing out the window, as if they were cruising by his driveway. "The ones who are drug dealers. They're driving around Trenton or Jersey City and one of them cuts the other off. They start shooting at each other. We read about the incident in the paper and think, how stupid! But you weren't any smarter."

I took another look out the window at his backyard, which was now barely visible in the twilight. I was sitting absolutely still in my chair, but my head was spinning. In 10 minutes, the man had me down cold.

I understood why Shoshanna would be drawn to him, why people wanted to spend their weekends with him. I decided that the most valuable commodity in the world wasn't money. It was self-awareness. And we'd all do anything to get a little bit more.

"Okay, so what do you want to do with yourself now?" he continued. "Do you want to be a trader again?"

"I can't be a trader again," I said. "I lost my license."

"We're not talking about reality. We're talking about your dreams."

I hesitated answering. I understood that it was supposed to be some kind of therapeutic exercise, but I didn't want to reconnect with dreams that couldn't be fulfilled.

"Take your time," he said. "It doesn't cost anything. You might even learn something."

"You want me to tell you what I wish could happen if everything went my way?" I asked.

"Yeah. If through some magical power, you could do whatever you wanted to do right now. Go ahead and dream. If it was up to me, I would..." he said, pausing to throw up his hands. "You fill in the blank."

This time it didn't take me very long.

"I'd play shortstop for the Chicago White Sox," I said.

"I mean an *adult* dream," he said, growing suddenly impatient. "Let me answer the question for you. You'd want to be a trader again, right?"

"Sure," I said.

"What kind of trader were you?" he asked.

"I was an options trader."

"What kind of options did you trade?" he asked.

"Equity options."

"Listed or OTC?"

I stared at him. It was a bizarre moment. What did he know about options?

"I traded both listed and OTC," I said slowly. "OTC when I was dealing with clients. I traded listed options when I wanted to lay off my risk."

"I know the game," he said. "You dump the deal on the client's desk, build in a big spread, then hope he doesn't realize how badly he's getting ripped off."

We smiled at each other for a while. I was smiling like a guy who was completely confused. He was smiling like a guy who had just told the funniest joke in the world.

"Who are you?" I asked. "How do you know all this stuff?"

"I worked on Wall Street in the '90s," he said. "I was Steve Bacon's chief Treasury trader. I did six months in Allenwood. That's when I got religion."

"Then you became a rabbi?"

"Jewish Theological Seminary, Class of 2000," he said, pointing to a diploma on the wall. "You think I bought this house on a rabbi's salary?"

I stood up to take a closer look at the diplomas: B.A. from Haverford. MBA from the University of Chicago. I had to walk around his office to reorient myself.

"I thought this was some sort of Jewish halfway house," I said.

"It is," he said. "I live here. I run lunchtime services for people who work on Wall Street. And on weekends, I run retreats for young adults looking for something spiritual in their lives."

"Where are your kids?"

"They spend weekends with my ex-wife. They live in a house across the street."

I ended my little tour of his office and sat down.

"So let's discuss why you're here," he said. "I assume it's because you wanted to earn some brownie points with Shoshanna. You wanted to demonstrate your willingness to accept some of her culture."

"I was trying to be open to it," I admitted. "Maybe it was a lost cause."

"But it was hard to be open to it? Is that what you're saying?"

I told him about the lox-and-bagel Judaism I was brought up in: presents on Hanukah, one Passover Seder with my Dad's side of the family. And my general lack of interest in spiritual issues.

"So what's your level of interest in Judaism now?"

I couldn't decide if the true answer was "somewhat interested" or "not at all interested." I decided to hedge my bets. "I've screwed up a lot of things in my life," I said. "I'm distracted and confused these days. But Shoshanna isn't. She knows what's right and what's wrong. I wanted us to be on the same page."

He considered my words, but didn't nod approval.

"Shoshanna is an interesting woman," he said. "Most of the time I get people coming in, struggling to find a way to become more spiritual. She was going the other way, trying to find some balance between the spiritual and the secular."

We looked out the window as a delivery van pulled up across the street. It said "Weinstein and Son, Kosher Butchers, Passaic New Jersey." A black guy got out of the truck carrying two heavy packages.

"Like most people, she came to me in a transition period," he said. "It was right after 9/11. She'd broken up with her boyfriend and had a fight with her family. She was living with her girlfriend on the Upper West Side. I asked her if she wanted to teach classes on weekends to the secular kids that come here. It seemed to help her."

The doorbell rang downstairs. There were three voices. Dmitri, the deliveryman and an older female voice. They were all arguing about the lateness of the delivery. Elsewhere, somebody else was unstacking metal folding chairs.

"Everybody comes here for answers," he said. "Shoshanna wanted me to tell her what to do. But I don't do that. If you eat a salad in a non-kosher restaurant, does that mean you can eat fish in a non-kosher restaurant? If you hear that your old boyfriend slept with somebody in Israel, does that mean you can sleep with somebody, too? I'm not Ann Landers. People can decide for themselves."

I felt a sudden, blinding flash of sexual hunger, for the smell of her hair, for the heat of her body, for the buttons on her pajamas, for sex with all its confusing, harrowing limitations.

Red light, yellow light, green light. Yellow. Red. I was adrift in my memories for a few seconds.

"I want to marry that woman," I declared when I came out. "I have to marry her. I'm tired of my life. I want a new one. With her. Right away. And I want you to help me."

He studied me as if he were a neurologist, trying to figure out why I had headaches and he was considering all the different possibilities. He leaned back and looked at me from a slightly different angle. Then he closed his eyes and peered at me through his eyelashes.

"I don't buy it," he said finally. "I get guys coming in here twice a month who fall in love with Jewish girls and say they want to convert. They never last. It's the same with parents. They don't practice a thing, but they send their kids to religious school because they think it will help bring certain values into their lives. It doesn't work that way, either. The kids figure out the game sooner or later. It only works when the parents have some kind of genuine interest themselves."

"Isn't there something I can do?" I asked. "Isn't there something you can teach me?"

"You don't have the slightest interest in religion," he said. "You're just a fool in love. You're welcome to stay for the weekend. But I think you'd be wasting your time."

I felt an urgent question welling up inside me: "What kind of sex are Orthodox girls allowed to have before marriage?" I asked.

He laughed, then smiled coyly.

"Let me tell you something about Orthodox girls," he said. "They live in a carefully circumscribed universe, but some of them are curious about the secular world. The clothes, the guys. It's exotic, it's sexy. But when it comes time to settle down, they choose something a little more familiar. They don't want to spend their life in that culture."

"She did," I said. "Her best friend married a secular guy. That's what she wants. Or what she wanted. We were going to meet in the middle."

"I assume you know that Shoshanna is not big on gray," he said. "She likes black and white. And you committed a multi-million-dollar felony. You weren't convicted of it in a court of law, but you were guilty of it just the same. She's never going to marry a felon."

"What about you? I asked. "Didn't you commit a felony, too?"

"I paid my dues," he said, smiling. "And as much as I might like to, I'm not going to marry her, either."

"Well, I paid everything — almost all I had — in a settlement," I said. "I gave up my career. Isn't that enough?"

"No," he said. "After I was charged and convicted, I helped the feds go after the other guys in the Treasury market. And I wrote instruction manuals and ran training sessions while I was going to rabbinical school. You can't really pay back all the millions, so you've got to do something else instead. Being fired frees you to do things you couldn't do before."

"Such as what?"

He shook his head. How could somebody who appeared to be an intelligent human being miss something that was so obvious?

"You've got to stop running around on your own," he said. "You've got to work with the SEC. They can find out who took the other side of those trades. They'll know what firm it came from, maybe even the particular trader."

"Just call up the SEC?" I asked. "Look up their number in the phone book?"

"Why not?"

"I don't think they'd be very happy to see me. I broke a lot of their laws."

"Good point," he said. He opened a Rolodex and started calling. "I'll have to come along."

I remembered my first and last visit to the SEC's offices in the Woolworth Building. It was a cheery little meeting at 4 p.m. on December 24. Also attending were my lawyer, the bank's lawyer, the grim SEC enforcement officer who handled my case, and his assistant, a tall, equally grim young woman with an Indian accent. She gave me forms to sign and accepted my check for $612,329.32.

"Hi, Sharon," the rabbi said, swiveling around in his seat before he spoke into the phone. "This is Larry Zimmerman. Does Mitch have any time free Monday? I think we need about an hour or so.... Great. Tell him I'll call him at home on Sunday."

If he wasn't wearing a long pointy beard, I'd have sworn we were back on Wall Street. Rabbi Zimmerman sounded like a guy who wanted to make a quick appointment and get off the phone. Maybe it was the tension in his voice. Or maybe he had a subtle rabbi accent that he could switch on and off at will.

He took one of his business cards from a box beside his phone and wrote something on the back. "They want to see us Monday at 2 p.m. They're in the Woolworth Building, 15th floor. Okay?"

"Sure," I said, clutching the card tightly in my hand.

"When you get home, e-mail me a detailed memo about Tim Scott. What you found, all your contacts with the police, the works. I'll need it Sunday morning."

We heard the van pulling into the gravel driveway downstairs and Dmitri helping people with their bags. The rabbi quickly took his cell phone out of his pocket and turned it off. Then he shut down his laptop.

"Shabbat is here. I've got to go deal with these kids. You got any other questions?"

"How am I supposed to get home?"

"Dmitri will call you a car," he said. He buttoned his jacket and ran his fingers through his beard, as if to reassure himself that he was Rabbi Zimmerman again. He shook my hand warmly and gave me a final surveying look. "Do something good for the world. You'll feel better about yourself. The jobs and the girls will come later."

Then he walked me to the bottom of the stairway and disappeared into the kitchen.

The sky was a deep blue when I walked outside. The driver pulled up on the gravel driveway just about where Shoshanna had parked. I gave him my address in Battery Park City and looked back at the house as we pulled away. The big curtained windows facing the street were ablaze with opaque yellow light. With the car windows open, you could hear the sound of the highway a few blocks away.

So one chapter in my life closes and another begins. No job, no girlfriend. But with the SEC's help, I might be able to find the person on the other side of those trades.

My stomach twitched. Then a little swoon. I tapped the driver on the shoulder.

"On second thought, take me to 22 Anne Street."

Chapter 16

This time there was no guard, although an empty coffee cup and a copy of *El Diario* suggested he was taking a break. I wanted to go through the building more thoroughly. The offices of the Catholic Charities Mission on the second floor had been locked and a sign directed FedEx and UPS deliveries to another address on Anne Street. Down the hall, the nameplate had been stripped from the office of the derivatives magazine.

Most of the other rooms looked like as if the tenants had moved out since our last visit. I went through the rest of the floors one by one, shaking an occasional door handle, not looking for anything in particular. Everything was consistent with a building being vacated a few weeks ahead of its demolition.

The Thai restaurant didn't look much different. As before, no women in the room. But this time, that detail was telling. At the largest table, five Wall Streeters were having a drink after work. Relaxed, slouching in their chairs in front of bottles of Thai beer, nibbling rice crackers. Was this the Anne Street Group?

Then I saw a familiar face: the guy who wore the black suit at the funeral the other night. I couldn't remember his name. Tim's friend, the trader. I remembered our conversation in the alley behind the funeral home. Maybe Tim's partner in crime? Possible, I supposed, but not very likely. His murderer? Not this guy. But what about the other guys at the table? My instinct told me not.

I decided on a generic guy-to-guy bar approach. I got a beer, then sauntered back his way. His name came to me as our eyes met. Todd.

"Hey Todd, got a cigarette?" I asked.

"Hey, how ya doing?" he said, smiling in recognition, but trying to remember my name.

"Dave. Dave Ackerman."

"Yeah, we met the other day," he said, introducing me to his buddies and pulling up an empty chair.

The eyes of the group were on me for an instant. I was suddenly aware of my mismatched sweatsuit. Maybe I was just back from the gym.

I had interrupted a discussion of where to take an out-of-town guest this weekend:

to a well-reviewed avant-garde thing at the Brooklyn Academy of Music or a killer production of "Turandot" at the Met. And what was the best way to get sold-out Met tickets if money was no object?

Todd scooted his chair a foot or two back from the table, an invitation for us to chat separately. He looked less authoritative in business casual than he did in his black funeral suit, and his round shoulders made him even less imposing. He was an easily recognizable B-school type: the short, aggressively friendly guy who got along with everybody but was never assumed to be leadership material.

"So what did you and Ross do after the funeral?" Todd asked.

"Not much. We walked downtown and ended up at Dark Star."

"Oh yeah?" he said, his eyes brightening momentarily. "How was it?"

"The usual scene," I said. "We had a bottle of wine."

"Ross never liked me," he said. "He had some fantasy of Tim as his ideal love match, and I was ruining it. He was always knocking on the door at the wrong moment to show us one of these Japanese prints he'd found in some bargain bin."

I recognized something familiar about his smile. It was the same overloaded grin I'd get from women who were attracted to me but knew they didn't have much of a chance. Clearly he felt more than a touch of pride about his affair with Tim.

He seemed to be good-looking enough, as far as I could judge, but I suppose his short stature put him lower in the pecking order. Maybe my body, which had a certain currency with women, had a higher exchange rate with gay men. Okay, I thought. If that's how the cards are dealt, let's play them.

I could easily imagine him as Tim's lover. A certain kind of raffish cynicism. Aggressive if you put him on a trading desk, perhaps, but not violent. Still...

"Ross showed me the townhouse where he and Tim lived," I said. "The basement door had a police notice on it. Ross said he walked by Tim's apartment on Friday morning and saw him under a sheet."

"Ugh," said Todd, wincing with disgust. "That's not the way I want to go."

"Me neither," I said.

"Some of these kids..." he said wistfully, staring at the door to the restaurant, as if he were waiting for one of them to walk in. "I had a couple bad experiences with hookers myself. It's an addiction like anything else. But I stopped. You just don't know what kind of ghetto trash you're bringing home."

"That's how it is," I said. "When you have more money than you need, you find all the wrong ways to spend it."

"I don't know how much time you spent with Tim," he said. "We were only involved for a few months in 1998. And then for a couple of weeks after 2000. By then, he was into crystal. His boys got younger and his drugs got stronger."

I nodded appreciatively, as if that matched my own memories.

"He had the Puerto Rican hooker-of-the-month down to a science," he said. "He'd put them on retainer, on call at $500 a week, which most of them preferred. Then he'd get tired of them. Plus he had a dealer who always came through with great shit. A former broker who'd leave it in his bedroom drawer."

I just smiled and shook my head. "He was into some bad stuff," I said. "It was a little too much for me."

"My feelings exactly. On our last night we got off a couple times, did a little this and that, and I fell asleep on his bed. Then I woke up at five in the morning and found him on the couch, completely belted up, with a Puerto Rican hooker sticking a needle between his toes. Enough of that shit. Go ahead and kill yourself, if that's what you want. I'm not going to watch."

"It's a damn shame," I said.

He stared off at a corner of the room, watching some little movie playback in his head. "But when things were good, they were *intense*," he said punching his palm. "In the eighth-floor handicapped bathroom, near the library." For a few moments he was lost in sexual reminiscence. Then he gazed appreciatively at my torso. "But I'm sure you know all about that."

It was time to break the news, but I wasn't sure how far I wanted to go. "Tim wasn't really a friend," I said. "He was more of an acquaintance. I was working on the trading desk. I was hired to investigate a trading scam he was running."

"A trading scam?" he asked.

"Yeah," I said. "Did you know anything about it?"

He looked away, and hesitated a second. He looked back at his friends, then at me. He leaned over the table and lowered his voice.

"Who hired you to investigate?" he asked. "Was it a board member?"

I peered down my beer bottle to stall for time. What did I have here? The possibilities spun out of control.

"I'm afraid I can't tell you," I said, trying to smile. "It's a state secret."

"I know which board member," he said. "It was Marquette."

"It could be Marquette," I said, trying to sound mildly amused. "That guess is as good as any."

I racked my brain, trying to recall Richard Marquette's face on Shoshanna's list of board members. I was pretty sure he ran an investment management firm in Greenwich. Red Hawk or Black Falcon or some other bird of prey.

"A trading scam," he said again. Some kind of emotion knitted his brow momentarily, but I couldn't tag it. Then he stood up and moved to a table out of earshot of his buddies, and motioned me to follow. "So how did it work?" he asked.

My guess was that he was playing dumb. Was he the guy who tipped off the director? If so, he might know how it worked. And he might know something about Tim's partners.

"It involved options," I said, trying to calibrate how much to tell him. "Tim was pretty well positioned on the derivatives desk. He had an early look at all the customer trades before they were executed. He told his partner, who bid up the options the bank needed to buy."

"What kind of options?"

"CBOE options on individual stocks, two or three years out."

"I bet there's no liquidity in those things," he said. "You could never do that in govvies. We'd be all over those spreads."

He suddenly made an eerie transformation from B-school wimp to govvie trader. Options traders like me viewed govvie traders as rough-and-tumble sonofabitches with weaker wits who fought each other day in and day out for a few basis points a trade. I could suddenly imagine Todd at his trading turret, a phone glued to each ear, punching the buttons on his squawk box.

"How did he pull that off without getting caught?" asked Todd.

"He *did* get caught," I said. "I caught him. Or I was about to catch him. Then he was murdered."

His smile turned sour pretty quickly. He was putting it all together. "So you think his death was related to..."

He didn't finish his sentence. He turned around and looked at the gang of four people at his table. They had just ordered another round of drinks and were looking at menus.

"I know who hired you to investigate," he said. "It was Marquette. You don't have to tell me."

"Why are you so sure?" I asked. "There are 18 people on the board of directors."

"I know it was Marquette because I told Marquette."

"Oh," I said noncommittally.

"You don't believe me, do you?" he asked.

I shrugged.

"Anyone who gives more than a thousand bucks to the Gay Men's Health Crisis gets invited to a Christmas fundraiser at the Pierre."

"Okay," I said.

"Marquette was standing right next to me. After a couple glasses of champagne I got up the nerve to take him aside. I told him that somebody had a little scam going on the derivatives desk and that he ought to look into it. I wrote down a diagram on a cocktail napkin. Then I zipped out of there before he could ask me any other questions."

"A diagram," I said.

"Yes."

"What did it look like?" I asked.

"It showed the trade flow and how the information was spun out to somebody else before the trade was completed." He picked up a paper napkin on the table. "About the size of this one. But cloth."

I smiled. "We studied that diagram for hours," I said. "But I'm not sure you'd call it a little scam. It was worth about two or three million bucks a year. That's why the bank hired me. I had special expertise."

"Because you were a trader and you were gay."

"Something like that," I said.

"And you're cooperating with the police?"

"Sort of," I said. "The bank isn't really keen on having the police stomp around the trading floor, trying to find out who's gay and who isn't. But we're pretty sure Tim's partner was somebody outside the bank. What did Tim tell you about this scam?"

"He didn't tell me anything."

I waited just long enough to make it clear that I felt his answer was inadequate.

"A few minutes ago, I asked if you knew anything. You told me 'No, not much.' So what's 'much?' "

"It was just something Tim mentioned in passing," he said. "He invited me to have a drink. He told me he had a little scam going and asked if I was interested. I said no. That was it."

"But I need the details. Where did this happen? Here? In a bar?"

"I told him I didn't want to get involved. Then I felt guilty about the whole thing. For weeks I was back and forth. Should I tell somebody? I decided to keep my mouth shut. Then I ran into Marquette at that party. End of story."

"That was the right thing to do," I said. "But you're a gay trader, a former lover, who left the bank a few months before the scam started. You're a perfect fit for the police profile. They'd be all over you in a minute."

"Do you think I was involved in any of this?"

"No."

"Then what are you trying to do? Threaten me?"

"No," I said. I held up my palms in a gesture of promise. "But I want to know everything that happened."

He looked at my hands in a disinterested way, as if he were trying to determine my age by tracing my lifelines.

"The details are not going to help you. We met at a bar in a tourist hotel in midtown. But there were no tourists."

"When was this?"

"Just a couple months after the Trade Center."

"Okay, November 2001. So that's a pretty bad time. You just heard you were going to be screwed out of your bonus."

"Ours were cut in half, but it's the same idea. Everybody was scrambling for some way to make up the difference. So he says here is a no-risk way to make some money. He sketched the outlines but he was skimpy on details. I thought he had a good shot at pulling it off. But I didn't want anything to do with it."

"So you turned him down."

"To be honest, I was more excited about the fact that I was having a drink with Tim three years after he dumped me. But the implication was that if I did this, it could lead to something really good. Then I asked him if it was illegal, and he said, 'Sort of.' That's when I said no."

"Did he ever say who was on the other side of the trade?"

"No. We didn't get that far."

"Do you think he was working with a group or with one person?"

"He didn't tell me any details. After I said no, he lost interest. A little chatter to make it polite, then he was outta there. I went home completely depressed."

His friends started hooting at the punchline of some joke. He didn't want to talk to me anymore, but he didn't seem eager to rejoin the conviviality at his original table, either. Instead, he settled back into his chair, musing. "So you didn't really know Tim," he said. "You were just investigating him. You weren't his friend or his lover."

I nodded in agreement simply because it was true.

He was lost in reminiscence for half a minute. And, I suspected, mourning.

"When you're young, your friends are more important to you than when you're older," he said grimly. "You don't know who you're going to fall in love with. So you end up in bed with all these different people. And you look back and think Wow! They were completely different from who I've got now. So when somebody from your past calls you up, from a time when you were on fire..."

I felt uncomfortable sitting there beside him, exposed to a personal sorrow that I didn't share.

Then he snapped out of it. "He's dead. That's it." He got up to leave.

"Can I call you if I need more information?"

He took tore off a strip of a paper from a menu and wrote his name and phone number.

"One more question," I said. "A quickie. How was this group involved?"

"What group?" he asked, a bit bewildered.

"This group," I said. "The Anne Street Group."

"You're kidding. You don't know about this place?"

I shrugged my shoulders.

"But you walked in here," he said, genuinely confused. "So you'd have to know about this place."

"Tim was on some e-mail list. It mentioned this address."

The wheels spun again until they reached a conclusion.

"So you're not a faggot," he said, with weary recognition. "You're just acting like you're a faggot."

I showed him my palms again, but defensively this time, as if to say: Hey, it's just a job, man.

"You should be ashamed of yourself," he said, getting up from the table. "This is a nice little place. It's an alternative to the bars for people who work downtown. Now they're going to tear the place down. And you're a real asshole."

"I've got nothing to be ashamed of," I said. "I caught Tim and now I'm going to catch the guy who murdered him. I gotta do what I gotta do."

Chapter 17

It was raining hard on Saturday morning, and the clouds were so dark it felt like evening. I was procrastinating about the job ahead of me: a memo to the rabbi that would explain the whole story so he could forward it to the SEC. I'd have to go through all the files, sort through the facts, and summarize the most likely theories to explain them. The files were in Shoshanna's apartment, in two boxes beside her dining room table. I had the key, but I hesitated.

I felt like a cat burglar as I entered her apartment. A combination of flowers and new carpet smells hit me as I looked around. Everything as she'd left it to go out for a jog.

My farewell tour. In the kitchen, an empty juice glass. A butter dish and a spoon in the sink. On the floor of the bedroom a silk camisole, eggshell blue, size XXS. Against my better instincts, I picked it up and marveled how the whole thing collapsed into a puddle in my hand.

Put it down, you jerk.

It would be raining in the Catskills, too. And what was Shoshanna doing? I imagined her having breakfast with a dozen 12-year-olds who thought she was the coolest thing: an Orthodox girl like them who was making it in the city. Were you allowed to spend a half hour with a blow-dryer on Shabbat? Not out there. So her hair would be frizzier. Maybe she'd wear it in a bun. Or even a ponytail. That would be interesting. *Stop, Dave. Stop.*

I tried to gather the documents I'd take to the SEC on Monday. The detailed trade confirms, with the specifics of each trade, would be particularly useful to anybody who wanted to trace the trade back to its roots.

As I picked through the files at her dining room table, I tried to summarize the certainties, in rough chronological order: Tim and his accomplice engineered a scam at the bank. At some point, Tim tried to convince Todd, his former lover, to expand the scam by joining them. Instead, Todd gave a trade-flow diagram to bank director at a gay fundraiser. A guy named Marquette. The director ordered the bank's investigation. Then everything got fuzzy. Tim is found murdered shortly after we challenge him. But by whom?

Shoshanna's file on Robert Marquette confirmed that he ran a big money-management firm in Connecticut. His wife was the vice chair of the Westchester County Republican party and the town manager of Old Greenwich.

I wasn't sure what all this meant. Marquette ordered the investigation, so he wouldn't have been involved in any kind of trading cabal. When he found out about the fraud, he told Lewis to investigate, and Lewis hired us.

Was Marquette gay? Todd met him at a fundraiser for the Gay Men's Health Crisis. So... pretty good odds.

I imagined Todd's pale round face and his little rectangular glasses. He certainly had the technical skills to be Tim's accomplice. But then he wouldn't have told the board member.

Well, maybe he didn't. Maybe he was lying to me at the Thai restaurant. Todd had three things going against him: He knew Tim, he was gay, and he was a trader. He could be bigdick99. If this, then that. If that, then this.

So why not call the director? Robert Marquette had two addresses, one in Old Greenwich, one on East 51st Street. When I tried the 51st Street number, the call was picked up on the first ring by somebody who liked to keep a phone handy. A deep gravelly announcer's baritone, the kind used to sell beer.

"Mr. Marquette, my name is Dave Ackerman. I was working on the Tim Scott investigation. I'd like to talk to you for a few minutes."

A short pause.

"You were the guy who was fired on Friday?"

"That's right."

Another pause while he thought things over.

"And you want to talk to me. Why?"

"You may be getting a call from the police very soon. I want to give you a heads-up."

I could hear a hand covering the mouthpiece, then a hacking cough, and possibly an expletive.

"What's your number?"

A few minutes later, he called with a time and a place: Sunday at 10 a.m. in his apartment on East 51st Street.

Marquette lived in a nondescript modern building a few blocks west of the United Nations, the kind financial types bought if they wanted a pied-a-terre close to Grand Central and their offices in midtown.

He was in his late 50s, and wore black sweatpants and a white polo shirt, the better to show off shoulders that had done some hard time in the gym. The mini-blinds were half drawn, but the apartment had a commanding view of the East River, where a cement ship with a huge crane was drifting by.

My gaydar meter went wild. An attractive teenage boy was watching MTV in the living room in pajama bottoms: medium build, washboard abs and long hair in a ponytail. Boytoy looked like he was recovering from a long night.

Marquette directed me to a dining room that had been converted into a study with double doors. A coffee thermos and a few empty mugs sat on a sideboard, but he didn't offer me any. He left one of the doors open so he could keep an eye on his friend.

"I'm sorry to bother you on a Sunday morning," I said. "I was..."

"Why don't you first tell me what you're trying to do," he interrupted. He was the kind of guy who liked to seize hold of a conversation and keep the weight on his side.

"I'm trying to do a little more work on the Tim Scott investigation."

He nodded and smiled tightly. "I believe the bank's investigation is closed."

"That's correct."

"And you're not working for the bank anymore."

I nodded and smiled back. "That's also correct. I was relieved of my duties last Friday."

"So you're acting on your own?"

"I'm acting on behalf of some other people," I said.

He hesitated for a few seconds, struggling a bit, but his curiosity got the better of his pride.

"Who are you working for?" he asked.

"A governmental authority," I said.

"Didn't you sign an agreement not to disclose anything at the bank after your employment ended?" he asked.

"Yes, I did."

"So you're violating your employment agreement. Is that what you're telling me?"

I was getting a little tired of all this. "The bank broke the law by not reporting the crime. You're a director of that bank. You were involved in the decision to investigate the crime and the decision to not report it to the authorities. Or so I assume."

That shut him up for another few seconds.

"So you're acting as an investigator on behalf of the SEC."

I didn't answer. According to Todd, Marquette was simply a bank director who got tipped off about the trading scam. But if Todd was lying, he could be a lot of other things. As a big-shot money manager, he could even be the guy who ran the show. He knew all the options guys at the leading investment banks, and he had inside knowledge of how their trading operations worked. Was he just the one who was tipped off about the trading scam? Or was he much more involved?

"You're not wearing a wire, are you?" he asked.

"No," I said raising my arms. "Go ahead and search me."

"I don't care if you are. Lewis said if I told you the truth you guys would go away. Is that true?"

"I will," I said. "I can't speak for anybody else."

"I've got nothing to hide. Tell me what you want to know."

"It's pretty straightforward," I said. "I've heard that you were the one who ordered an investigation of the derivatives desk."

"My wife and I were attending a charity fundraiser. Somebody approached me who knew I was a director of the bank..."

"How did he know?"

"How did he know what?"

"That you were a director," I said.

"People know who I am," he said proudly. "When you're a director of a global investment bank, a lot of people want to talk to you. They usually want to sell a big contract to the bank and think you can push things along. Or they want a job for their niece. It happens all the time."

"What did the guy who approached you look like?"

"Medium build, in his 30s."

"Not much hair? Little rectangular glasses?"

"That's right. He'd had a few glasses of champagne. He pulled me aside. He told me there was some kind of scam operating in the bank's derivatives desk and I ought to have somebody look into it. Then he disappeared into the crowd. He didn't tell me his name."

"So you launched an investigation because of something he said?"

"He was drunk, but he didn't seem like a flake. He knew how the trades were passed from one group to another. He had a napkin wrapped around his beer bottle. He wrote it all down on the napkin. I wasn't sure how to take it. The guy could be lying, or trying to embarrass somebody. Either way it was my duty as a director to report it to the corporation counsel. Ed took the whole thing very seriously. They put an auditor on the case immediately."

"But it wasn't an official audit, was it?" I asked.

"No," he said. "Ed Lewis wanted to keep it a board-level investigation since it started with a board member's inquiry. After a couple weeks, he called to tell me that the girl wasn't qualified enough to evaluate the option strategies the derivatives desk used. He wanted to hire a consultant."

Somebody rang the buzzer. We watched through the doors of the study as Boytoy let in a petite young woman his own age, bundled up in a vintage army jacket and a series of long scarves. Boytoy gave her a deep French kiss.

"Excuse me," Marquette said, getting up to close the door.

Now I was the one thrown for a loop. Maybe Boytoy wasn't a boytoy.

I took a quick glance around the study: There were touches that betrayed a feminine hand. Some dried flowers in a vase a bit too conventional to be gay. Some photos in leather frames clustered on a bookshelf. One of them was a receiving-line photo of him and his wife with Ronald Reagan. Snap snap. Thank you very much. But Reagan was shaking his wife's hand, not his. And another photo of a squinting 8-year-old boy in a pool.

"There's not much more to tell you," Marquette said, refilling his coffee mug. "Ed Lewis was in charge of the investigation. He called me once he hired you. Then I got another call a few days later, when the guy was found dead."

"Did you and Lewis discuss what to do at that point?"

"The police were quite sure it was part of a series of S&M murders in Chelsea. The guy liked to pick up prostitutes. Maybe the fraud was designed to support some kind of sex habit. But that was the end of the fraud investigation as far as we were concerned."

"And then you fired us."

"Well, I think you two got yourselves fired. You went back to the police and tried to convince them that the two crimes were related. I don't think they bought it for a minute."

There was a knock on the door. The teenager and the girl appeared in the doorway bundled to go out.

"Dad, we're going for brunch with one of Nancy's friends," he said. "Are you staying here?"

"No, I'm going back tonight. We've got a dinner party."

"Are you keeping the Lexus here?"

"No, I'll drive it back. You ought to call Liz before you go out. She's mad that you left last night without telling her."

The boy tossed some car keys to his dad and closed the door behind him.

"I've got a few more questions," I said. "You said you attended this fundraising event with your wife. What charity was it?"

"It was a cancer group," he said, keeping his composure.

I took a coffee mug from the table, poured myself a half cup and stirred in four packs of Sweet 'n Low, one by one, just for fun.

"The Gay Men's Health Crisis is certainly very concerned about AIDS," I said, "But I don't know if you'd call it a cancer group. In any case, it's not the kind of event a Republican politician would normally go to."

"I was mistaken," he said, looking me in the eye. "I must have gone there alone."

Then something extraordinary happened. He walked across the study to the bookshelf, and started scanning the spines of the books. He pulled a book out halfway, seemingly at random, then shoved it back in. He was just stalling.

When he turned around to face me, I saw a different person. His posture slackened, his eyes were softer, and new lines appeared on his face.

"I'm glad you've found a new career as an investigator, Dave," he said. "I think it suits you. But just realize one thing. Whatever you're doing now, you owe to me."

"How's that?" I asked. He returned to his chair and settled into it slowly, as if he was suffering from back pain.

"When Ed was looking for a derivatives consultant to help that auditor, I picked your resume out of the pile he showed me," he said. "I'd heard about an options trader who blew out last November. When I saw your resume, I connected the dots. A lot of people did what you did, but they don't get caught. I thought you needed a break. If you've got a new career with the SEC, I'm glad."

A big yellow barge stacked with multicolored shipping containers floated by on the river. We both stared at it for a while.

"Thank you for giving me another shot," I said. "I owe you one. But I owe even more to Tim. I don't think he was a particularly great guy. But he was murdered. Maybe he deserved a big fine and a suspended trading license. That's what I got. Maybe he should have gone to jail for a few months. But he certainly didn't deserve to die."

Marquette nodded in agreement.

"And you owe him, too," I continued. "You started the investigation into this fraud. You understood what Tim did, but didn't want to report it, even after he was killed. Then you had us fired when we tried to pursue the investigation on our own. The police are wrong, and you know it. This guy was murdered by an accomplice in his scam. You just don't want to admit it because you've got your life nicely arranged. And this would force you to tell everybody that you're gay."

He stared at his coffee mug for a while, then out the window, then directly at me. "Yeah, you're right," he said. "I've got my life nicely arranged. I've had a lover for the past 12 years. I've got a wife who knows. We've been through that a long time ago. I've got a business partner and he knows. I've got a home in Old Greenwich where I spend time with my family. I've got an office where I work. And I've got this place, where I stay during the weekdays. But if you start dragging me into an investigation of a gay S&M murder, everything could fall apart."

His eyes wandered to the collection of photographs on the bookshelf. I guessed that he was looking at the photo of the boy at the pool.

"No, my son doesn't know," he said. "I'm not sure how he would take this. He's a little fragile."

He looked like he had a lot of thinking to do and wanted to be left alone.

"I'm sorry, but I've got to ask you a few more questions," I said.

"Go ahead," he said.

"Did you know anything about a restaurant on Anne Street? It's called Thai Village."

"Never been there."

"Never been asked to a meeting there? Something called the Anne Street Group?"

"No."

"Have you ever received any emails from bigdick99@aol.com?"

"No," he said, wincing at the name, then stiffening a bit. "I'm not into S&M. I'm a very conventional guy. I'm an investment manager. I just happen to be queer. Are you finished?"

"Yes," I said, putting my coffee cup back on the sideboard.

"What are you going to do with this information?" he asked. "Am I going to get a visit from the police tomorrow?"

"I don't think so," I said. "It's up to the others and I don't call the shots."

"Well, I just hope you guys keep it as quiet as you can. Because if this thing goes the wrong way, it could hurt my wife's career. It could hurt my marriage. And my son."

He started walking me to the door.

"I suppose it's time to get this out in the open once and for all," he said, talking more to himself than to me. "I'm pretty tired of the whole thing."

Then he grabbed my arm by the wrist.

"I'm only doing this to help the murder investigation," he said, tightening his grip to make sure I understood. "Nobody cares about the money this guy stole. Do you understand that?"

I told him I did. When he let go of my wrist, we shook hands.

Chapter 18

On Monday, I made my second visit to the SEC offices in the baroque Woolworth Building on Broadway. Nothing had changed since my very expensive Christmas Eve meeting. An assortment of government lawyers and their support staff lingered in the elevator bank, some looking professional, some a bit ragged. But I saw a familiar-looking man standing in front of me in the line to the reception desk.

"Hi, Dave," he said.

It was Rabbi Zimmerman, minus the beard. He had a sharp camel-hair blazer, a fresh haircut and a complete shave. He had been transformed into a generic Wall Streeter in his mid-30s, and a handsome one at that.

"Nice jacket," I said, feeling the fabric.

"I haven't been clean-shaven since I got out of Allenwood," he said, stroking his chin. "It feels great. Thanks for inspiring me."

The rabbi appeared quite nervous while we waited in the 14th-floor reception area. The SEC offices could have passed for a law firm if it weren't for the imposing government seals and the intense security at the door.

Mitch Cavanaugh, the senior SEC enforcement officer, stepped into the waiting room and looked around.

"Is that Larry Zimmerman?" he asked incredulously.

"Shaved it off this morning in honor of you," the rabbi said.

"We gotta take a picture or something," he said. "Are you planning to get out of the rabbi business?"

"No, that's going fine," he said. "It was just time for a change."

The rabbi introduced me and chit-chatted with Mitch about former colleagues as he led us to a nondescript conference room. Before the door closed, we were joined by his assistant, a young black guy wearing a bow tie and suspenders.

Mitch took some files from his assistant and then whispered some instructions. The assistant started taking notes on a fresh legal pad.

"I looked at your memo, Dave," he said. "Interesting little scam this guy had going."

He radiated competence and authority, and set me instantly at ease. He pulled the memo I'd written the rabbi and scanned it quickly for a second or two.

"So this guy was tipping off his partner by purchasing out-of-the-money options?"

"It was a code."

"I understand. Very clever. Never seen that before. How did you figure that one out?"

"We did a lot of digging around, going nowhere. Then I tripped over it almost by accident."

"Good work," he said. "That's the way it always happens. And this guy was killed the day before you were going to turn him in? The cops think he was killed in an S&M scene. But you think he was killed by his trading partner."

"Or partners."

"And whoever it was made it look like he was gay to put the cops off the scent."

"No, it turns out Tim really was gay. But I'm pretty certain that he was killed by his accomplice or somebody connected with some larger trading group."

"And you wanted us to find out who was on the other side of the trade."

"Exactly."

"I got it," he said, putting the paper back in the folder.

"The detective certainly didn't. He was completely clueless."

"Not his beat," he said. "I don't know anything about murder investigations. He doesn't know anything about securities fraud."

The lesson was clear: Criticism of other law enforcement officers was not appreciated.

"And you think this guy and his accomplice stole about three million from the bank?" he asked.

"We found about three million in bad trades. But it could be a lot more."

"You should realize something from the start," he said, closing the folder. "We can find who was on the other side of the trade. That's easy. And we can charge whoever it was with serial securities fraud. But we don't have the authority to charge anybody with murder."

"I understand."

"And where's this other auditor? The girl who was fired with you."

I looked to the rabbi for help.

"She's taking a few days off," he answered.

"She's not interested in pursuing this investigation with you?" he asked.

"That remains to be seen," the rabbi said.

Mitch pushed the file away from him. Then he looked up with an apologetic smile, like a bank officer turning us down for a car loan.

"I'm sorry, guys," he said. "No can do. It's a nice little $3 million case. But we've got limited resources."

"But there was a murder," I pleaded. "This could be the tip of an iceberg. If they could pull off the scam at one bank, they could be doing it at a dozen!"

"Maybe. But maybe not. We can't afford to go chasing after every interesting lead we get. We're way overextended. I've got 24 people assigned to WorldCom. That's a $3.8 billion scam. I've got other people dealing with Tyco and the cable companies. The Bureau loaned us 28 investigators but we're still underwater. I can't pull one of them off to work on this case."

"This is not just a financial scam," the rabbi said slowly, summoning all his clerical authority. "There was a murder involved. A murder that may go unsolved."

Mitch had no quick answer for that. His assistant squirmed uncomfortably in his chair. Then Mitch looked at his palms and sighed, as if he were reading some sort of crib sheet.

"That's true. It probably will go unsolved," he said finally. "I wish I had somebody to assign this case. But I'm fresh out of guys."

"We've got to find a way to do this," I said, the desperation rising in my voice. "It won't take much of your time. I grilled one of the bank directors yesterday who authorized the investigation in the first place. I know some of the victim's friends, his former lovers. The cops don't understand how options work. If the killer goes free..."

It was the wrong thing to say.

"Finish your sentence," Mitch said.

I shook my head.

"You want to *really* know whose fault it is?" he asked. He stood up and leaned on the desk, resting his weight on his palms. "If the corporation counsel at the bank had actually followed the law and called us in to trace the case, we would have been able to nail these guys before they knew what was happening. Instead, this idiot let you play Dick Tracy. And you let these guys know they were being watched. And as a result, somebody gets murdered."

He was right. It was easy to forget, but impossible to deny. Directly or indirectly, my inept actions had contributed to Tim's death.

His assistant spoke up for the first time: "What about Stan?"

Mitch thought about that idea for a while.

"When is he due back?" he asked.

"Next week. He doesn't go back out to California until the 12th."

He thought about it some more, and seemed to be on the verge of capitulation. Then he exhaled loudly.

"Okay, there's a guy named Stan Donovan. Former FBI Depository Institutions investigator. Very good. He's assigned to L.A. for a savings and loan thing next month. But he's got a couple weeks before then. He'd love to do a little case like this."

"Sounds like he's our man," the rabbi said, eager to close the deal.

"There are a million reasons why I shouldn't do this," Mitch said, staring directly at me. "The biggest one is you."

He pulled out a beat-up file folder with a big number stamped across the top. I recognized it instantly. It was my SEC file. The first document in the file was a copy of the settlement I had signed last year. It contained my detailed first-person confession of everything I had done wrong. I had spent several days working on it and it made for good reading. He started at the first paragraph and then couldn't stop.

"Incredible," he said, looking up with horrified amusement. "You dump the losing options trade into your client's portfolio at 11:04 a.m. Felony wire fraud. Then you go out to have lunch?"

I knew enough to keep my mouth shut. I had been through this drill before.

"Then at 12:34, your client calls you on your cell phone while you're sitting on a park bench, and you tell him it was all a mistake. That's a nice touch. Very kind of you."

He made us wait while he read through my entire confession. Occasionally he'd snort or shake his head at further proof of my base criminality. The rabbi and I looked at each other in distress. We were losing him.

Then, quite suddenly, Mitch looked up at me with a new face: the judgment was gone and had been replaced by intense curiosity.

"So why did you do it?" he asked. "How could a smart guy like you do something so stupid?"

I looked at the rabbi, as if he were my lawyer and we had rehearsed this answer many times before.

"I was jealous of the guy who sat next to me," I said, looking directly into Mitch's eyes. "I was jealous of his talent. He was a superstar trader. And I wanted to be a superstar, too."

I had answered the question truthfully. I was ready to levitate. I had wings on my back and I could fly around the room.

The rabbi smiled, but Mitch squinted at me warily. He was trying to judge the sincerity of my hard-won personal confession. He was not an easy guy to fool. Maybe it was something he didn't hear that often in the SEC. Maybe he took it for what it was.

"I get it," he said, leaning back on his chair and nodding appreciatively. "So that's why you decided to change careers and become an auditor for that investment bank.

You wanted to make up for your crime in some way. It was like penance."

That wasn't quite accurate. In fact, it was completely wrong, but I nodded anyway. The rabbi nodded.

"In that case, I guess I owe it to you, Dave." Then he turned to the rabbi. "And to you too, Larry, since you brought him in here today."

He got up and pulled his assistant to the door, muttered some instructions and sent him down the hall. Then he went back to the conference table and pulled out another piece of paper from a file. It was some kind of computer printout with trade details.

"After I read your memo, I had somebody trace the trades," he said. "The accomplice was working out of a trading shop downtown."

"What firm?" I asked.

"TradeSpace," he said.

"Ugh," I groaned, reflexively.

TradeSpace was one of these workplaces for day traders that was very popular during the tech boom. You walked in, gave them a few thousand bucks in collateral and then started trading whatever you felt like. They gave you the trading turret and the data feeds, and you supplied the brilliant ideas.

When I lost my job, a lot of people who didn't realize I had also lost my trading license suggested I set up shop there. It was a perfect place for Tim's accomplice to use for a freelance scam. He could just sit there all day, watching the options screens for his cue. Then he makes a few trades, and the money goes straight into his bank account.

"I talked to the owner of TradeSpace this morning," said Mitch. "We've had a few run-ins with his customers before, so he's eager to cooperate. He's got 84 guys working there, and it's going to take him a few days to figure out which workstation executed this particular set of trades. But that's okay, because Stan isn't going to be back till next week."

"You're assigning Stan to the investigation?" the rabbi asked, eager to nail it down.

"I suppose so," he said. "In spite of my better judgment, I'm going to tell him to spend a couple weeks on this case before he goes out to California. If he can't wrap it up in two weeks, we'll just turn the file over to the cops. And we'll have to hire Mr. Ackerman here to be a trader at TradeSpace."

"As some kind of investigator?" I asked.

"No, as a nobody. You're not going to do anything. You're just going to sit there. We'll give you a little trading money to keep you busy. You'll keep your eyes and ears open in case Stan wants you to do something. If Stan has any sense, he won't use you at all. But it might be helpful to have somebody on the ground when he begins next week. You might as well start tomorrow."

"Does the owner at TradeSpace know about this?" I asked.

"I just told my assistant to talk to him," he said. "I wouldn't worry about him co-operating. And I wouldn't be surprised if he put 10 grand in your trading account to get you started."

"But I don't have a trading license."

"Good point. I've got to get you a temporary Series 7 on my authority," he said, writing a note to himself on the cover of my file.

"So once we nail the trader, we can start looking to find the other members of his group?" I asked eagerly.

That was another mistake. He winced and closed the file.

"I'm beginning to regret this already," he said. "Everybody wants to be a film director. And everybody wants to be a detective. Stan's job will not be glamorous. He has to prove that the guy at TradeSpace conspired with the dead guy to break 10b-5 of the Securities Act of 1934. If Stan thinks it's related to the murder, great, we'll contact the proper authorities. But that's all up to Stan. Understood?"

"Understood."

"And if you tell anybody — anybody — that you're working for the SEC, this relationship is over. You understand?"

"Understood," I said.

"This is not a whodunit. In a few days we're going to find out who the accomplice is. We just need a professional investigator to gather the evidence properly so the case will stand up in court. The evidence from this guy's trading system. The evidence on the other side from the bank. Then we need to tie it up in a nice neat package for the prosecutors."

He paused to indicate the meeting was drawing to a close.

"We've got to deal with some technicalities before I can let you go," he said. "Until Stan shows up next week, you'll deal with me directly. Any questions, you call me. But there shouldn't be any. You're just going to sit there and trade."

"I get it," I said. "I can do that."

The rabbi and I broke into huge grins, but Mitch ignored us.

"I'm going to send you up to the 15th floor to see Gary, my assistant," he said giving me a business card. "We've got to do some paperwork to make your role official. They've got to fingerprint you and give you some papers to sign and an ID so you can get into the office. Any questions?"

"Yeah," I said. "What if I make any money trading? Do I get to keep it?"

Mitch and the rabbi looked at each other. Then it was Mitch's turn to grin.

"You've got to pay back the TradeSpace owner for whatever he fronts you."

"Okay, but what if I make more?"

"I don't know," he said, scratching his chin theatrically. "Larry, I think we need rabbinical counsel on this one."

"I think Dave ought to pay back some more of the money he stole from his previous employer."

"But he already signed a settlement agreement," said Mitch. "That's going to be tricky from a legal perspective."

"Okay, I've got a great solution," the rabbi said with a smile. "If he makes any money trading, he should keep half for himself, since it's the fruit of his labor, and give the other half to a charity. A Jewish outreach program in Ridgewood, New Jersey."

"Is that your group?" asked Mitch.

"That's right."

Mitch shook his head. "Once a trader, always a trader," he said. Then he pointed to an internal stairway that led up to the 15th floor.

I bounded up the stairs, but at the top, I stopped in my tracks. I recognized a face from my last trip to the SEC: the young woman lawyer with the Indian accent who took my check for $612,000. She was approaching the stairway holding some file folders across her chest.

I pointed my finger to stop her.

"Hi," I said. "Remember me?"

She didn't have a clue. She gave me an embarrassed look and a shrug. She was much taller than I remembered her. And very dark. A smile slowly crossed her face.

"Of course," she said, her face brightening with the recognition. "You're from the D.C. office."

"No," I said. "Try again."

I was filled with a strange kind of delight. The grim-faced woman who took all my money was smiling at me! A flirty smile, or so I thought.

"Don't you remember?" I asked. "Last December 24th at 4 p.m.?"

An appalled look crossed her face. She looked at the temporary ID label stuck to my jacket. Then she gave me a look of utter confusion.

"I've switched sides," I said. "I'm wearing a white hat now."

"Congratulations," she said, recovering her composure and shaking my hand. "Who are you working for?"

"Mitch Cavanaugh, special investigations."

She nodded her head appreciatively, indicating I was in some kind of hot unit.

"You'll find we make much less money here," she said, glancing down the stairs, eager to leave.

"I'm a volunteer at the moment," I said.

The name on her ID tag said N. Laksmikantham. I wanted her to keep smiling at me. I wanted to establish once again that I was not a criminal. I wanted to hang out with her and Mitch and his buddies and drink coffee at the SEC cafeteria and talk about financial scams. I wanted to be some kind of minor SEC hero. Or any kind of hero.

Chapter 19

When I introduced myself the next day at the front desk at TradeSpace, the receptionist had a folder ready for me. She gave me a card that would get me into the building after hours and a log-in password that would work at any open terminal. I could trade through my new account at their preferred broker, or use my own. All I needed to do was choose my cubicle. Then she gave me my opening account statement with a balance at the bottom. The owner of the TradeSpace had put $10,000 in my account. That was real money, money I could use to trade almost anything I wanted.

My stomach tightened a notch. It wasn't a bad feeling. It was familiar and kind of sweet. My body was under a certain kind of pressure again. It felt okay.

The main trading room was built on raised computer flooring that creaked when you walked on it. There were a few dozen bleached-maple cubicles that must have looked great in 1998 but had since lost their sheen. The place was only half occupied and the traders were exclusively male.

I made a quick tour to see who was trading what. I passed a few futures traders staring blankly at their screens. They were scalpers who went in and out of small trades all day long, betting which way the market would go in the next 60 seconds. Then there were the technical guys with arcane candlestick chart books on their desks: If prices dropped to a particular level, they'd buy, if they rose to another level, they'd sell. A few guys were looking at options screens, but I couldn't tell what they were trading or if they were making any money at it.

And then there were the complete losers. The day traders combing the *Wall Street Journal* and the chat rooms in hopes of riding that day's hot stock. Most of them looked like they were probably recently unemployed and trading away their 401(k) funds.

There was a drafty lounge at one end of the place with a couple of cracked leather couches, and a chattering CNBC screen. Five microwaves had been stacked like TV sets, ready for zapping a quick lunch. The place was already littered with coffee cups and paper plates from breakfast. Slobs, I thought. Traders are the same no matter where they work.

On the way back, I passed by one empty cubicle that made me stop. It had a calendar still open to the January 2001 page; Fire Ladies. Two homely blondes posing beside a Santa Barbara pumper truck with a tumescent hose in their arms. I decided this cubicle was as good as any. I turned the Fire Ladies calendar to the November 2001 page, and circled November 12, the day I blew out.

Then I typed in my password and became a trader again. But what was I going to trade? I browsed through the trade entry screens at the Chicago exchanges. The Merc had made a few tweaks to the E-mini contract in the intervening months. A better way to manage block trades. Nice.

Then I realized I wasn't in a bank, and I didn't have several million of the bank's money to play with. I had $10,000. A laughable amount when you thought about it, but something I couldn't afford to squander.

What the hell was I supposed to trade? When I started out 9 years ago, my first boss taught me how to scalp the futures markets. Ride it when things were moving up and sell before it went the other way. In and out in five minutes, three minutes, even one minute. Pick up your $50, pay the broker $5, keep $45. You lose some trades along the way, but you do it again and again until you put a little money in the bank.

Not that it was simple. The words of a floor trader I once knew kept echoing in my head: "If it was easy, everybody would do it." But after a couple hours of jumping on winners and losers, I was up $50.

I leaned back on my chair and exhaled a gusher. Then I felt a little sweat under my arm. A slow start. That was okay, too. There was a good chance Tim's accomplice was working a few feet away from me. Next week, when they traced the trade to the particular workstation, I'd know who he was. And that guy, in theory, would know something about Tim's murder. Or could even be his murderer.

When the New York Stock Exchange closed at 4 p.m., the mood of the place changed. You heard some groans and laughs, and the pop of soda cans being opened in the lounge. Some guys quickly packed their bags and headed straight to the subway. But a few started congregating in little groups to let off steam.

I tagged along with three guys who were going to the T.G.I. Friday's, where we were joined by a few others. It was like all my other post-work bar experiences: One or two hours. Two or three beers. The stocks with the biggest moves. Why 3M or U.S. Steel was heading for the roof. Why it was time to load up again on the NASDAQ. And what did you think of that rally right before the close?

Some traders were more knowledgeable than others, but when the talk turned to sports, everybody was a complete idiot. Why the Jets were going to come back strong next season. How the Knicks could still make the playoffs. What stupid manager made what stupid trade. I couldn't imagine any one of them being involved in a multimillion-dollar trading scam, much less a murder.

As I walked home, a recurring doubt hit me once more: The accomplice may have left town after Tim died. I always assumed we'd find him. But the guy might be in South America somewhere hiring a lawyer and looking at beachfront houses. If so, the SEC wasn't going to waste any more time chasing him. Then what? In a couple weeks, I'd be back ringing the doorbells at the temp agencies. And we'd be facing a dead end.

And who was "we"?

Shoshanna was out of the picture, taking middle-school girls for nature walks through the piney Catskill woods and contemplating her next career move. If she wanted to talk, she would have called me by now.

It was time to confront a painful fact: I was single again.

The next morning, I stopped at a Dunkin' Donuts on my way to TradeSpace and bought two dozen mixed, which I distributed as I walked around introducing myself. I was the new guy, and I was determined to make friends and influence people.

It wasn't a bad place to work. Nobody bothered you when you were in your cubicle, but if you wanted to waste time, there were plenty of opportunities. There was always somebody in the lunch room, nursing a trading loss with a cup of coffee or trying to find some excuse to procrastinate. If you wanted to take a quick break, you could stand outside your cubicle and chat with anybody passing by.

That I could do. But I couldn't help wondering which of the 80 or so guys in the office were gay. I guessed that there'd be at least one or two in the population. Maybe even five or ten. When you're looking for it, almost everybody seems suspect. Do I rule out the guys with kiddie photos taped to their wall? Or the one with the photo of Derek Jeter?

As I walked around the room passing out donuts, I tried to keep my mind in an open Zen state, waiting for clues to hit me. I'd say hello, offer them a doughnut, and then watch their eyes.

One guy was drinking from a Morgan Stanley coffee cup, as if to make sure we knew he came from quality. He was wearing a white shirt and tie under a white sweater. A prissy, preppy kind of look, with fancy loafers right out of the box, but not necessarily gay.

Another wore black jeans, a dark-blue dress shirt and had a flashy sports coat draped over a chair. Upscale downtown. He gave me a longer top-to-bottom glance. I thought his gaze stopped momentarily at my crotch, but I wasn't sure. Then he took a colored sprinkle, grunted a thank-you and went back to his screen.

One looked like he was hungry for something, possibly friendship. He wore jeans and a dumpy sweater, and wasn't more than 22. He turned out to be a former math nerd turned aspiring options trader. When he found out where I used to work and that I traded options, he was all over me. Another protégé, I thought, eager to learn. That was fine, but he didn't seem gay.

And so on.

It followed a pattern: A glance at me, then the doughnut, then a brief glance at my body to size me up, then back to the doughnut. Sometimes they looked a fraction of a second longer to see if I was an ego threat: How was I dressed? Was I stronger, thinner, younger? I suppose it was similar to how you checked out a woman. You give her the first hello, then you look down, trying to scan her body as discreetly as you can. But it's never discreet enough.

About 11:00, the receptionist delivered a FedEx box from the Securities and Exchange Commission. A cell phone and a couple batteries tumbled out of the bubble wrap. It was a bulky thing, a year or two out of style. I turned it on and tried to make a call but it didn't work. Then I saw some typed instructions taped to the bubble wrap. "Record: hold down the # button. Stop: hold down the * button. Rewind..."

I didn't think it would be a good idea to call Mitch from the office, so I took a walk around the block and called the cell number scrawled on his business card.

"What am I supposed to do with this thing?" I asked.

"It's a digital tape recorder," he said.

"I figured that out. But when do I use it? Is it like a wire?"

"It's got about two hours of recording time. It should help you remember any conversations you have. But we can't use it in court unless we do some more paperwork."

"Am I supposed to tape people I talk to? Nobody uses these big phones any more. It makes me look like a dork."

"This is the SEC," he said. "I'm afraid that phone is as high-tech as we get. You don't have to use it. In fact, don't do anything with it. Just sit tight until Stan comes back from L.A."

I managed to lose $850 that day through a combination of bad markets, poor concentration and sheer bad luck. When I logged off my screen at the end of the day my neck was stiff and my undershirt was soaked.

I didn't feel like spending another mindless evening at T.G.I. Friday's, so I started walking up Broadway toward Chelsea. It was one of my stranger urban expeditions. My gaydar was going nuts but my heterodar meter was also operational. With plenty of interesting people of both sexes on the sidewalks, it all merged into a strange kind of bisexual horniness.

I went into a Starbucks and decided to be more scientific about it: I'd give everybody, male and female, a five-second gaze to see what happened.

The evidence that came back was overwhelming. The women hardly ever returned my gaze. But the guys frequently did, even if they were deep in conversation with the guy beside them.

When I got my first lingering gaze back, I freaked out a little, and looked away. After my second gaze, I left. Gays seemed to have it easy when it came to pickups. Or at least I did. Women hardly ever gave me long lingering glances unless they were deep into their second margarita. I started practicing my stare on people approaching me on the sidewalk: Hmm, who's this? He's good looking. But so is she! Look at her!

Then I thought about Steve Carey, my former protégé who had died of AIDS, and his elaborate measures to fake a fiancée. I walked him home last year. Hadn't he lived nearby? I found his townhouse near the corner of 9th Street and Sixth Avenue. The top bell said Vanderfeldt/Carey. What the hell, I thought.

"Who's there?"

"A friend of Steve's," I said.

"Steve died in January."

"I know. I used to work with him. My name is Dave Ackerman."

There was no answer.

That's okay, I thought. Strange person ringing the bell. Doesn't know who I am.

Then I got a thunderous buzz that scared the hell out of me.

Steve's roommate turned out to be slim little guy with ash blond hair cut in a pageboy with thick bangs that ended just below his eyebrows. He looked as gay as they come: delicate, about 5-5, with a soft voice and a feminine way of carrying himself. In a ponytail and a thick sweater, he could pass for a thin young woman.

The apartment was furnished with wispy white drapes framing West 9th Street, a '30s-era couch, perfectly reupholstered in ivory cloth. It quickly became clear the color scheme was designed to set off the apartment's prize possession: an antique Hudson River landscape that blazed away in full glory in the center of a big white wall.

"It's just an early-20th-century copy," he said as I stared. "I picked it up in a yard sale right before he died."

The dining room table held some grocery bags he had been unpacking when I rang.

"I'm sorry to barge in here like this," I said. "I was just in the neighborhood and happened to walk by and remembered..."

Then I realized I didn't quite know why I was here. He picked up on the awkwardness, took my windbreaker and pointed me toward the couch.

"I wasn't working at the bank when Steve died," I said. "I didn't even know about his funeral."

"Steve didn't want me to tell anybody from work," he said. "He resigned from the bank a few weeks before he died, so you wouldn't have known."

He had a Boston accent and small blue eyes, which he opened wide when he talked. We sat there for a while, quite comfortable in the silence that accompanies condolence calls. A Siamese cat stalked up to him, rubbed his leg and then settled down in the center of the room, where it could keep its eyes on me.

"Steve really admired you," he said. "He said you were a very patient teacher. He was heartbroken when you left. He thought you were the only nice guy in the whole place."

"He was a good student," I said. "He never got caught up in the money thing. He was just an Army brat, happy to be making it in the big city. I think he mostly got off on the intellectual challenge... I just wish I could have said goodbye."

"I'm sorry, I didn't have your phone number...."

"No, it's not your fault, it's my fault. I'm the one who completely fucked up my life."

It was the wrong thing to say, and quite uncharacteristic of me. How could my own stupid problems compare with a guy who was dead?

"Steve had been positive since college, so it wasn't like we weren't surprised," he said. "But he picked up the flu one weekend, and everything started to unravel. He took sick leave for two months, then he resigned. He died a few weeks later. The whole thing was very quick. That was the bad part, but that was also the good part."

The cat and I had a staring contest for a while, until it blinked and walked out of the room.

"The AIDS thing was certainly a complete surprise to me and everybody else," I said. "Steve was the last guy we'd expect to be gay. Every Monday morning he'd come back with these stories about what he and his girlfriend did over the weekend. Running in the park. Bed and breakfasts in the Poconos. How much he admired her, loved her. They were going to get married as soon as he got some more cash together. They had the location picked out. It was in Puerto Rico, this quiet little place in the middle of nowhere. Her name was Jeanne. She worked in marketing at Anne Klein. I guess it was too romantic to be real."

The guy took out his wallet. At first I thought he was going to show me a photo. Then it became clear it was a business card.

Eugene Vanderfeldt
VP, Marketing
Anne Klein Studio

The room got blurry as my eyes welled up with tears.

"It's going to take me a long time to get over him," Gene said, putting the card back. "It's not like I'm the first person to have a partner die of AIDS. But that doesn't make it any easier."

I started talking about anything to change the subject. About the day I blew out. About my stupid temp jobs afterwards. About my assignment with Shoshanna. The details were just gushing out, I didn't quite know why. Maybe I really wanted to tell Steve about everything that had happened to me, and this was the next best thing. Gene didn't seem to mind. I suppose he liked being back in Steve's world.

I explained all the steps we went through to uncover the trading scam, and how we threatened Tim in our office before his last weekend. I told him about our shock the day we found he'd been killed, and what the police had found in the apartment. The only thing I left out was my relationship with Shoshanna.

Gene was particularly interested in the details of the murder. What kind of drug overdose was it? How was it administered? What kind of drug was it? GHB? PCP? Ketamine? Crystal? I didn't know many of the answers.

After a while he made us omelets and opened a bottle of white wine.

"So why isn't the detective interested in anything you found?" Gene asked. "Is he stupid?"

"No," I said. "He did his best to understand. He asked one of his Wall Street friends to help him figure out the trading stuff, but he's chasing his own theory."

"Well, there have been many similar deaths in the West Village that could fit that pattern," Gene said. "Mostly overdose deaths. Nothing new. They've been going on for years. Did this guy Tim like to pick up tricks?"

"Yeah, when he was flush," I said. "I think it was kind of a binge thing for him."

"I was never involved in the bar scene," he said, shrugging his shoulders. "But it's one of the dangers of living that kind of life."

"You're not suggesting it was an accident, are you?"

"No, but if I wanted to kill somebody like Tim and get away with it, that's how I'd do it. I'd love to find out what happened. And what about this woman? What is she doing now?"

"Which woman?"

"Which woman?" he asked. "The auditor. The one you're in love with."

"Did I say I was in love with her?" I asked.

"Oh, come on," he said. "It's obvious."

"It's all past tense. She's taking some time off."

That led to a discussion about the Lincoln Town Car, and our crazy drive out to the rabbi's house, and my rabbinical psychoanalysis. I didn't tell him exactly where I was working, but I explained that I was trading for myself while I waited for a government investigator to show up.

"So you think one of the guys in this trading place is gay, but you don't know who," said Gene.

"That's what I've been trying to figure out," I said.

I described the guys who I had suspicions about: the preppy guy with the Morgan Stanley coffee cup, and the guy with the black jeans and the snazzy sports coat.

"What kind of shoes were they wearing?" Gene asked.

"I don't know. Loafers? I'm not sure."

"You're hopeless," he said, then got a crafty look in his eyes. "You want me to come by and take a look?"

"No, no," I said. "I'm supposed to sit there and do nothing. But I want to pass as gay. It could come in very handy."

"You're supposed to look *gay*?" he said, incredulously.

"Well..." I said. "I'm eager to learn."

He stared at my clothes and my hair, shaking his head at the educational task ahead of him. "There are some gay men who dress like you," he said, charitably. "But I would-n't call it a classic look."

We started at the top and worked down, flipping through a copy of *Out* to get some ideas about my hair. I had to stay relatively conventional because I was working on Wall Street. But he pointed out some sweaters and shoes that could make or break my look. They looked hipper than anything I'd usually wear, but nothing you couldn't find on a heterosexual fashion victim on the men's floor at Bloomingdale's.

"I don't want to get too caught up in the clothes," I said. "Because it's more than just the clothes."

"That's true," he said. "There's no particular way you have to talk or behave. But your windbreaker has got to go."

"I've got a leather jacket at home," I said.

"There are leather jackets and there are leather jackets," he said, disappearing into the bedroom for a moment.

"I'm a size 50," I called out. "Steve's stuff is not going to fit me."

"Just try this on," he said, emerging with a brand new leather jacket, the tag still hanging from the sleeve. "I bought XL because Steve had long arms, but it was too big for him."

It was dark green with a covered zipper and a pebbly finish, a bit tight, but serviceable.

We looked in the mirror again.

"You're getting close," he said, handing me a hairbrush. "Pull it straight back."

A little mousse from a tube, a theatrically swiveled hip, and we both started smiling.

"Now there's a hunk," he said, ripping the tag off the sleeve. "Get some new shoes and you'll be fine. Fubus are passé this season, but they're the right message. They make them in a very light tan now."

He gave me a hug and waved as I walked down the stairway.

I liked Gene. I decided that his ash blond hair was a good look for him. Gay sex with some hairy ape — that was impossible to imagine. But a small, thin thing like him... I could see how he'd be attractive.

I tried to push myself farther: Could I imagine Gene as a sex object, with his shirt off in one of the ads I saw in magazines, his pants unzipped halfway and his belt unbuckled? No, no, no. Too far, too fast for me.

On the way back home, I stopped at a place in the Village and bought a new pair of shoes, a sweater and a leather blazer. Then I checked myself in the store mirror: Not a bad looking stud.

The visit with Gene had sharpened my thinking. He had asked a lot of questions about the murder itself, and made me realize how ignorant I was about the details. I had never seen the police report, and the cop hadn't told us much.

Ross, Tim's upstairs neighbor, was the only one I knew who had been to the murder scene. When I got home, I gave him a call and agreed to stop by his place the next day around dinnertime.

Chapter 20

I brought my Chicago White Sox pennant to the office the next morning and pinned it prominently above my Bloomberg screen. My cubicle was a few feet from the kitchen, and well positioned to attract spontaneous conversation.

Almost on cue, half a dozen guys stopped by to tell me what they thought about the deficiencies of my team. As we approached the NYSE opening, however, they all went back to their cubicles and I was alone once more with my empty trading blotter.

A dozen proverbs popped into my head in the guise of business strategy: "Once burned, twice shy." "No guts no glory." "Nothing wagered, nothing lost." "A bird in the hand is worth two in the bush." "Fools rush in where angels fear to tread."

The futures scalping was a lot of work for not much payoff. I was playing with the house's money, but I didn't feel right blowing through it as quickly as I was doing.

I looked at the *Journal*. Chatter about a new war in Iraq. This or that company was rumored to be in play. Why not take a shot on some oil stocks? Got a hunch, make a bunch. I looked at the numbers and dismissed the idea. The futures were too tough. I wouldn't be able to have much effect on my P&L.

Then I remembered: I wasn't a bank trader. I was working for myself. A 200-buck payoff wasn't enough for the bank, but it was fine with me, thank you.

I spent $850 for options on five stocks that I thought might move between now and lunch.

As I was watching the trade twitch this way and that, I got a call on my cell phone from Gigi, Shoshanna's friend. Did I want to have lunch? I didn't ask why, but I suspected she was on an all-too-familiar mission: The dumped guy gets a condolence call from the best friend. You have drinks, she explains how her friend really cared about you, thought you were warm, friendly, sexy, whatever. But then, the inevitable punch line: Let's face it, the relationship wasn't the best for either of you, and it's time to move on.

All right, I thought. Let's get it over with.

At 11:42, Donald Rumsfeld made some more threatening remarks about Iraq at a Washington press conference. That gave my stocks a little bump downward, and pushed my contracts into the money. I clicked sell. Suddenly I was 80 bucks richer. Pathetic. I closed out my other trades, and then dashed uptown to meet Gigi.

The place Gigi chose turned out to be a kosher steak-frites place filled with young women who seemed to make their living dressing up. The men's uniform of choice was a tweed jacket, a hooded sweat shirt and a knit yarmulke.

I was a few minutes late, but Gigi was in a mood to forgive. To her credit, she sped quickly through the consolation script and jumped directly to what she really cared about: taking credit for putting the two of us together.

It was an astonishing bit of storytelling. It appeared that Shoshanna and Josh, her previous boyfriend, broke up when Shoshanna started working at the bank and moved to Battery Park City. Then he left soon after to go to Israel on a post-graduate program that managed to combine American tax-law courses with religious instruction.

"Our friendship took off again as soon as Josh left," she said. "But what does he do a week or so after he gets to Israel? He sleeps with somebody we know. 'That's great!' I told her. 'Now you can do the same with somebody else. You'll feel a lot better.' But right after that we had September 11. She had to camp out on my couch for three months while they cleaned up her apartment building."

"Are you telling me I was just in the right place at the right time?" I asked.

"Shoshanna doesn't think like that," she said. "Everybody was a basket case in those days. Then right after she moved back into her apartment, she gets this weird new assignment: Somebody's stealing money from the bank, but they don't know how. Then she meets you. It was obvious she was attracted to you. You seemed like a good guy. So I told her to seduce you. I thought it would be good thing. But she agonized about it forever. Whether to do it, how to do it, when to do it. I told her: 'It's not rocket science. Just bring the guy up to your apartment. He'll do the rest.' After that I got daily reports. You were patient with her. She liked your body. You were racking up a lot of points. 'Just do it,' I told her. 'If it doesn't work out with him, it'll work out with somebody else.'"

She stopped for a moment, realizing she was sounding a bit callous.

"I'm sorry if I've hurt your feelings," she said. "I just tell people the truth. That's the way I am."

"It may have started out as a casual thing," I said. "But it grew into something a lot more serious. I can't speak for her, but I was completely smitten. I still am. I proposed marriage at least once."

"That was very sweet."

"It wasn't *sweet*!" I said, raising my voice. "I meant it! That night we had at your apartment, with you and Ken and the rack of lamb and the kids bouncing on the futon... That was going to be my new life!"

Our neighbors gave us a look: How cute. Two lovers having a little fight.

"I was right," Gigi said, with a self-congratulatory smile. "You were a good thing for her."

I gritted my teeth. If this was consolation, I'd prefer to suffer my grief alone.

"So what did I do wrong?" I asked, trying to calm down and be civil.

"What did you do wrong?" she asked incredulously, before dropping her voice to a loud whisper. "You're a *felon*. Or you would be if you hadn't settled out of court. You stole over a hundred million dollars! You're the kind of guy she tries to put in jail!"

"It was one mistake! And I didn't steal it, I lost it. Why do I have to be judged all my life on what I did on November 12, 2001?"

She gave me a deeply empathetic look, but there was something professional about it. Then I remembered: She was a genetic-diseases counselor. She spent her day advising people, consoling people about their medical conditions.

"I'm sorry," she said. "Believe me, I pleaded your case. But it was a lost cause. I think the real problem was that you lied to her about it."

"I never lied. I just never told her the complete truth."

"So it's a sin of omission. Those are much more common than sins of commission. At least that's what I was taught in religious school."

We had reached the end of this discussion. She had managed to finish her salad, but my steak lay uneaten in front of me.

"Shoshanna is very deep," she said, picking out one of my fries. "She's very biological about it. She was always asking me: 'Do I want this man to be the father of my children? What are his strengths and weaknesses?' That's not the way I work. I married Ken because I loved the way he smelled. I got pregnant on our second date. But it all worked out for the best. And it'll work out for you... eventually."

She reached across the table and gave my hand a big squeeze.

"I'm an amateur matchmaker," she said, warming up to her new topic. "And you're a good catch."

Then she took out a book of 4 x 6 photos she kept in her purse, and flipped through it, picking out a few good ones to show me.

"This woman works on Wall Street, too," she said. "She works with 401(k) funds. Not too religious. Or at least willing to be flexible."

The snapshot revealed a modestly attractive woman sitting alone at a restaurant table set for two. She had a forced smile and was disfigured by the red-eye from the flash. But what was the context of this photograph? Did Gigi take the photograph to include in this pitch book? I was appalled, and my face must have betrayed me.

"I'm sorry," I said, handing back her photos. "I don't have a particular thing for Orthodox girls. I had a thing for one particular Orthodox girl."

"I understand," she said. "But I keep trying. I've made two matches so far. One of the guys was somebody secular like you. If I get one more, the Talmud says I go to heaven."

"I didn't realize that's all it took," I said.

"My mother has made 19 successful marriages. And not one divorce. She's a genius."

I realized I should have expressed more interest in her photos. She was miffed that I didn't want to date any of her friends.

"I'm sorry it didn't work out with Shoshanna," she said. "I really wanted it to. I like you and Ken likes you. But you should realize you were not the first secular guy that hit on her."

"I didn't hit on her!" I said. "She hit on me! And she didn't tell me she was Orthodox. Isn't that a sin of omission, too?"

She considered that moral quandary a half second before deciding it was irrelevant. I, a felon, had questioned the moral integrity of her best friend. I was no longer such a good catch.

"I don't understand what you're complaining about," she said, looking around for her bag and waving to the waiter. "You got some great sex out of it. Isn't that all you guys care about?"

Ross lived in the fourth-floor studio apartment in Tim's building. Most of his tiny living room was taken up by a huge thrift-shop couch and an equally huge collection of opera LPs that warped the shelves of his bookcases. The place was a cluttered mess, and smelled of Lysol and cat litter.

"So whatever happened to that guy you were in love with?" he asked, pouring me a glass of red wine.

The question took me by surprise. When we met after the funeral, I must have told him a few things about Shoshanna and switched the pronouns.

"What did I tell you?" I asked. "I'm trying to remember."

"You said you were in a new relationship and that you were completely in love. But you weren't sure it was mutual."

"Oh, yeah," I said. "It wasn't. I got dumped last week."

"Ouch," he said, wincing with commiseration. Then he reached out to squeeze my hand. "But you'll recover. If you're single, I've got a very cute guy I could fix you up with."

I broke into a huge smile.

"What are you laughing about?" he asked. "You don't think a fat slob like me would know any really hunky guys?"

"You're the second person who's tried to fix me up today. And I'm still stuck on my last lover."

"That's your problem, honey," he said in an accent that was part queen, part black. "It's time to move on."

"What's he look like?" I asked. "Thin? Big like me? What's he do?"

"Well, first of all, I assume you're Jewish because your name is Ackerman. He's Jewish, too. And he has a thing for bears like you."

He dashed off to get a photo in case I changed my mind. He flipped through a series of drugstore processing envelopes until he found the snapshot: Ross and this guy were sitting around a picnic table at Jones Beach, eating hero sandwiches. Tall, dark hair, small wide-spaced eyes, sort of like Matthew Perry. I thought he was rather attractive. I suppose I was developing a taste for this kind of thing.

"What does he do for a living?" I asked.

"He just made partner at a Wall Street law firm. The one in the Chase headquarters building."

"Do his law partners know he's gay?"

"Oh, yes," he said. "He doesn't make a big thing about it, but he doesn't hide it either."

"Do you know any investment bankers who are openly gay?"

"Sure," he said. "I've got a friend who's a librarian at Lehman."

"That doesn't count; a librarian is a traditionally gay role. Do you know any traders other than Tim? Or mergers and acquisitions guys? Institutional salesmen?"

"I don't really hang around with that kind of crowd. I usually end up with fat opera fags like myself."

Ross decided to play me some of his favorite arias — the 10 recordings he'd take to a desert island. Quite enjoyable, really, although opera was not my cup of tea. After Madame Butterfly suffered through a very slow death, I decided it was the right time to segue to another.

"I see somebody took the police notice off the door downstairs," I said.

"That happened last week," he said. "The guy in the apartment below mine said he saw workmen here a couple days ago."

"Is there any way we can get in there?"

"In where? You mean Tim's apartment?" His eyes lit up.

"Yeah," I said. "I'd like to know more about what happened."

"I don't know if there's anything left to see. They've probably cleaned it all up."

"I just want to get the layout of the place. We're not interfering with a police investigation."

He turned around and started rummaging through a junk drawer in his kitchenette.

"He gave me a set of keys, but that was in 1997," he said. "I'm sure he's changed the lock since then." He found a glass jar full of old keys and sorted through them.

"This might work," he said, staring at a key that matched the one from his own door. "But it might be the key for my storage place in Queens. God knows what I'm keeping out there. I've been paying $69 a month for years."

We walked down the stairway to the first floor. I wasn't eager for anybody to see us breaking into the apartment of a guy who had been recently murdered.

"If we hear somebody coming, just start walking out the door," I said.

"Are we violating any laws if we use a key?" he asked.

"This is illegal," I said. "Trust me. I'm a felon."

Ross gave me a quizzical look, then tried to insert the key into the lock. It didn't fit.

"Too bad," he said, looking a bit relieved.

"Are you sure the door is locked?" I said. "Let me try."

I turned the handle and gave it a shove.

The first things I saw were some five-gallon cans of paint and spackle, canvas drop cloths and a portable ladder, stained with several colors of paint. These were folded neatly just inside the door. The rest of the room was dark, but we were overwhelmed by an unmistakable odor.

Cat pee.

Or maybe human pee.

We stood in the hallway with the door open, hesitating.

"Are you coming in with me?" I asked.

I saw a floor lamp just a few feet away and turned it on. Ross followed me and closed the door behind us.

The lamp illuminated a modest living room a few feet above street level: hardwood floors, an Oriental rug, tan leather couches and a coffee table with art books. A spiral staircase with a spindly iron banister led downstairs. Another hallway led to a small eat-in kitchen. Not the place I would live if I had any real money.

"The bottom floor is a lot bigger," Ross said. "Should I lock the door?"

"No," I said. "We'll be out of here in a minute. But I wouldn't touch anything here if I were you."

There was a plastic zip-lock bag and several rubber bands on the coffee table, beside a large book of Egon Schiele reproductions. The entire table had been sprinkled with fine black fingerprint dust. The plastic bag was empty and was marked "EVI-DENCE." The same dust covered some of the surfaces in the kitchen, the arms of the couch and the banister of the staircase.

I walked down the steps to the basement slowly, without using the railings. The urine smell became stronger. The bottom floor had a low-ceilinged room that functioned as a home office and den with an aging leather sofa, a big TV and a small grove of ficus plants that were losing their leaves. The desk was covered with fingerprint dust and had a laser printer, but no computer.

Another five-gallon can of spackle and some crusty spackling tools sat in the center of the room. Apparently, the painter had taken one good look around and split. Beside the open door to the bedroom were a couple empty amyl nitrite poppers. I could see a few more on the floor just inside.

The bedroom was the biggest room in the apartment and faced a small backyard garden, still ringed by Christmas lights, which you could see through artfully customized burglar bars. The room had wall-to-wall white shag carpet, an antique brass bed and two antique oak dressers. The bed sheets had been stripped off the mattress, which had a large oval urine stain in the center.

The dressers looked unnaturally empty, and were covered with more dust. On the other end of the room, somebody had gone through the wicker hamper, dumping the dirty clothes on the ground.

"Are you coming?" asked Ross from upstairs.

"One more minute," I said.

I saw another empty evidence bag on the floor, and a torn paper envelope that once held a pair of disposable medical gloves.

Nothing here. Not anymore.

As I walked home to Battery Park City I asked myself: What was I expecting to find? Some weird piece of evidence the cops had overlooked? This wasn't about looking for fingerprints. Shoshanna and I had done the brunt of the detective work a few weeks ago. And the SEC was going to connect the dots in a few days.

There's nothing I don't know about these traders, Markowitz had said.

He knew all about Stu Lister's scheme to pump up his bonus. Or rather Shivakumar knew, and alerted him. Did Shivakumar know about Tim as well? *A trade can be a signal. For somebody who understands the numbers, a signal of future intentions.*

I had to walk by the bank on my way home. My company pass card had been taken away from me by the security guard in Lewis' office, but I still had my first temporary pass card. I took it out of my wallet and stared at it. A photo of me dated April 8, 2002, the day I met Shoshanna. A long shot but worth a try.

I arrived at the entrance to the bank at 10:29 p.m. One guard was standing at the reception desk and another was stationed at the metal turnstiles directly to the left. If my card worked, the little green light in the turnstile would click on and I wouldn't have to talk to either of them. Just another employee who left something upstairs. No need to act too friendly.

I waved the card in front of the turnstile. A red light. I tried it again. Same thing.

The guard came over and waved the card over the turnstile scanner and jiggled it once or twice.

"Shit," he said, and motioned me over to the reception desk. "Let me look this up."

I could have made a mad dash for the exit, but I figured that would really set the alarm bells ringing. Stick to the script. He typed my name into the computer at the reception desk.

"Ackerman, David," he read. "It says you're no longer working here."

"Yes, but I'm still a temp," I said, pointing to my card to give my claim more authority. He looked at the card, then at the other guard, who seemed to be the one in charge.

"We can't let you in unless somebody vouches for you," the other guard said. "Is there somebody upstairs we can call?"

"Normally there would be," I said. "But it's 10:38 on a Wednesday night." Then I smiled. "I left the keys to my apartment on my desk. Can you guys loan me a sleeping bag until tomorrow morning?"

That got me two smiles. The guard punched a few buttons on his keyboard and a visitor's pass with a bar code sputtered out of the label printer.

There was a three-man crew of floor polishers on the fourth floor near the entrance to the audit offices: one to ride the machine and two others to stand by and watch. My cubicle was just as I'd left it when I was summoned suddenly to Lewis' office a week ago. All I had to do was turn on the PC, and pray my login and password still worked. *The username is case sensitive. Is the "Caps lock" or "A" light on your computer on? If so, hit "Caps lock" key before trying again.*

I tried Shoshanna's sequence: "scassuto" and "powderpuff."

No dice.

I looked around the deserted audit cube farm. I was too close to give up now. Twenty or so auditors, each with logins and passwords that let them go almost anywhere on the company intranet. All I needed was one.

Then I remembered an old trick: I looked under all the keyboards and found two Post-its with usernames and passwords. The first one was out of date, but "dcooper" and "marbles" were the magic keys that opened the golden door.

Then it was a matter of finding Shivakumar's network drive. There were three Shivakumars at the bank but "Mehta, Shivakumar" worked in risk management. He had organized his projects by date, so it was a relatively simple matter to find the files referring to any investigations he'd done on Tim.

By painstakingly checking the data in a series of files, I could re-create his efforts, day by day. I could see him patiently covering the same ground we were to cover a few weeks later. On February 12, two months after Tim's first trades, he had noted that some of the bank's equity-option trades weren't as profitable as predicted. A couple days later, he had traced the problem to equity-basket trades, and sent a memo to Markowitz, marked URGENT, alerting him to the problem. A day after that came a memo identifying Tim as the likely source of what he called "a portfolio data leak." But, as he admitted in his e-mail to Markowitz, he had no proof, only an overwhelming series of coincidences. Tim was probably leaking key portfolio data to people outside the bank, but how was he doing it?

Shivakumar had a much better command of the territory, so his investigation was much quicker than ours. But I could feel the frustration buried in his countless spreadsheets. He had looked at the same e-mails, looked at the phone calls, looked at the Web site visits and finally at the videos.

Then he gave up. Or else he was stopped. Markowitz clearly knew about Tim's scam and was letting Shivakumar keep a running tab of how much it was costing the bank. But he didn't pursue the investigation any further.

I copied the files onto a memory stick and waved goodbye to the guards. Then I walked back to Battery Park City.

It was too late to call Mitch at the SEC, but surely he should know about this. And what did all this mean? Markowitz was clearly part of some kind of cover-up. But what kind?

And did that make him a suspect in the murder?

Chapter 21

"How did you get this information out of the bank?" Mitch asked the next morning.

"I snuck in."

"How?"

"Bluffing. And I found somebody's password on a Post-it."

"You like playing spy, don't you?"

"Mitch, I think this may change everything. At the very least, we know that Markowitz is covering up a crime."

"And at the very most?" he asked.

"I don't know. I'm not in law enforcement. What do you think?"

"E-mail me those files and I'll have somebody look into it. But let's make something clear. We already have an investigator. I don't want you doing his job, because you could screw up the whole case. Ruin the evidence trail or something else technical. Just stick to trading. Enough to keep you busy. Go out drinking with the guys after work and listen to the gossip. Can you do that?"

I certainly tried. A few hours later, I was sitting in a circular table in the back of T.G.I. Friday's. Everybody was talking about the lopsided Knicks victory the night before. Then a futures trader named Paul started to argue a patent absurdity — that the Celtics in the '70s were the greatest team in basketball.

The challenge was deliciously easy for a rabid Chicago Bulls fan. My command of basketball statistics was something of a parlor trick, but it was no fun if you simply recited them from memory. You had to use them as part of an argument, which usually came down to: "Your team sucks." Paul actually knew a lot about the Knicks, and made a noble effort. We recited win-loss numbers, home-away numbers, point-spread numbers and then stats on each major player. It was the team of his youth versus the team of my youth, but in the end I won simply because I had Michael Jordan on my side.

At one point a monster jukebox near us started up, forcing us into smaller conversational groups. I got another beer and moved over to the other side of the table where Shelby and Mark, two guys whom I had met before, were comparing notes about martial arts.

Shelby was explaining the virtues of *naginata*, a Japanese martial art, in a rich Southern accent. He said that it taught etiquette, respect, patience and self-confidence. From what I could tell, it also allowed you to bash your opponent over the head with a six-foot stick. Mark had sampled a few of the more oddball martial arts as well, but was drawn back to taekwondo because of the Bruce Lee-style jump kicks.

"What about you?" Shelby asked me. "Did you ever do any martial arts?"

"Wrestling in high school," I said. "That's a martial art, isn't it?"

It turned out that the three of us had been high school wrestlers. Mark and Shelby had both competed in the same 160 weight class, but they looked quite different: Mark was tall, dark and lanky, and Shelby was built like a blond fireplug.

Mark also took wrestling a lot more seriously. Shelby and I were suburban kids who spent a couple years on the wrestling team, but Mark was a working-class kid from Queens who went to SUNY Buffalo on a wrestling scholarship.

"You pussies could drop out of wrestling and still go to college," said Mark, daring us to knock the chip off his shoulder. "I had to stick with it or end up in my father's bakery. By senior year I hated wrestling. You know why?"

"Too many salads," I said.

"That's fucking right," he said, shaking his head with disgust. "Seven years of eating salads. I can't even look at that rabbit food anymore."

He had a double-sided accent: It was pure Queens when he was worked up about something, but it flattened out quickly when he tried to impress us talking about his big East Side apartment or his Lexus. It soon became clear that Mark's good-natured gibing was only the tip of an enormous iceberg of class resentment. There was something of a caste system in the trading business. With luck and hard work, borough kids like Mark could push their way into jobs as securities traders, but rarely into white-shoe firms like Goldman and Morgan Stanley. In most cases, they ended up spending their careers on the cash desks. Options guys almost always came from privilege.

Shelby was no exception. He struck me as a good-natured kid from Virginia who did all the right things, got a job as a yen trader, and then fell off the gravy train during a round of cutbacks. He was getting married in the fall to his girlfriend, who lived in Georgetown and worked for the Senate Agriculture Committee, but he didn't seem too worried. He thought it was only a matter of weeks before he would be employed again, and was using his time at TradeSpace to learn something about equity-options trading with his 401(k) portfolio.

He also seemed to be spending a lot of time at the gym, judging by the pumped-up shoulders on his 5- 6 frame. I suggested a few equity-options strategies I thought he might be able to pull off, and he gave me some completely ridiculous advice about a regimen to increase the definition in my biceps and triceps.

We soon established a little fraternity of our own. Lubricated by pitchers of beer, the conversation moved effortlessly between three topics: wrestling, weight training and securities trading. Mark had traded Treasuries at Bear Stearns for a while and claimed to be making money on the spread between cash Treasuries and the futures. I was moderately curious about how he did this, but he wasn't eager to reveal his tricks. He also shared Shelby's obsession with muscle definition, though he had a narrow-shouldered frame that would never bulk up no matter how many cans of protein supplements he threw down his gullet.

At one point we veered briefly into politics. Shelby was a Genghis Khan Republican who tried to start a pointless battle with me, a middle-of-the-road Democrat, about eliminating the capital gains tax. Mark was a libertarian who wanted to eliminate all taxes, and believed people should be able to buy whatever drugs they wanted.

"Even prescription drugs?" asked Shelby.

"Particularly prescription drugs," said Mark with a smile.

The evening passed quickly. Shelby turned out to be a terrific mimic, and his word-for-word reenactment of his wrestling coach's pre-game inspiration speech reduced us to drunken hysterics. Towards 9:00, the topic turned back to martial arts and, more specifically, the latest Jackie Chan movie, which Shelby had seen three times and was eager to see again before it disappeared from the last remaining Manhattan theater. We all made plans to meet the next night at a bar near the theater, and staggered out of T.G.I. Friday's like a bunch of frat kids.

The next morning I got in early, turned on my computer and tried to prepare myself for another seven grueling hours in the futures pits. I was too hung over to concentrate. My stomach started up like a washing machine, churning my Egg McMuffin into mush.

I put my head down on my desk and waited for my stomach to stop. I shoved my head into the crook of my elbow to darken the pink light seeping in from my eyelids. A flurry of memories, one worse than the next: from the horrors of September 11 through the morning of November 12, my last day as a trader, when I spent half an hour in a toilet stall trying to think up some way out of my disastrous option position.

In an effort to clear my head, I forced myself to focus on the day before everything started to go wrong. What was I doing on September 10?

I remembered it quite clearly. It was a Monday, and a pretty nice one at that. Clear and in the 70s. The White Sox were finishing the year a dozen games out of first place, and the Yankees were wrapping up another pennant race.

I had gone to bed at 10 the night before, shortly after Chris, my girlfriend, left for some film party in the West Village. Then she stumbled back in at 2 a.m., high and extremely horny, smelling of pot smoke, cigarette smoke and sweat. Before I was fully awake, she got out her favorite sandalwood lubricant, massaged me into a quick erection and we proceeded to work ourselves into a frenzy. Intense sex for at least an hour, punctuated by rest stops to stretch it out as long as possible. Of course, she could sleep till noon, and I had to get up at 5:45.

And what did I trade that morning? The futures were shaky before the NYSE open. A big number at 10:00. I decided to hold my little calendar spread through the number, nothing ambitious, because I was feeling a little tired. Ray Goodman was plotting his own crazy strategy two rows away, but he could have been on another planet. By the end of the day, the S&P Index had risen a few points. By playing with my models, I managed to pull $90,000 out of the market.

Reliving my days as a successful options trader gave me a moment of equilibrium. I sat up and looked at my Bloomberg screen with a calmness that I feared would soon dissipate. Today wasn't that much different from September 10. In fact there were a lot of similarities. Market moving sideways. Big number at 10 a.m. Exhausted. Dave Ackerman was still Dave Ackerman, more or less. What would Dave of September 10 do, given this market situation?

I opened up a fresh spreadsheet and started to reconstruct some of my favorite option models from memory, embedding cells with key ratios and sketching out potential scenarios, each formula an old friend. After a few minutes, I looked at my handiwork. It was like an aircraft of some kind. Something that would allow me to soar over the manual laborers in the futures pits.

But this baby needed fuel if it was going to fly. The key P&L cell — the amount of money I actually had left in my account — read $8,291. A pathetic number to Dave of September 10. How could I possibly duplicate my experience with so little cash?

Then a little voice somewhere in my head said: *Subtract a couple zeroes.* Sure. Turn your old $100,000 trades into $1,000 trades. Trade the way you traded in the past, but on a much smaller scale. It was a little tricky, but it could be done.

I went into my regular preflight routine. I had to assume the number today wouldn't be a big surprise and S&P would stay stable. The traditional way to make money in that situation was by selling options 20 points of either side of the market. Every old-fart options trader sitting on his balcony in Boca Raton would be doing that to make a few bucks before his 11 a.m. tee time. But if you puttered around with your months and ratios, you'd have something a little more interesting.

I had executed the strategy dozens of times before. Maybe hundreds. It was difficult to pull off, but a little boring to Dave Ackerman of September 10. It was the kind of trade that Ray Goodman would make fun of. It would never get you into the Options Hall of Fame. So, a calendar strangle, short February and long March. Then sit and watch it. And hope the market stayed calm.

It was time to call Jeff in Chicago. I felt a little awkward, because I needed his advice about market color, but I could only afford to trade a tiny amount.

"Hey, it's me," I said. "Dave."

"My man!" he said. "Long time no hear. I heard you had some trouble."

"That's behind me now. I want to ask you for a favor. I'm thinking of going a little slow at first. A few contracts at a time."

"Just a few?"

"Is that okay? It's sort of an experiment."

"Yeah, I guess. I'll tell the office you're just warming up."

"Thanks a lot. How's it look?"

"Goldman's getting out of a 4-way, so everybody's jumping on that spread. They're all pumped up."

"Perfect. Sell me 10 of those 4-ways."

"Okay, selling 10 only," he said. "Ticket 32. I'll call back with the fill."

The dial tone felt like a starting gun. Watch the prices, check the model, keep my ear to the rails. I was back once more in the world of mathematics and instinct.

I leaned back in my chair, took a deep breath and exhaled. This period, these next few days at TradeSpace, were a gift from the SEC. I'd never get another chance to trade. Half the money was going to charity. I might as well enjoy myself.

Things started looking good after the housing starts number came in. It wasn't quite perfect, because my trading system was clumsy and I had to keep mentally adjusting for the zeroes. I spent the morning glued to my chair, checking my models, adding a few options to one side or another to stabilize my position.

I had always traded this way. Things getting a little shaky? Ride it down a little. I didn't need a guru. I knew what to do. I had done it before. I just had to do it again.

The revelation was that there was no revelation. Let Ray Goodman and his aces race by above me in the stratosphere. I was the pilot of a UPS plane, making the daily package run from Denver to St. Louis.

At noon, my stomach demanded lunch but who needed lunch on a day like this? At about 2 p.m. my position started running into a little trouble. Dave of September 10 sold out, picked up $750, and bought a few calls on the NASDAQ just for fun.

I didn't dare look at my P&L number. It would be absurdly small to Dave of September 10. But to Dave of April 24 it was more than enough. I had succeeded once more, and my body was alive with the woozy rapture that only occurs when you rediscover a long-lost love.

I was born to be an options trader. Nothing else suited me as well. If I helped the SEC get this guy, would they give me my license back? Suddenly, anything was possible. If I could trade like this, I could marry Shoshanna. I could support a family. I could eat rack of lamb and drink Kosher Shiraz on the Upper West Side.

I met Mark and Shelby at 7:30 in front of a movie theater near Mark's house. The Jackie Chan film turned out to be a buddy movie about two cops, one Chinese, one black, which was long on clichés and short on the martial arts display Mark was hoping for.

"Sugar-coated bullshit," he complained, as we retired to a nearby bar. "The black guy couldn't kick his way out of paper bag."

"I could watch those jump kicks all night long," said Shelby. "But it was 10 percent fighting, 90 percent foreplay."

The conversation turned once again to weight training, and I found it all a little tiresome. They were both bodybuilders, trying to compensate for the bodies they'd been given: Shelby wore a polo shirt two sizes too short to show off his biceps and pecs, and Mark clearly wanted to bulk up his narrow shoulders. After giving me a few new tips on how to get the veins in my biceps to stand out better, Mark mentioned that he had a Bowflex Ultimate home gym in his second bedroom. Shelby was eager to see it, so we walked a few blocks to Mark's place.

It was a typical trader's apartment, decorated with the requisite leather couches, high-end audio equipment, and racks of CDs. He had a computer gaming center in a corner of the apartment, near the windows overlooking Lexington Avenue. The only thing on the walls was a collection of unremarkable underwater photographs of tropical reef fish Mark had taken during some scuba trips to the Caribbean. The second bedroom was a showcase of high-end sports equipment: The Bowflex gym stood on a rubber pedestal in the center of the room, surrounded by several top-of-the-line squash racquets, a bright orange surfboard and an Italian racing bike. In the corner two wetsuits, one for surfing and the other for scuba diving, had been dumped into some moving boxes.

"The straight squat bar is for glutes, hamstrings and quads," explained Mark, doing a few infomercial squats as we watched. "The lat tower is for back and shoulder muscles. And the pulley system allows you to change the angle of resistance for your upper body exercises."

Shelby put the machine through its paces for a few minutes before deciding he definitely had to buy one as soon as he started making some money.

"What's your highest bench press?" he asked Mark.

"I can max it out," said Mark. "It goes to 260."

"Oh, yeah?" I said, looking through Mark's shirt to his body. He had managed to build up his upper arms, but there was only so much you could do with those shoulders.

"That's only on a good day, after I've worked up to it," he said.

"Okay," I said. "Let's see you do 200."

"I can't do it cold," he said. "I need to work up to it. I just came back from vacation, so I'm off my form."

"Okay," I said. "Let's see you do 180. Right now."

Mark stripped to his t-shirt set the weight to 160 and jerked through a couple warmups.

Then he set it to 180, took a deep breath and made a gallant effort for a few seconds before giving up.

"Come back in a week," he said. "I'll be back up to my form."

We quickly retired to the living room, where Mark showed off his collection of high-end Scotch, which he kept behind a tacky locked glass-covered shelf. "My cleaning lady was taking a few samples," he explained, fishing out his keys and removing one of his favorite single malts.

Shelby seemed to be aware of the names of some of the brands, and soon they were discussing the different kinds of peat malt and obscure misty islands off the western coast of Scotland. The bottle of Glenmorangie was 15 years and cost $140, while Lagavulin Double Matured was $210, because it was aged in special oak casks that gave it hints of caramel, apple and sage.

"Oh, come on," I said when I'd heard enough. "There may be a difference between $15 and $50 scotch, but once it gets past $50, the differences diminish to nothing. You can't tell a $50 bottle from a $150 bottle."

"Not true," said Mark.

"You might not be able to tell the difference, but I can," said Shelby.

I proposed a blind taste test. I got Mark to tell me how much some of his bottles cost, and marked them with Post-its. Then Mark and Shelby covered their eyes with tube socks while I set up a series of 15 or so Dixie cups on the table labeled A through F.

It was good fun and a great way to get stinking drunk very quickly. Mark immediately mistook a $20 Crown Royal for a $120 Royal Lachnagar Special Reserve. Shelby, as I suspected, couldn't even tell the difference between Scotch and bourbon, and their sense of discrimination went downhill as we drank more. Then Mark and Shelby got into an age-old discussion about intoxicants. Was the high you get from good Scotch any different than the high you got from bad scotch or wine or beer?

They represented two types of Wall Street guys I didn't have much contact with. Working-class guys like Mark often felt cast adrift when they became successful: They couldn't go back to their homeboys, and they didn't fit in with the Ivy League types at the top firms. So they hung around with each other, taking limousine trips to Atlantic City and cultivating sophisticated tastes for cigars and Scotch and whatever they thought was classy. Mark was a bullshit artist — the kind of guy who enjoyed entertaining because it allowed him to show off how much money he made.

Shelby was a little harder to read. Plenty of guys from the South found their way to jobs on Wall Street, but they never seemed to stick around very long. When they hit their 30s, they sold their townhouses in Park Slope and took jobs at super-regional banks back home. A few months of unemployment had done a number on Shelby's psyche. The more he drank, the more he looked like he was going to let loose with some kind of personal confession I didn't really want to hear.

"You guys want to switch to something else?" asked Mark.

"You have any bottles of Latour you're hiding?" asked Shelby.

"I've got a case of Lafitte '92 and a killer bottle of Graham Vintage Port from '69," he said. "But I was thinking of something else."

"I'll stick with this Laphroaig 15," said Shelby. "I bought fancy Scotch when I was working at Credit Suisse. But it doesn't feel right when I'm not making any money."

"You're not making any money now?" asked Mark.

"No," he said. "I'm not making any money and I'm not afraid to admit it. I've spent two months at TradeSpace knocking my head against a wall before I realized something: It's simply not possible. Are you making any money? Real money?"

"I'm doing okay," said Mark.

"But are you making as much as when you were on a trading desk?"

"I'm doing okay," he repeated.

"What about you?" he asked, turning to me for confirmation.

"I'll be honest with you," I said. "I spent my first few days getting nowhere, scalping in the futures markets. It's hard. You don't have the volume, you don't have the deal flow. But yesterday I started working on some option trades and I did okay."

"As much as you'd make as an options trader?"

"No," I admitted. "But enough to get by."

"That's what I'm trying to say," said Shelby, looking to us for confirmation. "The best traders, people like you, may be making enough to pay the bills. But you'd have to pull off some kind of scam to make any real money at TradeSpace."

My heart skipped a beat. What was going on here? The usual trader bullshit or something more? I had my fake phone in my left pocket and the extra battery in my right. I reached into my pocket and pressed the record button. It started humming.

"What kind of scam are you talking about?" I asked.

"I don't know," said Shelby. "You could probably make some money if you had access to a bank's system and you had an account at TradeSpace."

"But you're not working for a bank anymore," I said. "How are you going to have access to their trades?"

"Well, you've got to have a partner on the inside."

I realized I was not going to get a decent recording with the gizmo in the pocket of my jeans.

"Okay, how are you going to do that?" I asked.

Shelby stopped to think, but he looked too drunk to plot any serious bank fraud at that point. I moved the recorder from my jeans to my shirt pocket in one quick gesture. Neither of them seemed to notice. Mark, meanwhile, was smiling like a goofball, obviously eager to see what stupid idea Shelby would come up with so he could shoot it down.

"I don't have the specifics of how I'd do it," said Shelby, after considering it for a few seconds. "But I'm sure if I thought about it, I'd find a way."

"Well, I have thought about it," I said, "and I haven't figured out an easy way to do it."

"All I know is that I'm getting married on October 3rd," said Shelby, putting down his drink. "If this job at Lehman doesn't come through, I'm completely fucked because I'm not going to make any money at TradeSpace. Nobody is," he said, casting his glass in a drunken arc. "You two may be the exception. But how many people are making more than $10,000 a month?"

"Hal says he's making money in pairs trading," said Mark.

"Bullshit," said Shelby. "He's a fucking liar. Hal made 10 grand last month because the market happened to be going his way. Anybody could have made money in the Treasury market last month. He probably lost $20,000 the month before. All these people thought they were geniuses and now when the markets aren't going up all the time, they wonder what the problem is."

I decided to stop drinking and clear my head. My assignment was to make friends with fellow traders, but neither of these guys stuck me as nefarious enough to commit a financial crime. So why was I spending a Saturday night in a tacky apartment getting drunk with a couple of bodybuilding nerds I didn't really like? The whole thing was depressing.

"So what's a big options guy like you doing at TradeSpace?" Shelby asked.

"What do you think?" I said.

"I don't know. You must have had some kind of problem."

"That's right."

They waited for me to start my explanation, but I wasn't going to oblige them.

"It's a long story," I said, finally. "I did something wrong. I got greedy. I got fired."

There was an awkward pause until they realized I was not going to tell them anything more. I didn't feel like telling them the truth, and couldn't think of a good lie. The party was winding down.

"You guys hungry?" asked Mark, eager to play host. "What about some Thai food?"

That sounded okay, and Mark went to his kitchen to get some menus.

While we waited, Shelby perused a narrow bookshelf beside the stereo, and I looked idly through his CD collection. Lots of metal from a decade ago, then a lot of trance and jungle stuff of more recent vintage.

"*Jesus Christ!*" whispered Shelby, staring at a picture in some kind of heavy coffee table book.

"What is it?" I asked.

He shook his head and passed the book to me.

A photo inside showed a well-built and well-oiled naked white guy on his hands and knees, his mouth open to accommodate the tip of a large black cock, which looked at least ten inches long. There was another matching large black cock inserted in parallel fashion into his other end. The owners of the cocks had been cropped out of the left and right frames to give the photo a certain artsy symmetry.

I handed the book back to Shelby, who gave it another stare, then shoved it back in the bookcase.

"Did you know that Mark was..." He couldn't finish the sentence.

"No," I said honestly.

We glanced at the other titles in the bookshelf, which held what appeared to be an expensive collection of gay erotica. I looked around the room for cues that I was in a gay guy's apartment. Nothing. He certainly fooled me. A gay guy without the decorator gene.

"I'm getting out of here," he said. "This stuff gives me the creeps."

A second later, Mark came back into the room with four menus fanned out in his hand. He stared at us for a moment. Something had happened in the interim, but he couldn't quite figure out what.

"We can choose from three different Thai places," he said. "And here's an Indian restaurant for good measure..."

"I'm sorry, Mark," said Shelby. "I've had a little too much to drink, and I've got to get up early."

"That's cool," said Mark, nodding and looking at me.

"I'm starving," I said. "Let's go for Indian."

"Okay," Mark said, his eyes flipping down to my crotch. He took a step closer. "I'm hungry, too."

Chapter 22

Once Shelby left, everything changed. A genie whisked away all the air we had been breathing and replaced it with something warm, steamy, and intimate.

Mark and I stared at each other through the mist, our hands at our side, a foot and a half between us. He had thick black hair, cut short like a helmet, and deep brown eyes. A piercing stare, a little glassy from booze. Not a bad looking guy, I thought, if you liked Mediterranean types.

"He saw your porn collection," I said. "It freaked him out."

"Oh," Mark said.

He made a movement, the slightest twitch in my direction. Instinctively, I put my hands in my pockets and tried to relax into my role. But what was my role? A word popped into my head. Coquette. Of course. I knew this dance. I just had to do it backwards.

This time, I was the object of desire. He couldn't embrace me with my hands in my pockets. I didn't have to sleep with him. I didn't have to do anything with him. I could tease his prick all night long. I felt enormously powerful in an entirely new way.

His right arm rose slowly, index finger extended, as if he was pointing towards my neck. Then he placed it on my sternum, with the lightest possible touch, and ran it down my chest to my belt.

I smiled and shook my head, slowly and deliberately.

"I'm not going to fuck you tonight," I said. "Let's start from there."

He shrugged. "Your call," he said.

"I'm in a relationship right now that may be breaking up," I said apologetically. "It's probably over, but I'm not sure."

"You're not with him tonight," he said.

"Let's sit down and have another drink," I said, pointing the way to the couch.

I could have sat on the easy chair, but chose to sit on the couch beside him, one cushion away. I'd been on couches with dates before. All you had to do was keep both feet on the floor.

I shook the ice in my glass and looked at him expectantly, like some coed in a '50s movie. He poured me some more Scotch.

"So you're about to break up with this guy?" he said.

"He's in the Catskills on a retreat," I said. "We had a fight before he left. He came from a strong religious background, and he had some problems with sex."

"Catholic?" he said.

"Very," I said. "Big Irish family from New Jersey. He moved down to Battery Park City to get away from them. And like an idiot, I took a sublet down there a few weeks ago to be near him."

"A steamy fuck?"

"No. Not particularly experienced. In fact, he didn't really know what he was doing. But that didn't matter."

"What does he do?"

"He's a compliance person. Twenty-four or so. Small and thin. Great hair."

Mark gazed up at the ceiling, bored. The guy wanted to get laid. He didn't really want to hear about my boyfriend.

"In a couple weeks it's going to be over," I said. "Then I'll be able to do whatever I want."

"You can do whatever you want right now," he said.

"You're right," I said. "If I feel like it."

He looked at me the way I looked at women I desired: Direct. Conniving. Shamelessly hungry for a great fuck. I took off my shoes, curled up on the couch and hugged my knees. Maybe I was on the verge of changing my mind. Maybe I wasn't.

Women had their own ways of letting you know they wanted you. They were slinky. They smiled. They ran their hands down your back. They moved their face close to yours and waited for a kiss. But outside of porno magazines, they rarely looked at you with the same wanton, open-mouthed, I-want-to-lick-you-everywhere gaze.

It was my turn to be slinky, I decided, as I glanced at the bulge in his jeans.

As a heterosexual, your attention is fixed on the opposite sex. You are always on. You watch the endless parade of women in the street. Big hips. Slim hips. Tank tops. Blouses. Red hair. Black hair. And then their ghosts as they drifted through your dreams at night. You are always connected by an endless chain of desire to a group of people who were hopelessly different. You accept the glacial pace of seducing them — the talking, the waiting, the foreplay — as a given.

But if you were gay, you didn't need women anymore. They were not particularly important. You could fuck people just like yourself, people who wanted to have sex the way you did. BAM, BAM, BAM. One after another. No waiting, no compromise. You were free!

The whole thing made a lot of sense.

We stared at each other across the leather couch. He sat cross-legged on two left cushions, his arm outstretched. I sat on the far right cushion, hugging my knees, the one empty cushion serving as a demilitarized zone between us.

As the coquette, it was my job to keep the conversation going.

"So how long did you work at Bear Stearns?" I asked.

"Five years," he said.

"Did you tell anybody you were gay?"

"Are you kidding?" he said. "They had no clue for four years. Then this idiot I was going out with left a message for me. He had a real queeny voice. I told him not to call me at work. That's when they started suspecting something."

"Is that why you got fired?"

"No," he said, shaking his head. "It was the fucking euro. You don't need a Deutsche mark trader if there are no more Deutsche marks. What about you?"

"They never suspected a thing," I said, thinking about my friend Steve and how he fooled us all. "I'm big on sports scores, so that counted for something. I had a boyfriend named Eugene who worked in marketing. So I turned him into Jeanne, my fiancée. Every Monday morning I had a cover story. What we did over the weekend. How we were getting engaged. I had a woman record an outgoing message on my answering machine. The usual shit."

"You can get by in a trading room because you don't see those people socially," he said, taking off his shoes and throwing both feet on the couch. "If you were in mergers and acquisitions, you'd have to take clients out to golf events. You'd have to invite them over for dinner. 'Are you married? How many kids do you have?' You'd be completely fucked."

His feet now extended onto the third cushion, a few inches from me. I was hugging my knees, but I couldn't do it forever and he knew it. I had to either stretch out and intertwine my legs with his, or else swivel and put them back on the floor.

"Have you been in this apartment long?" I asked.

Putting both legs back on the floor would be a little too much. I needed something else.

"About five years," he said, watching me carefully. It was time for the flirt to make a move.

"It's a nice place," I said. I swiveled my legs off the couch, planted one foot on the floor and crossed the other as casually as I could. Then I extended my hand across the couch, within inches of his.

It didn't work. The genie whisked the magic steam out of the room, and replaced it with the normal stuff.

Mark yawned and looked at his watch.

"So I'm not going to get lucky tonight," he said.

"Not tonight," I said.

I didn't want to leave just now. Maybe he was Tim's partner. Maybe he had some gossip about him. In another half hour I'd know more. I had to do something to heat things up again.

I got up off the couch wandered into the gym room. The bench press was set at 180. I pulled out the metal flange so it was set to 160. Then I stripped down to my V-neck t-shirt and started doing reps.

Brace. Breathe. Push.

Brace. Breathe. Push.

At 10 reps I was sweaty.

At 20 I was breathing hard, but I kept my pace.

Brace. Breathe. Push.

Brace. Breathe. Push.

I saw him standing in the doorway out of the corner of my eye. Maybe he was moving his hands in his pockets, maybe he was just watching me. I was going to pay for this little episode with sore arms for a week, but I kept going, filled with narcissistic pride. I was a fucking hunk. I knew it and he knew it. On Monday I was supposed to start working with the guy from the SEC. If Mark was the one who killed Tim, we'd nail him.

"One hundred," I said, letting the weights drop with a satisfying thud.

"Bravo," he said, "30 reps at 160. I'll never get close to that. You want something to drink?"

"Sure," I said, wiping the sweat from my forehead.

He tossed me a bottle of Poland Spring and a white gym towel, and stared as I chugged it and dried off my chest and arms.

I caught a glance of myself in the mirror. I was glistening with sweat, maybe not a *Men's Health* cover, but pretty damn good.

He seemed to think we were making progress. He pulled a CD from his shelf and adjusted the volume. The music was an eerie trance thing, with a steady backbeat and distorted electronic voice that repeated some undistinguishable phrase every fourth bar. Maggy the Grape? Rowing the Lake? I suppose you could think of it as romantic. Or at least seductive.

"What about something besides the Scotch?"

"Like what?" I asked.

He opened a round cookie tin on his coffee table. Inside were a few prescription bottles, a plastic pipe contraption, and a small baggie of pot.

"I found a great Internet pharmacy in Malaysia," he said. "You can get anything you want. China White. Halcyon. Ecstasy."

"Anything?" I asked skeptically. "Like cocaine?"

"No," he said. "Pharmaceutical coke will always be hard to get. But have you ever done Dilaudid?"

He tossed me a prescription bottle. Alpha-methylfentanyl. Little pale yellow caplets.

"Not tonight," I said, putting back the bottle and reaching for the bag of pot. A quarter ounce of dark green buds. Pot was something I could handle.

He filled the pipe, which turned out to be some kind of high-tech bong, packing the tiny bowl with the eraser end of a pencil, then took a hit and passed it to me.

"Sure you don't want to try any of these?" he said, shaking a couple pills out of the bottle and popping them into his mouth.

"Maybe later," I said.

The air in the room changed once more.

A brief wave of nausea, followed by a kick in the forehead. My head separated from the rest of my body and took a pleasant stroll around the room. Everything was still in the same place. Me. My body. Mark. But we were all separated by the music, which flowed around us in happy wisps.

He stretched out on one end of the couch and released a sigh. I stretched out from the other end, and our socks touched. It felt oddly familiar, like something I might have done with Shoshanna, except his legs were much bigger. Or something I might have done when I was 15, sitting in my friend Howard's den after a Nintendo session, talking about the Bears' new fullback. No big deal. Foot to foot. I could handle that. Except this time the guy had a hard-on. It occurred to me that the musical phrase itself might not be one particular phrase, but might keep changing just to confuse me.

"What about you?" he asked. "Did you ever get any action at work?"

Had I missed something? I had to stop spacing out and concentrate.

"I fool around a little, but not at work," I said. "I usually get into these monogamous relationships that last a few months. Then they peter out."

That was not the right thing to say. Not much of a turn-on. But I had to keep my eyes on the prize. I was here for a reason, and I was in a free, reckless mood.

"You ever heard of a guy named Markowitz?" I asked.

"Sure," he said. "Everybody knows him. He's a big shot derivatives trader. Is he straight?"

"Not according to somebody who worked for him. Tim Scott. Did you know Tim?"

"No."

"He died a couple weeks ago. Picked up the wrong trick in a bar."

"Never heard of him," he said, shrugging. "You got to be careful. You ever fuck Keith Edwards? He's an options trader."

"Where's he work?" I asked.

"Goldman. He's the king of NASDAQ options over there."

"Must be a pretty talented guy."

The music modulated down a half octave, and the phrase turned into abstract series of distorted breaths.

"Bullshit," he said. "He just went to the right high school."

"The right high school?" I said. "Are you serious?"

"Absolutely. How do you get into the training programs at Goldman or Morgan Stanley."

"You've got to go to the right business school."

"Right. It's got to be a Top Ten B school: Wharton, Stanford, Chicago. And how do you get into those schools? You've got to do 4.0 at a top undergraduate program. And how do you get into one of those?"

"It's very competitive," I said.

"That's right. If you're from a shit high school in Queens and you bust your balls to get a 4.0, you know where you end up? Queens College. And then there's no way you're going to get into Stanford Business School. You're already off the track."

He grabbed for his whiskey glass, but missed, spilling the ice on the carpet.

"So you spend six years on the shit track as a Deutsche mark trader. And then some idiot invents the euro and there's no more Deutsche marks."

He stared at the whiskey glass on the carpet, but didn't get up. There was a lot of truth in what he was saying, but a lot of self-delusion as well. Trading was a meritocracy, for the most part. If he was a really good Deutsche mark trader, he wouldn't have lost his job. They would have found something else for him to do. By the same token, I knew plenty of Ivy League types with only a modicum of talent who made a lot of money by just doing their homework.

"So what's your story?" he asked, getting up to pour himself another drink. "How did you get a big options job at a big investment bank?"

"I got into a training program after I graduated from Columbia Business School."

"See, what did I tell you? And where did you go for undergraduate?"

"Dartmouth."

"And how did you get into Dartmouth? Did you go to private school?"

"No. I went to a public school on the North Shore of Chicago, which is a pretty wealthy area. But I had to bust my ass in high school to get the grades. And I busted my ass at Dartmouth."

"Yeah, but your parents paid for your education at a private university."

"That's true."

"Just proves my point. And how did you lose your job?"

"I did something stupid," I said.

"You were going to tell us a while ago and then you stopped."

"I didn't want Shelby to know," I said.

"What a little cunt," he said, then started to mimic his Southern accent. '*My fiancée works at the Senate Agriculture Committee. My fiancée lets me drive her car. My fiancée lets me suck her tits.*' "

He laughed at his own wit.

"She's got his dick on a string. She wants him to move down to Virginia? What kind of job is he going to find in D.C.? A complete loser. I bet he isn't even 5-5. Guys that short have something wrong with them. A big chip on their shoulder. You know what I mean?"

I smiled and nodded along.

"The whole bunch at TradeSpace. Complete wage slaves. Every one of them. They put away a little in their 401(k)s and they think they're rich. But they'll never make any real money. They just want to make enough to pay their mortgages and raise another bunch of spoiled brats just like themselves."

He filled my empty glass with a couple inches of Scotch.

"At least you took some chances," he said, eyeing me intently. "So tell me how you blew out. I want to hear."

I sat there a moment, thinking of what to say through the fog of dope and booze. Why did I leave my job? Why did I stop trading? Everybody was always asking me the same thing. This time the truth wouldn't work. But a new story began to take shape in my mind. A standard scam. I made a show of hesitating.

"It was pretty simple, actually," I said. "I set up a phantom company with a guy I knew in the back office. Nothing fancy. It sounded like the subsidiary of a big client. Then we moved the winning trades in the fake account and the losing trades in the real account."

"Who was your partner?"

"Just a kid in trade admin. He had permission to make corrections in the accounting system. It worked pretty well for six months, then we got greedy. Every trade in one account was a winner. We didn't add enough losers. So the auditors found out. They grabbed my partner and said they'd throw him in jail unless he told them everything.

That's how they got me."

Mark nodded along, eating every word.

"It worked out okay in the end," I said. "Neither of us wanted to go to jail, so we cooperated. Both of us got fired."

"And that's why you're at TradeSpace," he said.

"Yeah. Nobody's going to hire me. So I'm trying to learn from my mistakes. Make some more money and get out. I've still got the proceeds from one account they didn't find. But I'd do it differently now, because I'm stuck on the outside. I've got to work with somebody who's already in."

Mark looked away and shook his head.

"What's wrong?" I said. "Do you find what I said appalling?"

"No," he said, shaking his head. "Judge not, lest ye be judged. It's just not my kind of thing."

"You never really thought about committing some kind of financial crime?"

"Not really. But I want to get out of this business, too. I'm sick of trading. I've saved a lot of money. I sell dope on the side. That's a high margin business, especially for the designer stuff. But I can't do that forever. Eventually they catch up with you. I really want to do something else."

"Like what?"

"Like nothing. Hang around on the beach somewhere cheap. Surf. Drink. Fuck. Get high."

"Where are you going to do that?"

"Anyplace but New York Fucking City," he said. "I've been doing some research. I'm just hanging around until I sell my apartment. I hate this town. I hate working for these fucking banks. Living this double life. It's like high school all over again. You think people are talking about you behind your back, but you're not sure. You come into work in the morning and find a Playgirl centerfold taped to your monitor. Fuck that shit. They buy you, they buy your dignity. And you sell it to them. Willingly."

Sometimes people surprise you. Mark was a little deeper than I thought. An asshole and a bullshit artist. But also a working-class guy closing in on a common Wall Street dream: Make a lot of money, save a lot, retire at 40. Most guys ended up making a lot and blowing a lot.

He might be able to pull it off. But he didn't strike me as the guy I was looking for. I sighed and tried not to look disappointed. Maybe he was good for some gossip.

"So who else in this place is gay?" I asked.

"What place? TradeSpace?"

"Yeah."

"There are some people who drift in and out," he said. "One guy looks like a *GQ* model. Tall, blonde. Really cut. But he comes and goes. Sometimes you see him for a couple days, then he disappears. Then a couple of obvious closet cases. If I had to cruise TradeSpace for action, I'd be in bad shape."

"Sounds like a pretty transient group," I said.

"A lot of guys at TradeSpace are on their way out," he said. "They work on the street a few years, get tired of taking the bullshit, then they do something else. I know one guy who became a stock broker. Got all his clients from people he met at gay bars. Makes a ton of money."

"Maybe I ought to go to Zurich and pull out some cash for him to invest," I said.

"Is that where you have your money?" he asked. "Switzerland?"

"Yeah."

"Are you kidding?" he asked. "The Swiss will never give you cash to put in a suitcase. They'll want to wire it to another bank. Then the IRS will want to know where it came from."

"I guess you're right. I ought to move it somewhere else."

"Switzerland is okay if you don't touch it, but the IRS has all sorts of hooks into those accounts now. One of these days they're going to come after you. You need a place that doesn't have an extradition treaty with the United States."

"That assumes I'd want to leave the U.S."

"Yeah, let's assume that," he said. "Because you'd have to become a resident citizen of another country to get protection from extradition. So where are you going to do that? St. Kitts and Nevis are beautiful, but they changed their banking laws a year ago. The Philippines is tricky, but it's a fucked-up Catholic country with a big Muslim problem. Then there's Nauru and Niue, but then you'd be stuck in the middle of the western Pacific."

"So where would you go?"

"The Seychelles."

"The what?"

"The Seychelles Islands. They're off the east coast of Africa. A big offshore banking center. A hundred thousand people on 115 islands. They speak English and French. Plenty of gay tourists from Amsterdam and Germany. If you become a citizen and invest $5 million in government securities, you have immunity from criminal prosecution. They can't make you forfeit your assets. They can't extradite you."

He reached for his baggie and repacked his pipe with the end of the pencil. A stubby pencil. With a date written in red marker near the eraser.

My legs got weak.

He pulled hard on the little pipe and held it in.

"Let me get this straight," I said. "You can commit a crime here in the U.S. and then move to the Seychelles and be completely free?"

"It doesn't apply to crimes of violence or drug crimes," he said, exhaling a thin stream of smoke. "But you only committed a financial crime. You're safe as long as you give up your U.S. citizenship and buy $5 million in government securities. They pay you shit interest rates on your money, but it goes a long way over there. For $100,000, you can buy a mansion on the beach. Servants are cheap. Great surfing. Sailing. Wind-surfing. Beats this fucked-up town."

"But I'd have to live there," I said. "I'd have to move."

"Are you kidding?" he said. "Leave this fucked-up city? Sit around on the beach, surfing all day long? Versus what? Hanging around here? At TradeSpace?"

"Yeah, but it takes $5 million. I only have half a million in Switzerland."

"Well, that's your problem," he said. "But it's something to think about. You gotta have a dream."

After weeks of searching for Tim's partner, it didn't seem real. He wasn't some sinister figure with a menacing grin. He was gay. He worked at TradeSpace. And he was an expert on good places to live if you wanted to avoid extradition to the U.S. So get the fuck out of his apartment, you idiot!

I picked the pencil out of the cookie tin and gave it a close look. "What happened on 2-12-02?" I asked. "A lucky trade?"

"Just something a friend gave me," he said. He took another long drag, a little cross-eyed this time, as if it were difficult to pull the air through the pipe.

"The Seychelles," I said. "That's your dream."

"White sand beaches. You get up, surf all day. They've got a couple gay bars in Praslin. Get high. Fuck your brains out."

"What's stopping you?"

"Nothing," he said. "I'm selling this apartment in two weeks. With what I've saved, that will put me over the top. The closing is May 10. I already bought a one-way ticket. I was out there a couple weeks ago. On Grande Anse, on the west coast of Mahe. Three good days of surf. There were a couple of good breaks nearby. One of them was a point break called Coetivy. The other was a reef break at a beach down the road called Beau Vallon."

He offered me a hit, but I declined.

"You know anything about surfing?" he asked.

"A little," I said.

"The point break was a right, and the beach break was a left. For three days the beach break was going off four to six feet glassy. One of the longest lefts I've ever ridden. I must have spent 10 or 15 seconds in the curl. I came out, cut back, did a drop knee turn, cut back, walked to the nose. Pulled a cheater five, and held that for about 20 seconds."

I could imagine him sitting at his desk at TradeSpace, watching the screens, waiting for Tim to buy an obscure out-of-the-money option.

I could imagine him jumping on the signal, bidding up the price just before the bank's big trade, then cashing out and watching the money pile up in his TradeSpace account. Wouldn't it be great if making money were that simple?

"If you really want to hit it, you can charter a day trip to the outer reefs. Then you're talking 20 or 30 feet. Hawaiian."

I could imagine him getting a panicky call from Tim the Thursday we threatened him, then trying to figure a way out of their mess.

The recorder was still humming in my front pocket. The extra battery was in my back pocket.

"I'm a pretty good surfer, but not like some of the guys I see out there," he said. "It's going to take me 10 years of practice to get as good as them."

To hell with New York. You go to the Seychelles. Convert your money to government securities, buy a mansion and live out your life free from extradition. And then Shoshanna and I fuck it all up by stumbling onto a strange pattern in Tim's options trades.

All that I could imagine. But how could he kill somebody? Somebody he worked with? At some point he'd have had to restrain him. That would be easiest when Tim was asleep. Then he'd have to get enough drugs into him to overdose. An injection or two in the arm, in the middle of the night. Dead in a few seconds. Bind him with surgical gloves. Throw some poppers on the floor to make it look like an authentic S&M fuck gone awry.

It didn't sound that hard. Half an hour's work and you were done. Walk out the basement door. Lay low for a while, making sure nobody suspected you of scamming the bank. Or of murdering your partner.

Then tiptoe out of town. And fly out to the beach of your dreams.

It was time to leave. I could feel the recorder humming.

"Mark, my man, I've got to go," I said, rising from the couch and stretching as slowly as I could. "That dope of yours is too strong. I've got to get home before I pass out."

"You sure you don't want to stay?" he asked, giving me his best bedroom look.

"I'd love to," I said, stroking his right arm and returning his gaze. "But give me another week to settle things with my ex."

"Like next weekend?"

"Sure," I said.

"Like next Friday night?"

"Next Friday night."

"Okay," he said, running his fingers down my chest. He stopped at my belt buckle and gave it a soft tug. "It's a date."

I started shaking as I walked down the hall to the elevator.

Dave, are you nuts? Are you fucking crazy?

I walked out of his apartment building and then four blocks in a zigzag fashion, looking behind me at every corner. I tried to get hold of myself. *Chill, Dave.* The bad guy is not coming after you with a knife. He has no idea you're the law. In fact, you're not the law. You're just helping Mitch at the SEC build his case. So call Mitch and tell him what happened.

Mitch didn't answer his cell phone, so I tried his home number. He was watching TV and sounded like he'd had almost as many drinks as I'd had.

"You're not going to believe this," I said.

"What?"

"I found the guy. I just stumbled onto him. I spent a couple hours in his apartment."

"I thought you were going out to the movies."

"Yeah, but one of the guys turned out to be gay."

"What makes you so sure?"

A young couple stared at me as they walked into the subway. I was talking too loud and crashing from the pot high.

"The Seychelles Islands," I said. "He's going to go there. He's leaving in a couple weeks, after he sells his apartment."

"I don't understand."

"He works at TradeSpace. And I got it on tape."

"Dave," he said. "Listen to me. Did this guy mention anything about the specific scam you were investigating?"

"He talked about trying to find somebody, a partner, on the inside. No, wait, that was the other guy. He didn't mention any scam at all. But he's got $5 million. And he's got moving boxes in his bedroom."

"What other guy are you talking about?"

"There were two guys. They were both high school wrestlers. We all were. One of them was straight. The other guy, Mark, is the guy we want. He's got a lucky pencil Tim gave him. And he had all this gay porn on his shelf."

"Are you stoned or something?"

"Actually, yes. But it all happened. The whole thing fits..."

"Stop," he said. "Let me make sure I understand. You had a conversation with a guy you think is the partner of the guy who was murdered."

"Yes."

"Did you tape this conversation?"

"Yes."

"Did this guy say anything incriminating?"

"He mentioned the Seychelles Islands. He's going to move there in a few weeks. It grants you immunity from prosecution for financial crimes."

"The Seychelles Islands?" he asked. "No shit!"

As Mitch mulled this over, the newspaper guy was unloading a box of Snapples and asked me to move a few feet away.

"Okay," said Mitch. "So Mark mentioned the Seychelles and said he was moving there. Did he mention anything specifically about the crime you were investigating?"

"No."

"He didn't mention anything about the guy who was murdered."

"No. He claimed he didn't know him."

"So what you have on tape doesn't establish anything. And this guy has no idea you're investigating a crime."

"He doesn't want to kill me, he wants to fuck me. I'm gay. I mean, he thinks I'm gay. He's hot for me."

"Okay, okay," he said. "I get it. If this is the guy, it puts us a few steps ahead. But we've still got a long way to go before we have the evidence to nail him in court. The tape isn't worth much."

"But he could split any time. Nothing's stopping him from getting on a plane tomorrow morning."

"That's right. But he doesn't know we're after him. And it's going to take a couple days to establish he's the one and build a case for an arrest warrant. That's why I don't want you running around playing cop. That's not your job. My investigator is coming in on the red-eye from San Francisco tomorrow. We've got a conference call scheduled for Sunday night."

"At 9:00."

"Right. You've done a good job, Dave. Maybe we can wrap this up in a hurry. Maybe even by Tuesday. But don't do anything more. Don't contact this guy. You're not in any immediate danger. Just go home and relax. Take a long bath. Get some sleep."

I took the subway home and found myself looking at the women in the subway car with drugged interest. A tall leggy one with red horn rims and a fat boyfriend. Three drunk blondes in bridesmaid gowns. A curvy Hispanic in a jean jacket reading a novel on her way uptown.

Mitch was right. I'd found Tim's accomplice, but my tapes wouldn't prove anything. On Monday morning the SEC would take over the investigation. They'd pull all the evidence together and arrest Mark before he split. They might want me to stay close by. But they might not. They might not need me at all.

I was exhausted. Victory at last. I should have been pleased, but it was something of a letdown. I would no longer be the center of the investigation. I wouldn't even be able to confront him, accuse him, lock him up in handcuffs. It was somebody else's bust now, and a routine one at that.

When I got back to Battery Park City, I collapsed on the couch and listened to the tape. A lot of barely intelligible mumbles interrupted by clinking ice in Scotch glasses and loud scratches when the recorder rubbed against the fabric in my front pocket. A big pause during my sweaty workout. Then the two of us, talking quietly. Mark talking about his life, giving me advice about the Seychelles. All his stuff about surfing. But nothing really incriminating.

My arms were aching from the effects of my 30 bench presses. Mitch told me to take a long bath. Why the hell not?

There was a bottle of Badedas Aura Foaming Bubble Bath with Extract of Horse Chestnut under the sink but I was not an experienced bubble-bath taker. I'd put in way too many capfuls, and it puffed up into a structure resembling the High Sierras.

But it did the trick. I sat back and began thinking about my life. Three weeks ago I'd walked into that investment bank looking for a job. I'd fallen hard for a girl, moved down to Battery Park City, uncovered a trading fraud, and had a few odd sexual encounters along the way. I'd started and ended a promising new career as a forensic auditor. I'd survived an abbreviated psychoanalysis with a trader/rabbi, and made a brief tour of the gay world. And I'd solved a murder.

What did I have to show for it all? A temporary badge at the SEC and a great new leather jacket.

After the SEC gig, I'd be back throwing more resumes at people who didn't want to see them. The romance was over, and I still had five months left on my sublet. Maybe I'd see Shoshanna in the elevator with some other guy. That would be a lot of fun.

As I slipped deeper into the perfumed foam, I resolved never to get within 100 feet of a weight-lifting machine.

I resolved never to fall in love with any Orthodox women, or formerly Orthodox women, no matter how great they looked.

I resolved never to listen to songs about moondances...

Or unzip a zippered white Columbia sweatshirt...

Then I heard a truck in the distance. A buzzing truck. A big semi. Insistent. Coming my way.

I woke up and found myself in a lukewarm bubble bath. The buzz was the doorman. A delivery? In the middle of the night?

I pulled myself out of the bath, dripping a quart of water onto the bathroom floor. I wrapped myself in a towel and walked to the intercom beside the door.

"Mark Costas is here," said the doorman.

"Okay," I said. Mark who? Then I bolted awake. Mark. Mark. I should keep him downstairs. Have him wait in the lobby. See what he wanted. I buzzed the doorman back and waited for him to respond.

"Could you please tell Mark to wait for me in the lobby?"

"He's already in the elevator."

"Okay," I said. "No problem."

Not so bad, I thought. The guy's horny. Meet him at the door. Go out to a coffee shop. Order rice pudding and talk all night.

I was standing in my towel, still dripping wet. I dried myself, threw on some jeans and a t-shirt. And shoes, of course. If I was going to go out, I'd need shoes.

Plus the leather jacket. I looked at myself in the mirror. Another spaced-out gay stud going out on the streets at 2 a.m. What about something to protect myself if he pulled something funny? I had my aluminum baseball bat in the closet. You can't greet a guy at the door that way. Don't exaggerate the situation. Mark has no idea who you are. But where were my shoes?

I don't remember him actually ringing the bell, but I'm sure it happened. I opened the door and Mark walked past me holding up something like a badge. For a second I was confused. Oh shit, I thought. Maybe this guy is a cop.

"You left this, asshole," he said, slamming the door behind him.

He held it right up in front of my face. A cell phone battery with a label that read

"PROPERTY OF THE SECURITIES AND EXCHANGE COMMISSION."

I saw the sucker punch in very slow motion, a copper ring embedded in his clenched fist, coming at me so slowly that it would have been easy to get out of the way. All I had to do was lean back a bit for it to whistle past me.

Then I was on my back looking up at him. How did I get here? The soles of his shoes seemed several inches high. He raised one shoe and kicked me in the groin. I blacked out for a moment, and awakened myself with my own groans. While I was curled up on the floor, trying to spoon-feed air into my lungs, I heard him doing something behind me. Making noise. Knocking over the halogen lamp. He tied my two legs together with something. Lamp cord? My hands were free, but I was frozen into a fetal curl, breathing in short sips.

Then rip, rip, the sound of duct tape, around my legs a couple times. At that point, I could see him standing over me, but he was hyperventilating — he was cross-eyed from the effort. He was stoned on some heavy shit.

We stared at each other, both catching our breath, plotting our next moves.

I still had my hands. I rolled over, wincing with pain, and grabbed the leg of the table by the door. I tried pulling it, but I couldn't get it to fall. That gave him time to grab my legs and flip me on my stomach. A classic reverse nelson from high school wrestling, but it was child's play with my legs bound. Another couple rips and my hands were taped together behind my back.

I yelled as loudly as I could, but I couldn't get any wind behind it. Then I rolled over on my side, just to do something. He made a clumsy attempt to gag my mouth with another piece of tape, wrapping it around the back of my neck. Messy, but it worked. A second piece around my mouth. Then another piece over my eyes. Darkness.

I went slack.

I tried to collect my thoughts. I could hear him wheezing. Some light was leaking out from two holes where the tape met my nose, but that was it. I was still weak and nauseous from the kick in the balls. But the mouth gag wasn't perfect. If I worked my jaw a bit, I might be able to... no, that was impossible.

I could still yell for help. If I could get myself to the wall, which was probably about five feet to my left, I might be able to kick it and alert the neighbors. Then start yelling like crazy. That was my best shot. But I needed to gather my strength.

He was doing something about 10 feet away. At the dining room table? The scrape of the chair, a zipper. "Fuck with me, I'll fuck with you," he mumbled more to himself than to me.

There was an interval, a minute or so, when I heard nothing but his steady breathing. A small click. A hiss. A cigarette lighter. But he wasn't lighting a cigarette.

I thought about a cave. Some nice cave I could crawl to where he couldn't see me. Wait this thing out. Whatever he was doing, he was doing in a hurry. I heard the chair scrape again and his footsteps coming towards me. Move, Dave. MOVE!

I started rolling to my left. I hit a table leg, and then found the wall. Then I raised my legs, the pain shooting from my groin, and started kicking the wall as hard as I could: "*HELP! STOP! HELP!*"

Then I felt a little pinprick.

It felt great.

The little blobs of light between the tape filled with colors — the Glen plaid colors you'd find in some golf pants. And then the rush began. The closest feeling was skiing downhill. Or maybe it was more like being pulled by something. Water skiing. Or riding something. Like surfing. Riding this enormous force.

Wow.

Chapter 23

Something was pressing down painfully hard on my mouth. And my face.

I opened my eyes. Almost daylight. An oxygen mask, held by a black woman with a pale crescent scar over her eye. She was crouching over me with a chattering police radio that was way too loud.

My shirt was unbuttoned for some reason.

"We got him," the woman said. "His eyes are open."

Who's got who? I thought. They were talking about me.

"What time is it?" I asked, but my voice was muffled by the mask. I heard a siren in the background.

"What time is it?" I demanded angrily when she removed the mask. "Tell me right now!"

Then they all started laughing.

I woke up in a small windowless room wrapped like a mummy in thin hospital blankets. A plastic tube was blowing oxygen up my nose and a doctor was attending to a whirring machine.

He looked up and asked: "How do you feel?"

A severely thin man, slightly stooped with soft, kind eyes.

"Nod your head if you understand me," he said.

I nodded.

He looked at his watch and said "In case you're wondering, it's 11:34." Then he smiled.

Morning? Evening? It didn't matter.

It was our little joke.

At some point, I began playing a little game: Who what when where why.

Who: I knew who I was. Dave Ackerman.

What: Too confusing.

When: 2002. Nighttime. Probably.

Where: New York City. Probably.

Why: Too confusing.

But that was enough. I had situated myself in space and in time. An achievement.

I knew I had been moved from wherever I was to intensive care because I could see beyond the open curtain to another patient across the way. Most of the room was in darkness, but there was a table beside me with a brightly lit Styrofoam bowl of applesauce on a Styrofoam tray.

In the abstract, it glowed like a dessert featured in a gourmet magazine.

Chef Andre has made the finest applesauce, a simple concoction that he prefers to serve in a white Styrofoam bowl.

Then I woke up again. With the curtains parted, I could see the rest of the ICU beyond: some areas intensely lit, others dark. A body in a white sheet was wheeled by, like a floating mummy. The overhead lights above me were turned off. It must have been evening, or night, but a speaker by my desk was summoning nurses here and there.

How stupid! If they wanted you to sleep, why would they keep waking you up?

The first memory about what happened wasn't a thought, it was a feeling, and not even a feeling but a memory of a feeling. To have a guy close to you, breathing hard beside you, a guy's body, clothed but sweaty, male muscles, force behind the skin, pushing against yours.

High school wrestling. Flip. To move a body against gravity, you had to stay close to the floor. A guy wrapped around you, pulling and pushing you, breathing hard in your ear, trying like hell to get you on your back. Heavy, but not like a woman's weight at all. A woman's body was at rest. This was an entirely different kind of physical contact.

I could remember what he looked like but I didn't remember his name.

I woke up, blinked a few times, and the new nurse stepped away to do something else.

Suddenly, I put it all together in a sentence.

I was killed… almost killed… by a guy who had a surfboard … and you have to catch him... right away!

I repeated that a few times to practice it. Did it obey the rules of grammar? Of logic? Yes.

I was almost killed... by a guy with a surfboard. You have to catch him right away!

The next time the nurse came around I pointed to my mouth.

She stopped, took my pulse.

"This guy tried to kill me!" I said.

What came out of my mouth was forceful expression of some kind, but completely garbled. I might have been an old man making a senile pronouncement about the weather. She patted my hand compassionately and took my pulse.

I closed my eyes and the ICU curtains closed and then parted again like a theater stage. Except the curtains had clear netting at the top.

A man appeared, stage center, who studied me and bent over to talk.

"Do you know who I am?"

I nodded. The cop. His name was just a bit beyond me, but I got the concept. He was talking with exaggerated elocution and much too loudly. As if I were demented. I wasn't demented. I was just a little confused. He had something in his hand, just below the edge of the bed.

"The guy who hit you... the doorman said he looked something like this."

They were not mug shots. And not drawings done by a police artist. They were something in between. Done not by an artist, but a computer's idea of what he looked like.

Whose name was...

The right build, more or less. But his shoulders were sloping, not broad. And the face was wrong: a generic truck driver with a broad flat nose. Or a comic book punk. Then another sheet of paper with the same guy wearing a baseball cap.

I shook my head. "No," I said.

"But you knew this guy. You told the doorman to let him into your apartment. Were you trying to play cop?"

I shook my head violently to bring the message home. Which was a mistake. I remembered an odd but important fact: Your brain has the consistency of Jell-O, protected by your skull.

"What about this guy?" he asked.

The light was reflecting back at me from the white paper. I blinked. This cop was much too forceful. The nurses and doctors were on my side, but this guy came from another world. Where did he get all that energy? The guy on this page was slender with a thin Latin pencil mustache. Young. Skinny arms akimbo. Different culture. A down-scale gay punk. A gay punk hooker.

"Tim's neighbor saw this guy in the hallway of the apartment building. Five-nine, about 140 pounds. Stumbling like he had taken the wrong drugs. But he knew enough to walk to Sixth Avenue where he could get a taxi."

I had one of the names. The straight guy from Atlanta was Shelby. The one who had the girlfriend. And the guy who attacked me was...

"We think this guy was in the room when Tim took his overdose. Maybe it was somebody he hired for the night who took the same shit. Or he could be a killer. Or maybe it was some kind of threesome."

The guy with the surfboard had a ticket to the Seychelles. *Stop him at the airport!* I had to communicate that somehow. A message to the world outside my head. I had to speak.

"Do you remember this guy's name?" he asked, shaking the paper.

Which guy? I tried. I was too exhausted. I could see his weight machine, I could see the packing boxes in his bedroom. I could see his tight polo shirt.

"Muscles," I said.

The cop pointed to his bicep. "Muscles?" he asked.

"Yes." I said.

"Gay?" he asked. "Or straight?"

I remembered the pornographic photo from the guy's collection. A white guy pinioned between two black dicks. I was fading fast.

"Yesssss." This time I couldn't quite clip off the end of the word. It came out of my mouth like a snake.

The next time I woke up, I was in a regular hospital room. A teenage boy was in the other bed, accompanied by a grandmotherly figure who had taken up residence in the armchair beside him, knitting the world's largest sweater. She spoke to him in a language I couldn't place, neither Italian nor Greek. Both of his legs were in casts, and he answered her sullenly in English.

A new bowl of applesauce appeared beside my bed. Or maybe it was the same one. I reached for it and ate it with pleasure. I found the buzzer for the nurse.

"Please bring the cop here again," I said, when she appeared. The words dropped out of my mouth like magic. She was surprised as I was, and nodded violently. A good sign for this patient.

I marveled at my accomplishment. Speech! You opened your mouth and you were able to communicate thoughts in your head! Miraculous.

Then I closed my eyes and a few seconds later Mitch appeared at my bedside instead of the cop. Or a few hours later. I'd given up trying to figure it out. I didn't recognize him at first. Who was this slob? Not business casual, just casual. Rumpled khakis and glasses instead of contacts.

"How's the SEC's only clandestine agent?" he said.

I summoned up all my strength. And a smile. I had something urgent to communicate.

"The guy's name was Mark Costas," I croaked. "The guy who hit me."

"I know," he said. "We figured that out yesterday night."

"You gotta stop him! He's going to the Seychelles Islands."

He unfolded a thick wad of stapled paper from of his hip pocket and studied the pages. "That would have been a good idea yesterday. He took a 9:32 flight to Frankfurt Saturday morning. He's already there."

"What day is it now?" I asked.

"Sunday night," he said. Looking at his watch. "8:20."

Whatever air I had in my lungs escaped. Gone. That little sucker-punching sonofabitch. The anger cleared my head.

"He's staying on an island called La Digue," Mitch said, reading from his sheet. '...*About four hours from Victoria International Airport by schooner. Oxcarts are the primary means of transportation, which can take the visitor past vanilla plantations, a copra factory and, of course, the incomparable beach (star of Bacardi ads, swimsuit fashion shoots and countless honeymoon snapshots).*'"

I could see him clearly now: Mark Costas. Close-cropped dark hair. Narrow sloping shoulders. Narrow brown eyes.

"They said you got kicked in the nuts pretty bad," he said. "That's gotta hurt."

"It doesn't feel bad right now," I said. "I'm pretty drugged up."

We smiled at each other for a while in a stupid, friendly kind of way.

"I've got a lawyer flying to the Seychelles to see how to extradite him. $4,000 for tickets, and another $5,000 to pay a retainer to a Seychelles law firm. We're sparing no expense to defend our superspy."

"What are you going to charge him with?"

"Well, that's the problem," Mitch said, returning the papers to his pocket. "The option trades traced right back to Costas' terminal at TradeSpace. But he's a citizen of the Seychelles now so he can't be extradited for a financial crime."

"What about for murdering Tim?"

"That's a little tricky," he said. "We're dealing with two guys. Costas, the guy you let into your apartment, and another guy who somebody saw outside of Tim's apartment the night he died. That's the one the cop is chasing. There's nothing linking Costas to the murder."

"He tried to kill me! You can extradite him for that."

"In theory," he said, settling down into the visitor's armchair beside the bed. "You're alive, for one, so it would have to be attempted murder. But that's going to be hard to prove."

"Hard to prove," I said.

"You told the doorman to let Costas into the building. There were no signs of assault."

"He kicked me in the balls!"

"Rough sex."

"He tied me up with duct tape."

"Ditto."

"He tried to kill me with an overdose."

"No law against giving yourself a drug overdose."

"I gave myself an overdose?"

"Sure. After a little rough sex. The duct tape had been removed. None on your body when they found you. Bath towel nearby but no other clothes. Injection mark inside your left wrist. You're right-handed. Disposable needle and wrapper on the dining room table."

I was still a little slow. It took me a while to see where he was going.

"You invite him up to your place for some quickie sex and a drug cocktail," he continued. "He walks out past the doorman calmly, looking high as a kite but smiling after a good fuck. Then you take another taste and overdose yourself."

"No."

"Yes. That's what any decent criminal lawyer will say. That's what we're going to hear in Victoria, which is where they hold the preliminary extradition hearings in the Seychelles."

A wave of exhaustion descended on me. Like those lead blankets a dentist puts on you while taking x-rays.

"Which is not to say that we won't eventually get him here for an attempted murder trial," he said with a stoic sigh. "But it ain't gonna be easy. Or quick."

To hell with a trial. Just let me return the sucker punch with steel-toed boots.

On the other side of the hospital room, the grandmother started asking the teenager a series of questions. He answered her with a sullen "no" or with nothing at all.

"What language are they speaking?" I asked. "It's been driving me nuts."

Mitch cocked his head to one side and listened carefully.

"Maltese," he declared after a few phrases. "I heard some of it in Philadelphia when I was a beat cop."

"No shit," I said.

"Three years on the force. Then my uncle told me I could get hired by the FBI to work with white collar criminals if I had a law degree. It's been a nice break from my routine—dealing with a violent crime."

"Glad I could brighten your day," I said.

He didn't know how to take that remark. "No hard feelings?"

"No," I said. "It was my own damn fault. I tried to play hero. You warned me."

He made me go through the details of my night with Mark and Shelby, minute by minute, writing it all down in tight cursive script. He explained how he and the police had kicked open the door to my apartment Saturday morning when I didn't answer my phone and the details of the complex drug cocktail Mark had tried to kill me with. Apparently, I'd been saved by my sheer size.

Mitch had spent several hours with Nardulli that weekend, explaining how the financial scam was related to Tim's murder. An SEC investigator researched Costas' financial records and found another two million worth of trades we hadn't discovered. With Tim's share and his own, it was just enough to establish citizenship in the Seychelles, but not enough to live the way he wanted to live.

"He was waiting around for the cash from his condo sale," said Mitch. "The closing was in two weeks."

"But no direct link between Costas and Tim's murder."

"Nardulli is working on the assumption that it was committed by a third person who was observed at the scene of the crime."

"He's chasing a phantom."

"That's what I tried to tell him. The West Village is full of gay hookers stumbling out of apartment buildings. But he's the expert on gay homicide. Not me."

He checked his watch and got up to go.

"I've spent a little time with Larry and Susanna. They're eager to see you but I told them to hold off a while."

"Larry?"

"Larry Zimmerman. The rabbi."

"Oh yeah," I said. "I forgot about him."

"You forget about her, too?"

An ephemeral snapshot of Shoshanna appeared for a second in my mind's eye —

at her desk, looking for split ends. "Oh yeah," I said. "Her."

I woke up several times that night, anxious and exhausted. When the new shift came in at 8:00, I asked the nurse for some coffee. She returned with an extra large cappuccino from the coffee bar in the cafeteria.

"Your cousin has been waiting to see you," she said, warily watching the monitors. "Do you feel up to it?"

"My cousin?"

"Rick Markowitz."

"Oh yes," I said, nodding weakly. "Rick. Absolutely. I'd love to see cousin Rick."

Rick arrived wearing something strange — a smile. He put out his hand reflexively and then withdrew it when he saw the drip tube in my arm. He was dressed in his regulation business suit, but he'd assumed the stooped posture of a penitent. In another age, he would have had his hat in his hand.

"I had to come over to apologize," he said. "How you feeling?"

I shook his hand weakly.

"I'd like a head transplant," I said. "But I'm okay."

"I'm sorry that I had anything to do with..." He looked around the room at my neighbor and at the medical equipment. "With all this... trouble."

I nodded to accept his apology, even though I wasn't sure what he was apologizing for.

"Right," I said. "That's okay."

To make conversation he asked more specific questions: Was I in much pain? How long would I be in the hospital? Did I need anything? It was clear he didn't care a rat's ass about my recovery. He was simply glad I had survived.

My mind was beginning to work in its old grooves again. Something big was on his mind. I had accepted his apology. Now he was after something else. What had he heard about me? That I had a near-death run-in with Tim's former partner?

The teenager beside me was taking a nap, and grandma was clipping coupons from last weekend's ad supplement. We talked some more about my health, when I had moved from intensive care, how long I'd be here.

"It's my fault that you got beat up. That you were almost killed." he said.

"Your fault?"

"If I had listened to HR a few years ago, this would never have happened. They told me not to hire Tim. He was nothing but trouble at Credit Suisse. His boss said he was an asshole. But I needed to fill my equity trading slot in a hurry."

I nodded sympathetically. "Sometimes assholes make good traders," I said. "Sometimes they don't."

"That's right," he said. "I heard you traded options at my alma mater. Ismir said you were pretty good."

I smiled involuntarily. A slight shift in roles, Dave, the ignorant auditor beneath contempt, had now become a respected colleague, a fellow member of the options elite.

"Ismir told me you blew out on a huge four-way straddle. What happened?"

The question that refused to die. It was hopeless. I'd be forced to explain this mistake the rest of my life.

"Trader's Dilemma," I said wearily. "With a naked option play. The morning of November 12, 2001."

Professional shorthand, but it was more than enough. A loss so big you'd lose your job if they found out. So your only sensible choice is to double up on the bet and hold your breath.

He shook his head in commiseration. "I fell into that hole myself. My first year at Merrill."

"Yeah?" I asked. "What happened?"

"A stupid one-way bet on Treasury futures." He flinched at the memory. "The morning of March 12, 1992. The worst two hours of my life. Watching the three-year note sink like a stone. Half a million bucks down on my P&L, and I had the job only three weeks."

"Then what happened."

"Greenspan said a few magic words at a G7 conference and the market recovered."

We nodded our heads. Just two guys talking trade. I'd done it dozens of times in my other life with somebody like him. A quiet beer with my managing director after a crazy trading day. How did the desk perform? How did we handle the opportunities presented to us? Who performed well? Who fucked up?

"I think I know why you kept Tim around," I said. "In terms of trading desks, he wasn't the worst guy I've ever met. And once you get somebody trained to do things your way, you grow dependent on them."

"That's right," he said. "You work with what you've got. With the resources you have. You don't have time to wait for the perfect team of employees. The cash register has got to ring every day. Every hour." He opened his palm and traced the creases idly with his index finger. "Tim would show up Monday morning bragging about how he'd bagged this bitch or that bitch the night before. Maybe he was talking about guys. It didn't matter to me. He'd go into the bathroom, throw some water on his face, have four espresso shots and trade his ass off."

"You knew about the gay stuff."

He looked up at me and squinted, as if I had woken him up from a dream.

"I had an idea," he said. "He was getting laid too often for a straight guy. Nobody gets that lucky. I thought he might he bisexual. But I kept it to myself. I don't know what you and Susanna said to him, but it scared him."

"When?"

"The day you and Susanna showed up with that stupid report on Stu Lister."

I shook my head. "We were so full of shit."

"I'm glad we finally agree," he said.

I threw up my hands in apology. "We wanted to nail somebody. So we found some schmuck trying to inflate his bonus. But Tim was afraid we'd come after him next?"

"I'm pretty sure. He approached me after the close that Thursday. He'd heard you were going after Stu and I told him what idiots you were. Then he asked me if I knew anybody who had ever gone to jail for trading fraud. A strange question from him. I said one or two. That was it. Twenty seconds. But I thought: This guy's got something to hide."

A double knock at the door. Then a young woman with two ID tags and a metal clipboard, maybe a medical intern. Hair the color of a new penny, wearing some kind of dark green yoga outfit with a bare midriff and a stretchy top.

"Richard Leland?" she asked. "For occupational therapy?"

"I'm not Richard," I said. "But I'll sign up right now."

She smiled, and straightened her back as a way of acknowledging our bug-eyed stares. Then she closed the door, slowly, to give us a final view of her slim Spandex ass.

"Sweet Jesus," Rick said, chuckling and shaking his head.

"It was just a mirage," I said. "Ignore it."

I watched him looking at the closed door, as if staring would make her magically reappear.

"But you *knew* he was stealing from the bank," I insisted. "You *knew* about his scam."

The slightest change in posture. A little stiffness in the neck.

"Yeah?" he asked. A twitch in his eyes. Almost a blink. Not surprise. Just his worst fears realized. "And how did I know about it?"

"Don't be a jerk," I said.

"No, you're the one being a jerk. What are you trying to say?"

We stared at each other a while. A low-key war of wills. I looked away. Hell, I was the one in a hospital bed. I didn't have energy to burn. Then suddenly, from somewhere inside me, a bolt of anger.

"*Fuck you!*" I said. My arm shot out, knocking my empty cappuccino cup across the room. "We were out there busting our ass, digging through deal sheets, phone records, option models, e-mails, every kind of documentary crap, while you were sitting on a spreadsheet that estimated how much he was siphoning off of each deal. It was live and updated in real time."

He took a deep breath and started to respond.

"Don't try to deny it," I said. "I found it on Shivakumar's network drive. I've got a copy of the file somewhere..."

My voice trailed off as I reached back for the memory. Where was that damn thing? On my dining room table. And a digital copy in the memory stick on my key chain.

"I don't think you were involved in the scam." I said. "It would be small change for you. But for some reason, you decided to ignore it."

"You don't know what really happened," he said.

I rolled my eyes. "Okay, I don't," I said. "But even if you were aware of Tim's scam and didn't report it, you're in deep shit."

He shook his head and stared back with disdain. "You've got it all wrong."

"So what did I get wrong? Tell me!"

"I didn't have a clue about how it worked at first. That's number one." He began twisting his fingers in on each other, if he were washing one hand with another. "I could not figure out how the guy was signaling his trades. Shivakumar and I went through every possibility like you did. It drove us crazy. We thought it was some kind of signal. So we watched Tim every time he twitched his nose. Then we thought it was his cell phone. Or an instant message. Then Shivakumar figured out that he was using trades as signals. That was absolutely brilliant."

"And number two?" I asked. "The other thing I got wrong?"

He stood up suddenly and moved to the rack that held my intravenous antibiotics. He stared at the label with his hands behind his back, as if he was restraining himself from doing something violent.

"I didn't ignore it. I was going to nail him. But I was waiting for the right time."

"The right time?" I asked.

"Two or three months," he said. "I was up for a big job and I made a stupid mistake. But by then I was in Traders Dilemma. The same goddamn mistake all over again."

I felt a little heat in my groin. The pain began at that instant and ended only a few weeks later.

So, once again an infinitesimally small risk that explodes. He didn't have to tell me anything more. He was up for a job as SVP of Capital Markets in the next reorganization. A trading scandal on his own desk would blow that career move sky-high. So he sweeps it under the rug and waits. When Shoshanna and I come around, he doesn't tell us, hoping we'll go away. But now he's interfering with our investigation. He's doubled the bet. And when Tim gets killed, he faces an uglier choice: If he tells the truth to the bank and the cops, he loses his job. His career. So he doubles-up once more, betting that nobody will find out.

"The risk in Traders Dilemma just ratchets up and up and up," I said. "All by itself."

"It always does," he said. "But the bet is always better than the alternative."

I looked at him critically, as if I were choosing a character actor for an insurance commercial. Not such a bad guy. He had a certain fierceness I admired. And the arrogant fearlessness you needed to be a leader. Boldness of vision. Drive. I had a fair measure of those qualities. He had them in spades. A guy like that makes a bet against chance. A reasonable decision, given the odds. As a trader, he lives and breathes the odds. But it turns out to be a bet lost.

Rick's eyes softened. A guy in trouble.

"I need your help," he said.

I gave him a nod, a noncommittal one. Not to say yes, but to indicate I was going to listen carefully to what he had to say.

In his eyes... not quite a smile. Simply hope.

"Is it absolutely critical that you tell the bank about that spreadsheet?" he asked. "Would that really change anything?"

I treated it as a factual question. Was it absolutely critical? Who would it help? Who would it hurt?

"I'm not sure," I said. "I'd have to think about it."

He curled his lip and bit it. Trying to send a little message my way. Hey, we've all been in trouble. We all need a little help, a favor once in a while. He grabbed my arm desperately. "Don't make a decision just yet. Just promise me you'll think about it."

"Okay," I said and closed my eyes. "I promise."

He swiveled neatly on his heel. Then the saddest man in the world left the room.

The pain really kicked in when he left. Maybe it was some kind of change in my medication, but I was suddenly aware that something functional below my waist had been injured. A low-grade nausea that gave me little jolts of pain whenever I took a deep breath or moved my hips.

My nurse cranked up the codeine, but couldn't put me back on my old drugs unless a doctor approved. The codeine dulled the pain but made me woozy and emotional.

Rick and I were brothers in the trading profession. People treated all of us the same way. When they found out you were investment bankers, they always gave you a knowing nod. Somebody who only cares about money. You could hear their mind close.

Of course it was about money. But this business was also about the quality of your thinking. All the thinking it took to get to the top of your high school class. Then your college class. Then your MBA class. Thinking and thinking. Homework. Essays on the French revolution. Tests. Equations. Labs. Bad trades. Good trades. Opportunities. Risks. Years of concentration. One intellectual problem after another. Along with its own measure of creativity.

It was a craft, a trade, for better or worse. But once you joined the fraternity you found yourself isolated from the rest of human values. They, those other people, would never understand.

Wasn't that reason enough to cut him some slack?

Mitch arrived as I was finishing a cold pancake breakfast. He was gripping a manila folder tightly in his hand. I expected another mug shot, but this was something different—an elevator camera photo, taken with a fisheye lens from 10 feet high.

There was my buddy, Mark Costas, staring directly at the camera — aware of it, almost having a conversation with it.

"Look at the date and time," Mitch said, with a sly look in his eye.

It was in a little box on the bottom left: 11Apr02 20:42

"8 p.m., the night Tim died," I said.

"That's right. He's going up in the elevator to TradeSpace. He just had a five-minute chat with the doorman. About whether you could call Derek Jeter black or white since he's got parents of both races. Now look at this other photo."

A surveillance camera with a view of TradeSpace. Much grainier but there's Mark all alone in his cubicle. At 1:32 a.m.

"He spent the night at TradeSpace," Mitch said. "The whole night. Browsing gay porno sites. He took a nap from 2 a.m. to 5 a.m."

"All night?"

"For the alibi," he said. "To prove he wasn't there when Tim was killed."

I felt a headache coming on. "But if he was so determined to establish an alibi, he knew what was happening."

"That's right," he said. "So there's Mark and somebody else. A third person after all. Maybe somebody at the bank."

I did not want to hear this. I was already nauseous from the effort of moving my head to look at photographs. I was too thick-headed.

"I know what you're thinking," I said.

"What?"

"Markowitz and Tim."

"Yeah."

"But Markowitz wasn't involved with Tim's scam."

"You're sure?"

"He's up for head of capital markets. It's a big job at the bank. A few million bucks a year. He had to sweep this little scandal under the rug until the job came through."

"I heard the same thing over the weekend from somebody at the bank."

"Rick told me he intended to nail Tim later. Once he got the job."

Mitch cocked his head to one side. This was new information.

"When did he tell you this?"

"A couple hours ago. He came by for a condolence call."

Another piece of new information. One he didn't like. Information I hadn't volunteered.

"Either way, he knew about it all beforehand," Mitch said.

"Definitely," I said. "I have a spreadsheet he used to track the trade. I suppose that's obstruction of justice."

"Yes," he said. "In theory." He sank back into his chair with weary resignation.

"Why only in theory?" I asked.

"Because nobody's ever going to prosecute him. If I show that spreadsheet to the bank, they'll have to fire him. His banking career will be all over. But they'll never press charges."

He opened the top of his big legal briefcase and let the surveillance photos drop to the bottom.

"So we're back to the Puerto Rican hooker?" I asked.

"I guess so," he said. "Costas hired one. Or one of his pals hired one. Or..." He threw up his hands in disgust. "Not my beat anymore. I've got WorldCom to fry. You got any ideas?"

I shook my head a little too quickly, which made me dizzy.

"What do you want me to do about Markowitz?" he asked.

"Give him a pass," I said. "Don't tell the bank about the spreadsheet."

"Why not?"

I shrugged. "He made a mistake. What's the point?"

He scrutinized me carefully. With cop eyes. "You like this guy?" Mitch asked. "Is he some kind of friend of yours?"

"No," I said quickly.

He raised his voice at me for the first time. "Then why are you carrying his water?" It was not a question, it was an accusation.

I gave up. It was time to disappear under the covers and let somebody else deal with the world for a while. "Do what you have to do," I said. "I don't care any more."

He took out some forms from his briefcase. An eight-page employment contract, setting me up as a government employee. He explained that I was going to be hired by the SEC as part of a new unit that would track stock options granted by corporations to their senior management. The options math seemed like a no-brainer, but it was almost too good to believe. Plug in the numbers, adjust the model for this and that. A future.

"They're eager to have you start work soon," he said. "The hospital said you'd be okay in a week but wait until you feel up to it. Just report to me the first morning and I'll introduce you to your new boss."

He turned to go, then hesitated, as if he had misgivings about giving me the job.

"I appreciate what you did, Dave. But if you're going to be working at the SEC you need to understand something: We bust white-collar criminals. Guys like you and me. Guys with families and careers and Westchester mortgages. If you're going to feel sorry for everybody we try to nail, you can't work for us. Understand?"

I nodded. The first nod of a government employee. Of a federal enforcement officer. Or whatever I was now.

"When I get back to my office I'm going to tell the bank about what Markowitz did. He committed a crime. It's going to destroy his career, but that's not my problem. Or yours. You've got a new life with us. I don't want you to get started on the wrong foot."

We shook hands, but he didn't let go.

"I had a long dinner with Larry and Susanna last night," he said.

"Shoshanna, not Susanna."

"Shoshanna?" he asked. "The girl you were working with at the bank. The one who skipped out on you."

"I'm not sure that's what you'd call it."

He smiled. I could call it what I wanted, but I wasn't going to change his mind.

"I guess he's divorced, huh?" he asked.

"Who? The rabbi?"

"Yeah."

"I think so. Why are you asking?"

"Nothing," he said. "When I knew him, he was married and had two kids. Now I hear he's divorced."

I was missing something. "Is that some kind of tip?" I asked.

He shrugged. "I'd rather you heard it from me."

Chapter 24

That was the beginning of a long period of uncertainty and waiting. My bruised testicles healed by the third week; my bruised heart took longer.

My new job at the SEC served as a convenient distraction. I was assigned to a group auditing the executive-compensation programs of the Fortune 500. I was making a tenth of my previous salary, but I enjoyed my new role as a valued, if overworked, member of a law enforcement team.

The murder of Tim Scott reduced itself to a police case, and a tedious one at that. In June, Mark Costas was charged with attempted murder in New York State Court. The Seychelles law firm he hired threw up the usual roadblocks, but the State Department lawyer who was arranging for the extradition assured me I'd be facing Mark in an American court by fall.

Then in July, the constable in Seychelles reported that he had been unable to deliver the extradition summons to Costas on the island of La Digue. Costas' lawyer said he hadn't heard from Mark in two weeks. Later, we learned Costas had withdrawn most of his cash and flown to Frankfurt, and from there to places unknown.

Nardulli had never given up looking for the Hispanic male seen stumbling out of Tim's apartment building that night. I got a few calls from him in September, when he discovered a Merrill Lynch peso trader who admitting spending a couple nights with Tim in the late '90s.

Then the trail went cold.

In December, I attended a SEC Christmas party where three Indo-Pak SEC staffers dressed up in burkas performed a Supremes routine — "Don't Mess With Bill" — a tribute to the SEC's vice-chairman. Halfway through the number, they stripped to bikinis and started belly-dancing.

The star of the show was Nan Lakshmikantham, the tall lawyer I met on the stairway on the day I signed up to help Mitch. She was still married at the time but a couple months later I learned she separated from her husband.

Initially, I think she thought of me as a temporary post-separation boyfriend. Things began with a bang, as she tried to make up for several years of her husband's philanderings in one wild President's Day weekend. But a powerful and immediate body connection turned swiftly into something else — and surprised both of us. After a month, we started wondering why we weren't living together.

It was weeks before she introduced me to her two boys, aged 6 and 10. They were initially wary, but then embraced the opportunity to have an auxiliary American dad who knew how to imitate the professional wrestling moves they saw on pay-per-view.

Shoshanna, it turns out, found herself in a similar situation with Larry Zimmerman and his two kids. Nan and I attended a reception for people she worked with at the bank, but declined the invitation to their wedding.

There was a final flurry of activity in February when Nardulli arrested a Venezuelan hooker who had been implicated in another drug overdose case. But the DNA check didn't match. That seemed to be Nardulli's last effort.

Spring threw a sneak preview in the first week of March. That Saturday morning every parent in Manhattan decided it was a perfect time to get their kids out of their cramped apartments for a family outing to Central Park.

The tree limbs were still naked, but under blue 60-degree skies, nobody seemed to care. After an extended visit to the zoo, Nan's boys rediscovered the big pile of granite climbing rocks nearby, which was swarming with kids happy to be outside on any pretext. I tried to catch some rays on a park bench nearby while Nan sat beside me, nervously watching their ascent.

As I was dozing, I heard a strange sound: a determined warble that rose above the bird calls, as if carried by a warm breeze. It was somebody whistling, accompanied by an orchestra. I got up and followed the music down the path till I found an older gentleman standing in front of a portable amplifier, a stack of CDs and a derby hat stuffed with dollar bills. He was wearing a brown tweed suit with a bow tie and was whistling a song into a microphone: "A Pretty Girl Is Like a Melody."

"Issidro!" I exclaimed. "*Como sta?*"

He was starting his final chorus and raised his eyebrows in recognition. He looked smaller and rounder than he did in the bank dining room. A small crowd of parents and strollers was clustered around him, and he made a point of whistling directly in front of the toddlers who seemed the most bug-eyed. At the finale, he threw his arms out like an opera star and fell into a deep bow.

"Mr. Ackerman, my good friend!" he said, during the applause. He wiped his lips with a handkerchief.

"That was some real blowing," I said. "I can't believe you can do that."

He accepted the compliment and kept a discreet eye on the deposits in his hat. "Have you heard the good news about Ms. Cassuto?" he asked. "She's married now. To a rabbi."

"Yes," I said. "I saw her at a reception."

"Did you hear she's pregnant?"

"She is? Wonderful. I'm very happy for her."

Somebody threw a ten-dollar bill into his hat, and he offered them a CD.

"Would you like one?" he asked me. "On the house?"

"You gave me one in the bank dining room last year," I said. "I enjoy it very much. Especially 'The Flight of the Bumblebee.' "

Nan appeared around the corner with the boys in tow. They saw me talking to Isidro, but made a beeline for the sword-swallower act that was just starting nearby.

"Are those your kids?" he asked. "They're very fine boys."

"My girlfriend's kids. Not mine."

"But soon? Some of your own?"

"I don't think so," I said. "It's really up to her."

"Of course," he said, nodding. "That's always the way it is."

He threw a nasty look at the sword swallower. He couldn't start up another show now and was eager to chat.

"I never knew Susanna was Jewish," he said. "I thought Cassuto was an Italian name."

"I think it's one of these names that's sometimes Jewish and sometimes Italian."

"Italian Jews," he said, nodding.

We stood by ourselves, watching the upscale parade of grateful sun-worshippers. Once in a while, we caught glimpses of the flaming swords spinning above the heads of the crowd a few feet away.

"When you left the bank, they said you two did something wrong," he said. "I told everybody that you and Susanna did your job too well. That's why Markowitz had to leave at the same time."

"I've got a new job now," I said. "A better one. Working at the SEC."

"A government job," he said, nodding approvingly. "They have very good benefits."

"What happened to Markowitz? Where did he go?"

He shrugged his shoulders. "I heard he's working with his wife now. In Greenwich. A headhunting business. That's just what I hear at lunch."

Then he seemed to make a decision. If the sword swallower was going to steal his crowd, he'd just have to move elsewhere. He gave me a warm handshake and began packing his cart.

I started walking back to join Nan and the kids. As I waved to Nan, indicating that I was coming over, I felt a tug on my sleeve. It was Issidro grabbing my windbreaker.

"I have to tell you something," he said quietly. "But you have to promise not to tell."

He guided me a few feet away and lowered his voice. "Somebody said you were in the hospital. That somebody tried to kill you."

"What did you hear?" I asked.

"That Tim had a partner who tried to kill you and the police are still looking for him."

"That's true," I said. "More or less."

"I'm very sorry. I can tell you something about it, but you have to promise."

"Promise what?"

"Everything."

"You're not being very clear," I said, irritated. "What are you making me promise?"

"I didn't do anything. I wasn't involved. But I could get in trouble."

I sighed. It had been almost a year since I was attacked. Ten months since Mark disappeared. I wanted to be free of that period in my life, and the crime that I was convinced would never be solved. I was happy that day, happy about my new life. And the sunshine. I didn't want to be dragged back.

"Okay," I said reluctantly. "Just tell me. I promise."

He had a little leather bag that held his microphone. He zipped it and unzipped it as he talked.

"I wanted to come to you in the hospital. Maybe I should have. But I didn't."

I nodded. Okay, old man. Just tell me. Just get it over with.

"So I have to say I'm sorry," he said.

"Please stop apologizing," I said. "It all worked out for the best. Pretty much, anyway."

"My nephew Miguel and Tim," he said, twisting the microphone case in his hands. "They used to meet in the handicapped bathroom."

"Your nephew the waiter. Who served us the cappuccinos."

"Yes. After the lunch rush, on the 38th floor. First, $50. I warned him, but I couldn't stop it. Then at night, too. Or before work. For $500 a week. Too much for a 19-year-old kid. Whenever Tim wanted."

"So Miguel, he was like Tim's prostitute."

"Yes."

"Did your nephew know Mark Costas?"

"He thought Tim and Mark had a drug business. Because Mark was selling drugs to the traders. Maybe that's what they fought about that night. Something illegal. Tim would always take the drugs from a box he had in his bedroom. It was full of pills. But that night they used some different pills."

"Wait. Who fought about what? Who gave the pills to whom?"

"Mark was the drug dealer. But his drugs were no good. Or they were too good. Very strong. So they got very stoned and fell asleep. Miguel woke up in the middle of the night. And he figured Tim would wake up later. So he got into a cab and came home."

"Who are you talking about? Tim and Miguel?"

"Yes. That Thursday night."

A couple with a huge double-stroller filled with sleeping infants walked by his amplifier and stared at the CDs. He was about to approach them to sell them a CD but I held him back.

"What do you mean, 'the wrong pills?'"

"Miguel didn't tell me any of this until two months later. After Trujillo Alto. All I knew that night was that he came back at 2 a.m. and slept on the couch instead of his bed. He never did that. And his breathing was too fast. In and out. So I took him to the emergency room. I was out all morning at this hospital so they only had two waiters for lunch." Issidro started walking in a tight half-circle, kicking up dirt with his shoes. "Then I heard that Tim died that same night. I was afraid the police would find Miguel in the hospital."

"Miguel never talked to the police?"

"No. I sent him to Trujillo Alto for three months, back to my cousin's house. His aunt. No more drugs. Then he prayed to Jesus. And when he came back from Puerto Rico he started working at Chung Lo Palace in the Bronx."

"So your nephew was with Tim the night he died. After Mark and Tim had a fight."

"Miguel didn't do anything. They had the sex that Tim wanted him to do. He would get orders. Do this. Now do that. You know what I'm talking about. But he almost died from those drugs, too."

The sword swallower was finishing his act to a rich round of applause. I saw the boys running to Nan for money to put in his metal bucket.

"I think the police are looking for your nephew," I said. "At least they were. A few months ago."

"We heard that. That's why he hardly ever goes into Manhattan anymore. Chelsea. West Village. The bars. No more. You're not going to drag him into that anymore. I know you're not."

A cold gust blew across our section of the park, rustling the branches. Old Man Winter letting us know he was still boss.

"You're right," I said. "I promised."

"You're a fine man," he said. "If Susanna was serious about you, I knew you were a very fine man. I could tell when you came to visit me in the dining room."

He picked up his amplifier and put it into a folding grocery cart.

"Your nephew. Is he still living with you?" I asked.

"Yes. I gave him the big bedroom. He's working at a Chinese restaurant. The biggest Chinese restaurant in the Bronx. He has a boyfriend, a very nice young man. Very serious. They have their crazy times on weekends, but no more drugs. Just vodka. I should have kept better track of him. I told him: Don't mess with people in the drug business. Free samples. Bullshit. Nothing's free. Stay away. But you can't tell a 19-year-old what to do. They sleep where they want. Five hundred dollars a week was a lot of money. More than his pay. But I should have told him to stay away. Kicked him out of the apartment. Maybe all this wouldn't have happened."

He picked up the CDs and wrapped them carefully in a plastic shopping bag.

"He's here in the park with me," he added. "The two of them are trying to pick up a little money today."

"Your nephew?"

"Yes."

"Where is he?"

He hesitated.

"You're not going to say anything to him?"

"No."

He loaded the microphone case and his handmade sign into his grocery cart and started off toward the granite rocks. He seemed older than I remembered and walked with a slight limp I hadn't noticed before.

Miguel and his partner were just around the corner, standing in front of a crowd of their own. Just two Latin teenagers in makeshift clown outfits, and pretty sorry ones at that. They wore tie-dye t-shirts, two old hats and some pale clown makeup half-heartedly and inexpertly applied. But they had the requisite box of thin balloons, and they were doing a modest business turning them into poodles and swords.

The boys were already back at the climbing rock. I motioned to Nan to bring them over. When Neal, the 6-year-old, saw the balloons, he knew the drill. He smiled and grabbed the next place in line.

"A poodle or a sword?" Miguel asked him.

"A sword," he said. Then he looked at his mother for approval. "Please," he added.

Martin, the 10-year-old, stood off to the side. He clearly wanted a sword too but decided that he was too old for that now.

"How much?" Nan asked, when Miguel gave Neal the sword.

Miguel raised three fingers as he blew a thin stream of air into the next balloon.

Nan straightened up to her full 5-10, her bargaining posture. She would not be taken for a ride.

"Three bucks?" she said. "I'm not spending three bucks for a balloon."

"Just give him the money," I said. "Do me a favor."